THE INSTITUTIONS OF LOCAL DEVELOPMENT

IGU SERIES ON LOCAL DEVELOPMENT

Series Editor:
Fabio Sforzi

This series collects the main thoughts and research outcomes on local development carried out by the Study Group on Local Development of the International Geographical Union (IGU) and of scholars linked to it in purpose and in method.

Local development represents a major frame of reference for social scientists and policy makers which have an interest in the study of development and its implementation. In the past, development found explanation especially in economic terms, where real places were neglected. The Italian experience of industrial districts has focused attention on real places by proving that the advantages of agglomeration of economic activities exceed the purely economic effects to include trust, co-operation and governance. Then, the interpretation of development has to integrate economic with social, cultural and institutional foundations, emphasizing the importance of places as units of investigation and policy. These thoughts are the background of local development. In the concept of local development, places make external competitiveness for localised firms, and, at the same time, they satisfy the need for social integration of inhabitants. In this view there isn't 'one best way', but a multiplicity of ways of local development. These are as many and different as are the possibilities of amalgamation between economic growth (efficient combinations of knowledge, technology and organization of production) and social cohesion (dynamic maintenance of a values-system, related institutions and models of governance). The 'geographical turn' in the interpretation of development, which embeds economy in local society, points out variety and peculiarity of places as positive critical values for civilization. In the contemporary open world, the active defence of cultural diversity of places represents a way to mean globalisation; an alternative approach to that founded on cultural standardization and on oligopolistic practices which restrict competition. On the interpretation proposed here, local development and globalisation are interdependent so that between local and global there is a mutual interaction. Therefore, all those positions which tend to separate them or to set one against the other have to be denounced as unfruitful.

This series will host works on local development, both theoretical and empirical, which investigate specific places, stressing their making, strengthening, growth or decline. But this is also a series for local development aimed at stirring up research, debate and proposals on issues linked to the future of society considered in its place-dependent nature.

The Institutions of Local Development

Edited by

FABIO SFORZI
University of Torino, Italy

LONDON AND NEW YORK

First published 2003 by Ashgate Publishing

Reissued 2018 by Routledge
2 Park Square, Milton Park, Abingdon, Oxon OX14 4RN
711 Third Avenue, New York, NY 10017, USA

Routledge is an imprint of the Taylor & Francis Group, an informa business

Copyright © Fabio Sforzi 2003

Fabio Sforzi has asserted his right under the Copyright, Designs and Patents Act, 1988, to be identified as editor of this work.

All rights reserved. No part of this book may be reprinted or reproduced or utilised in any form or by any electronic, mechanical, or other means, now known or hereafter invented, including photocopying and recording, or in any information storage or retrieval system, without permission in writing from the publishers.

Notice:
Product or corporate names may be trademarks or registered trademarks, and are used only for identification and explanation without intent to infringe.

Publisher's Note
The publisher has gone to great lengths to ensure the quality of this reprint but points out that some imperfections in the original copies may be apparent.

Disclaimer
The publisher has made every effort to trace copyright holders and welcomes correspondence from those they have been unable to contact.

A Library of Congress record exists under LC control number: 2002028104

ISBN 13: 978-1-138-72006-0 (hbk)
ISBN 13: 978-1-138-72004-6 (pbk)
ISBN 13: 978-1-315-19399-1 (ebk)

Contents

List of Figures	vii
List of Tables	viii
List of Contributors	ix
Preface	xi

Part I: PLACE-SPECIFICITY OF COMPETITIVENESS

1. Local Embeddedness and International Competitiveness –
   The Case of the Swedish Music Cluster 3
   Daniel Hallencreutz, Per Lundequist and Anders Malmberg

2. The Local Embeddedness of Ethnic Entrepreneurship – Over-
   and Under-Embeddedness in the Israeli Arab Economy 29
   Michael Sofer and Izhak Schnell

3. High-Technology Clustering in Cambridge (UK) 51
   Philip Cooke and Robert Huggins

Part II: TRUST SHAPING COLLECTIVE ACTION

4. The Relations of Co-operation in Group Enterprises and
   Associations in Ghana – Exploration of Issues of Trust and
   Power 75
   Fergus Lyon

5. Social Capital and Development – Issues of Institutional Design
   and Trust in Mexican Group-Based Microfinance 93
   Marina Della Giusta

6. Constructing Alternative Circuits of Value – The Case of Local
   Currency Systems (LCSs) 115
   *Roger Lee, Andrew Leyshon, Theresa Aldridge, Nigel Thrift,
   Jane Tooke and Colin Williams*

Part III: SOCIAL CAPITAL IN THE PATHWAYS OF LOCAL DEVELOPMENT

7   Social Capital in the Development of the Agro Nocerino-Sarnese   141
    Anna Bull and Matteo Frate

8   The Emerging of Different Patterns of Local Development in the
    Third Italy   175
    Luigi Burroni

Index   *191*

List of Figures

Figure 1.1	The music cluster chart	7
Figure 2.1	A general model of mixed embeddedness	37
Figure 2.2	The spatial distribution of purchasing linkages	39
Figure 2.3	The spatial distribution of sales linkages	39
Figure 3.1	Aspects of the Cambridge IT cluster	68
Figure 6.1	A circuit of social reproduction	120
Figure 7.1	Relationship between cross-cutting ties and governance	151
Figure 7.2	ANS during 1980s: perverse networking	158
Figure 7.3	ANS's dynamics	166
Figure 8.1	Measures of political economy in Veneto and in Tuscany during the 1980s	178
Figure 8.2	Quantitative weight of different intervention of political economy during the 1990s	178
Figure 8.3	Growth of labour contracts for type of contract, 1991-1995	182
Figure 8.4	Wage levels per dimension of firms, 1995	182
Figure 8.5	Local manufacturing systems per type of firms, 1996	184
Figure 8.6	Territorial concentration of manufacturing activities (value of the location quotient), 1996	184

List of Tables

Table 1.1	Firms in industrial sectors related to the music industry 1999 (SE-SIC 92, 5-digit level), number of firms by employment size	9
Table 1.2	Supporting institutions	15
Table 1.3	The course structure of the BA in music management programme at Kalmar University	16
Table 1.4	Main industry and workers' organisations in Sweden	17
Table 1.5	Dressing the Swedish music cluster for international success – the Porterian 'diamond' at work?	19
Table 2.1	Branch specialisation index of the labour force in plants with three employees or more, 1992	32
Table 2.2	Selected characteristics of industrial plants by main branches, 1992	33
Table 2.3	Enterprises by number of markets and per cent overcoming barriers	40
Table 3.1	Shares of biotechnology and services functions	62
Table 5.1	List of variables	100
Table 5.2	Summary of trust patterns	108
Table 6.1	Monetary networks and Local Currency Systems (LCSs)	118
Table 7.1	Population and education, 1991	155
Table 7.2	Population and labour market, 1991	156
Table 8.1	Unionization in Veneto and in Tuscany, 1981 and 1995	181
Table 8.2	Number of local manufacturing systems in the two regions and percentage of employees, 1991 and 1996	183
Table 8.3	Model of governance of the two regions	186
Table 8.4	GDP per inhabitants, 1995-1999 (Italy = 100)	187
Table 8.5	Extra-agricultural employment rate in 1996	187

List of Contributors

Theresa Aldridge, Department of Geography, Queen Mary College,
University of London, UK

Anna Bull, Department of European Studies and Modern Languages,
University of Bath, UK

Luigi Burroni, Department of Political Science and Sociology,
University of Florence, Italy

Philip Cooke, Centre for Advanced Studies,
Cardiff University, UK

Marina Della Giusta, Department of Economics,
University of Reading, UK

Matteo Frate, Department of European Studies and Modern Languages,
University of Bath, UK

Daniel Hallencreutz, Department of Social and Economic Geography,
Uppsala University, Sweden

Robert Huggins, Newidiem,
Cardiff, UK

Roger Lee, Department of Geography, Queen Mary College,
University of London, UK

Andrew Leyshon, School of Geography,
University of Nottingham, UK

Per Lundequist, Department of Social and Economic Geography,
Uppsala University, Sweden

Fergus Lyon, CEEDR,
Middlesex University, UK

Anders Malmberg, Department of Social and Economic Geography, Uppsala University, Sweden

Izhak Schnell, Department of Geography, Tel-Aviv University, Ramay-Aviv, Israel

Michael Sofer, Department of Geography, Bar-Ilan University, Ramat-Gan, Israel

Nigel Thrift, School of Geographical Sciences, University of Bristol, UK

Jane Tooke, Department of Geography, Queen Mary College, University of London, UK

Colin Williams, Department of Geography, University of Leicester, UK

Preface

This book has its origins in the Conference of the International Geographical Union Commission on Local Development held in Trento (Italy) in October 2000. It collects a selection of papers presented at the Conference, in revised form. The papers are developed on the basis of theoretical and empirical evidence, and support a plural interpretation of the institutions in local development. Institutions are considered both as containers of socio-economic organisation and as socio-economic practices. What is prominent for this book is that all the chapters acknowledge the contextualised and instituted nature of local development. Local development is a process which occurs in places and in inter-places relationships, mediated by recurrent practices of varied constitution, from legal rules, public policies, and technological standards, to informal habits, codes of conduct, organisational cultures, and semantic or ideological conventions. But, there are also institutional entities like local authorities, local structures of political parties, entrepreneurial and trade union organisations which support and dynamically maintain those practices over time. Human agents of production act through such institutions, rather than as blind followers of rules or as fully autonomous actors. To stress the importance of places doesn't mean to restrict the attention to local institutions. Local development is as much the product of local institutions as of supra-local ones such as the offices of regional, national and international organisations, and of 'institutions at a distance', such as national policy regimes, international regulations, and the rules and practices of remote business elites.

The book has three parts. Part I calls attention to the importance of local embeddedness for industrial competitiveness. The analytical framework draws on the cluster concept to address the role of institutions both as 'milieu' and as 'specialised institutions' for local development. Part II explores issues like trust, institutional design and the potential of Local Currency Systems (LCSs) in shaping collective action. Part III deals with the social capital and its role in moulding pathways of local development.

The editor would like to thank Professor Ash Amin, from Durham University, UK and Professor Silvio Goglio, from Trento University, Italy, who acted as conveners, the Department of Economics which provided financial support and the Faculty of Law which hosted the Conference. Thanks are also due to Biagio Santaniello, at the Laboratory of Territorial and Urban Research (LARTU) of the University and Polytechnic of Turin, who prepared the camera-ready copy.

Fabio Sforzi
Chairman of the IGU Commission on Local Development

PART I
PLACE-SPECIFICITY OF COMPETITIVENESS

Chapter 1

Local Embeddedness and International Competitiveness – The Case of the Swedish Music Cluster[1]

Daniel Hallencreutz, Per Lundequist and Anders Malmberg

Introduction

This chapter focuses on the Swedish music industry which in recent decades has put out a remarkable number of successful music products on the world market, including Abba, Roxette, Ace of Base, The Cardigans, Europe, Meja, Dr Alban, Pandora, Jenifier Brown, Robyn, and Dj Mendez to mention but a few. The recent international success of these and other 'acts' has made Sweden one of the largest net exporters of popular music in the world after the US and UK (Burnett, 1997; Forss, 1999).

When a country over a range of years manages to continuously produce a large number of globally successful products – as well as of related services such as production companies, music publishers, video producers etc. – in a market characterised by fierce competition, it may be assumed that this is no 'one hit wonder'. In the case of the Swedish music industry, we may rather assume that there exists a 'milieu' for the production of popular music, which contributes to the international competitiveness. The overall aim of this chapter is to explore the sources of competitive advantage of the Swedish music industry.

Theoretical Framework

Despite disciplinary variations, recent work in evolutionary economics (Dosi, 1988; Edquist, 1997; Lundvall, 1992; Nelson, 1993; Nelson and Winter, 1982) and business studies (Enright, 1993; Porter, 1990; Sölvell *et al.*, 1991) have recognised that long term industrial competitiveness cannot be reduced to a question of cost advantages and internal economies of scale. Rather it has to do with the innovative capacity and the ability of firms to continuously upgrade their knowledge base in the interaction with other actors in their daily operations. In this sense, a salient feature is the stress on the *systemic nature* of industrial production, i.e. that economic actors should be regarded as interrelated rather than atomistic (Håkansson, 1987; Lundvall, 1992; Nelson, 1993; Porter, 1990; Saxenian, 1994; Whitley, 1992).

Among several approaches to the systemic nature of industrial production, the cluster concept put forward by Michael Porter (1990) has been particularly influential in business, government and – perhaps to a lesser extent – academia during the last decade. Following Porter (2000, p. 16), '[c]lusters are geographic concentrations of interconnected companies, specialized suppliers, service providers, firms in related industries, and associated institutions (e.g., universities, standards agencies, trade associations) in a particular field that compete but also cooperate'. Moreover, the competitive advantage of an industrial cluster is according to Porter promoted or impeded by the existence and quality of the four interrelated determinants in the now well-known 'diamond model', namely, a) factor conditions, b) demand conditions, c) related and supporting industries, and d) firm strategy, structure and rivalry. Put differently, Porter 'embeds' firms and industries in the diamond model in order to explain their capability to create and sustain international competitiveness. Thus, as stated by Porter (2000, p. 21), a competitive cluster is 'the manifestation of a diamond at work'.

Having described the determinants of competitive advantage, Porter adds *government* as an external factor influencing the diamond. Government refers to how the public authorities of a country influence the four determinants through various regulations and policies. *Chance events* are seen to play a role in shaping the environment for competing in particular industries. More specifically, chance events have 'little to do with circumstances in a nation and often largely outside the power of firms' (Porter, 1990, p. 124). Examples of such events are major technological shifts, wars, surges of world demand etc. In the context of the music cluster, at least two chance events can be identified. Firstly, digital recording technology has changed the preconditions for music making and recording (Cunningham, 1998; Hesmondhalgh, 1998). Secondly, developments of communications technology (i.e. Internet) have transformed the traditional ways of releasing and distributing music (Hallencreutz and Lundequist, 2000a; Rao, 1999).

The Porterian cluster concept has been criticised by economic geographers, who have stressed that it is superficial, simplified and too much focused on tangibles. According to Storper (1997, p. 283), for example, Porter merely regurgitates the obvious outcome of economic success as observed in a number of places. Another pitfall is the tendency to cram 'a great diversity of experiences into a single formula'. Amin (1999), in turn, argues that the Porterian perspective fails to properly investigate the sources of competitive advantage, lying in the character of embedded local social and institutional arrangements.

Recently, however, Porter (1998) has pointed out the importance of considering the socio-economics of industrial clusters for explaining sources of competitive advantage. On this matter, Porter (2000, p. 21) has argued that the degree and nature of 'personal relationships, face-to-face communication, and networks of individuals and institutions that interact' heavily influence the competitive advantage of an industrial cluster. Furthermore, Porter (2000, p. 21) stresses that: 'Formal and informal organizing mechanisms and cultural norms often play a role in the functioning and development of clusters'. Thus, in accordance with Amin and Storper, Porter acknowledges the embedded nature of industrial production.

This chapter explores the sources of competitive advantage of the Swedish music cluster. This is accomplished by extending the Porterian (1990) cluster concept to include the Granovetterian notion (1985) of embeddedness as developed by Zukin and DiMaggio (1990).

Structure of the Chapter

The remainder of the chapter is structured into four main sections. Firstly, the Porterian (1990) cluster concept and the notion of embeddedness are elaborated upon in an attempt to conceptualise the music industry as an embedded cluster. Secondly, in accordance with the Porterian approach (cf. Sölvell *et al.*, 1991), the chapter explores the system for production of popular music in Sweden. This is accomplished by dividing the industry into four categories, where we first focus on the core sectors of the music cluster and then turn to the role played by customers, related industries and, supporting institutions. By using these categories as a template, this section provides a systematic description of the *clustered structure* of Swedish music industry. Thirdly, in order to identify the sources of competitive advantage, the chapter examines the social and institutional arrangements embedding the production system for popular music in Sweden. This is accomplished by discussing the link between cluster characteristics and the Porterian diamond model in the context of Zukin and DiMaggio's (1990) typology of various forms of embeddedness (i.e. cognitive, cultural, structural and political embeddedness). Finally, a brief concluding section draws together the line of argument of the chapter.

The analysis of the Swedish music industry presented in the chapter is based on data from business registers (Market Manager, UC-select, and Statistics Sweden). Furthermore, the empirical findings presented draw on 76 semi-structured face-to-face interviews with firms, workers' organisations, industry organisations and spokespersons for the industry undertaken between autumn 1999 and spring 2000. Each interview, on average, lasted one and a half hours. The interviews covered two main topics: the interviewee's career trajectory on the one hand and present occupation and assignments on the other. The purpose of the interviews was twofold. Firstly, to gather information concerning the creation and development of industry specific knowledge (codified and tacit), and, secondly, to map the degree and nature of personal relationships (intra- and inter-organisational). In addition to the statistical data and interviews, background literature such as professional journals (e.g. Musikindustrin and its predecessor Topp40), hagiographies (e.g. 'Cardigans: been it') as well as articles in newspapers and weekly publications were important sources of information.

As already implied, the concept 'popular music' recurs frequently in this chapter. This concept is, as Middleton (1990, p. 3) puts it, 'riddled with complexities'. In this paper a broad definition has been adopted, including genres such as pop, rock, soul, funk, rap, reggae, techno, r'n'b, heavy metal etc. This definition derives mainly from the conception of popular music as music embracing genres that are recorded, mass distributed and commercially viable. Moreover, we have included genres which are commonly financed by free enterprise rather than public funding, as is the case with most art/classical music and to some extent jazz (Burnett, 1996, p. 37). Nevertheless, jazz, for example, has in reality a market share large enough to be considered as 'popular music' in Sweden whereas 'Goa trance', one of several sub-techno genres, is much more exclusive. Nonetheless, Goa trance is probably more likely to be defined as 'popular music' in an inquiry regarding definitions of popular music.

The Music Industry Conceptualised as an Embedded Industrial Cluster

There exists a number of different readings and interpretations of the cluster concept (Austrian, 2000; Enright, 1996; Feser and Bergman, 2000; Gordon and McCann, 2000). However, they differ in degree rather than in kind. In this matter, Enright (1996, p. 191) points out that 'terms with somewhat different meanings are sometimes used interchangeably, creating confusion and a need for more precise definitions'. One difference in accentuation concerns to what extent a set of interrelated and agglomerated industries must be competitive, preferably internationally competitive, in order to be defined as a cluster. The literature on clusters differs, furthermore, regarding the suggested appropriate geographical level of analysis. What degree of localisation should we demand from an industrial system before it can be regarded as an industrial cluster? Another difference concerns the demarcation of clusters when mapping linkages and dependencies. In this context, some scholars have focused primarily on input-output relations between buyers and sellers whilst others have incorporated related industries and supporting institutions (cf. Austrian, 2000; Enright, 1996).

According to Porter (1990), competitive advantage is created and sustained through localised processes – usually linked through vertical or horizontal relationships – in a firm's or an industry's home base (nationally or regionally). In order to capture such relationships, Porter (1990, p. 287) has developed an analytical framework by dividing industrial clusters into four broad core sectors, namely 1) primary goods, 2) specialised inputs into these goods, 3) machinery and other equipment used in making the primary goods, and 4) services associated with the goods or their production. In addition to these four core sectors, three other elements are included in an industrial cluster: consumers, related industries and supporting institutions (Sölvell *et al.*, 1991; Porter, 2000).

In the case of the music industry, we have identified five categories of *primary goods*, namely (cf. Forss, 1999):

- phonograms;
- published music;
- live performances;
- copyrights;
- music productions.

Turning to the *speciality inputs*, we have chosen to regard these as consisting of the human capital involved in the actual music creation, i.e. the abilities and skills of composers, lyricists, musicians, artists etc. As concerns the third core sector, *producers of machinery and equipment*, they include providers of studio equipment, music instruments, CD-pressing technology etc. Finally, the *associated services* comprise a great number of services directly supporting with the music industry (e.g. agents, managers, recording studios/engineers, publishers, distributors, and industry organisations). This structure is presented in Figure 1.1.

It can be seen, then, that the production of popular music involves a complex chain of operations. When a final consumer purchases a phonogram, it is the result of a chain of operations, extending from aesthetic production, through recording, to the marketing, distribution and finally, consumption of the goods (cf. the concept of production channels as put forward by Doeringer and Terkla, 1996). This production chain is, in turn – like all economic activity – embedded in a wider institutional context (Granovetter, 1985).

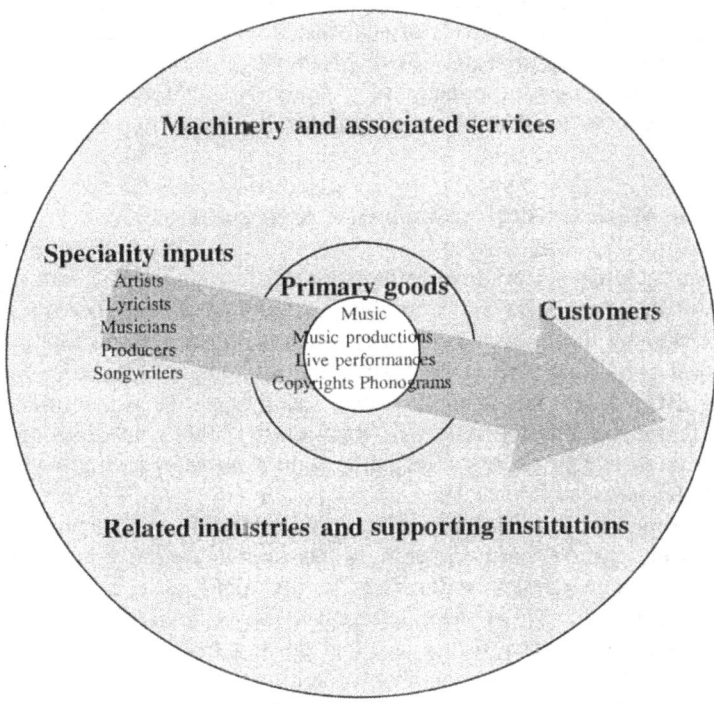

Figure 1.1 The music cluster chart

Discussing the concept of embeddedness, Zukin and DiMaggio (1990) distinguish between four forms of embeddedness:

- *Cognitive embeddedness* can be described as how different kinds of sources and consequences of cognition shape the behaviour (e.g. rationality vs. bounded rationality) of individuals and collective actors (e.g. organisations and firms).
- *Cultural embeddedness* refers to how shared understandings and meanings (beliefs, norms, conventions etc.) influence the form of organisational activity, structures and process.
- *Structural embeddedness* relates to the notion that on-going inter-actor relationships embed all economic activity.
- *Political embeddedness* refers to how power structures in an economy shape organisations, inter-organisational relationships, organisation strategies and outcomes.

However, when discussing these embeddedness dimensions, it is important to point out that they 'are not distinct kinds of embeddedness but rather different abstract dimensions of embeddedness which may actually all be involved in one concrete embeddedness relation' (Oinas, 1998, p. 53).

In the context of this chapter, it is important to acknowledge that embeddedness may be observed at various levels of analysis: from interpersonal relationships to industrial networks (Dacin *et al.*, 1999). Moreover, following Granovetter (1985) and other embeddedness proponents (e.g. Grabher, 1993; Zukin and DiMaggio, 1990) embeddedness is not by nature geographically limited to local relations.

The Swedish Music Cluster: An Empirical Assessment

There is no specific sector directly corresponding to the music industry in the Standard for European Industrial Classification (SIC 92, NACE Rev. 1). However, there are a number of sectors which, when taken together, seem to capture the four broad core sectors identified in the Swedish music cluster outlined in Figure 1.1. Following SIC/NACE classification, twelve sectors have been identified as being related to the music industry. All in all, there exist 15,000 companies operating in Sweden in these twelve sectors – including limited companies, trading companies and private businesses (Table 1.1).

It is important to point out, however, that many of these companies should be excluded, as they have either been wrongly classified or are not related to the music industry at all (e.g. painters and writers in SIC 9231 or companies producing talking books in SIC 2214). Moreover, there are associated services such as accounting, marketing, advertising etc., that are not included in the selection of sectors in Table 1.1, despite the fact that some firms in these sectors work primarily or exclusively within the music industry.

Approximately 2,500 of the firms in Table 1.1 are limited companies. A closer examination of these firm's articles of association, board of directors, homepages on the Internet etc. as well as list of members for industry organisations, show that roughly 1,500 of these can be defined as belonging to the four core sectors 'composing' the music cluster. Forss (1999) has estimated the overall employment in the Swedish music industry (including firms other than limited companies as well as self-employment) to be some 10,000 people.

Table 1.1 Firms in industrial sectors related to the music industry 1999 (SE-SIC 92, 5-digit level), number of firms by employment size

SIC 92		Number of employees						
		0	1-4	5-9	10-19	20-199	200+	Total
22140	Publishers of sound recordings	907	230	21	9	13	-	1.180
22150	Other publishers	434	165	35	16	7	-	657
22310	Industry for the reproduction of sound recording	48	6	3	-			57
24650	Industry for prepared unrecorded media	28	13	1	-	-	-	42
36300	Industry for musical instruments	122	23	7	3		-	155
51433	Wholesale (records, tapes, CDs and videotapes)	127	47	8	19	14	-	215
52453	Stores for records and videotapes	325	167	25	5	4	-	526
52454	Stores for music, instruments and music scores	271	120	19	1	2	-	413
52614	Mail order houses for books and media goods	73	6	3	2	3	-	87
92310	Performing artists, producers of artistic and literary works	8.865	901	85	19	34	-	9.904
92320	Theatre and concert hall companies etc.	459	253	59	37	44	7	859
92340	Dancing and other entertainment establishments	452	139	25	20	3	-	639
	Total	12.111	2070	291	131	124	7	14.734

Source: The official business register, Statistics Sweden.

Almost half of the 1,500 limited companies at focus here are located in the Stockholm region. This confirms the general picture that the music industry has a high proclivity to agglomerate in major urban areas (Hesmondhalgh, 1996; Scott 1999a, 1999b). However, a survey of business registers (Market Manager; UC-Select; Statistics Sweden) shows that a great variety of firms in the music cluster are located outside the Stockholm region. Hultsfred and Sundsvall are two cases in point. A common denominator explaining the origins and growth of these local agglomerations is the proactivity of real enthusiasts and to some extent local policy-makers.

The origins of the Hultsfred agglomeration date back to the 'Hultsfred festival' initiated in the mid 1980s. Initially being a fairly small festival, arranged by a few local real enthusiasts, the reputation and organisation of the Hultsfred festival have gradually grown. Today the 'Hultsfred festival' is the largest in Sweden (27,000 visitors in 2000) and by far the most internationally renowned. In tandem with the growth of the festival, a number of smaller companies operating in the music industry have established themselves in the tiny town of Hultsfred in the southeast of Sweden. Moreover, local authorities, educational institutions, third sector bodies etc., have promoted a number of educational programmes, most notable are the PIR programme (Performance In Rock), the DMD programme (Digital Music Distribution) and the BA-programme in music management (Jansson, 2000).

The Sundsvall agglomeration, in turn, can be traced back to a lively post-punk scene in the late 1970s in combination with the emergence of an institutionally thick support structure for music business in 1990s. According to Melin (1999) around 300 full-time jobs in Sundsvall are directly or indirectly related to the music industry. Of these 300 full-time jobs almost 20 per cent are accounted for by the self-employed (i.e. approximately 60 firms).

The agglomerations of Hultsfred and Sundsvall are not unique examples of popular music production milieus outside the Stockholm region. The Swedish music cluster is comprised by a great number of local agglomerations of music production (e.g. Eskilstuna, Lund, Malmö, Skellefteå, Umeå, and Örebro). Moreover, it is noteworthy that a great number of the internationally successful Swedish artists and groups initially originate from other places than the Stockholm region (e.g. Roxette from Halmstad, the Cardigans from Jönköping, Kent from Eskilstuna, the Wannadies from Skellefteå, and Jennifer Brown, and Ace of Base from Göteborg).

The Core Sectors of the Swedish Music Cluster

As noted above, the purchasing of a phonogram is the final link in a chain of operations, spanning from the aesthetic production, through recording, to the marketing, distribution and finally, consumption of the goods. This chain differs radically from the traditional uni-directional linear, or 'Fordist', production model. Negus (1992, p. 46) expresses the complexity of music production by stating that 'the sounds and images of pop can have multiple points of origin and may be altered considerably as different people become involved in the acquisition, recording, marketing and promotion of artists'.

Another prominent feature of this complex production chain is a general trend towards an increased division of labour. This is manifest in the fact that services previously undertaken by 'the majors' and larger 'independents' have come to be outsourced in order to spread risks and 'seeking out innovation from outside the company' (Hesmondhalgh, 1996, p. 481). Moreover, this outsourcing tendency has resulted in an increasingly vertically disintegrated production organisation that has enhanced the presence of small independents and created a labour market for project-based and freelancing jobs (Scott, 1999b). It is important to note that alongside this reinforced vertical disintegration, the 'majors' – i.e. the TNCs that dominate the global record industry – have tended to strengthen their control over several central functions, such as financial control and distribution (Hesmondhalgh, 1996; Negus, 1999; Sadler, 1997; Scott, 1999a). Thus, the five 'majors' dominating the global music industry are Bertelsmann AC (headquartered in Germany), The Seagram Company Ltd. (Canada), Sony Corporation (Japan), EMI Group Plc. (UK), and Time-Warner Inc. (US). These five giant transnational companies encompass a number activities ranging from leisure, entertainment, media, consumer electronics and manufacturing.

In the following subsections, we examine the core sectors (i.e. producers of primary goods, speciality inputs, machinery and equipment and associated services) of popular music cluster in Sweden.

Producers of primary products All of the five majors act locally in Sweden through fully owned subsidiaries. Since the early 1980s these corporations have strengthened their position in Sweden by acquiring a number of the largest independent record companies (e.g. Metronome, Elektra, Sonet, and Polar). Despite this trend of take-overs, there are still many independents operating in Sweden (e.g. MNW Record Group, Bonnier Music Group, and, Marianne Records). Burnett (1996) and Malm (1997) have estimated the number of record companies in Sweden to approximately 150 and 250, respectively. These estimations correspond fairly well with official business registers (Market Manager, Statistics Sweden, UC-Select) showing a Figure of 113 limited companies.

Turning to publishing companies, the Swedish Music Publisher's Association (SMFF) lists 69 members, which is the actual number of active firms. The majority of these companies are headquartered in the Stockholm region. In terms of music publishing, two intertwined trends may be identified. Firstly, there has been a great number of mergers and acquisitions of publishers by the majors and larger independents since the 1970s. Secondly, there is a tendency amongst publishers to diversify through incorporating segments traditionally performed by record companies such as A&R (Artist and Repertoire management) and promotion.

An apparent feature of the Swedish music industry during the 1990s is the growing number of internationally successful production companies, such as Cheiron, Sprinkler and Murlyn Music. Cheiron, for example, is a company run by a group of producers operating a studio in Stockholm. Cheiron has not only produced a large share of the internationally successful Swedish music acts (such as Ace of Base, Robyn and Papa Dee) but has also produced, remixed or written material for artists like The Backstreet Boys, Michael Jackson, Britney Spears, Celine Dion, Bon Jovi, and N'Sync.

The fourth primary product in the cluster, live performance, involves a dozen concert and live music entertainment producers/promotors operating in the Swedish market. EMA Telstar (since 1999 affiliated to the US company SFX Entertainment) dominates the Swedish market. Although EMA Telstar is by far the largest actor in terms of market share, it should be observed that there are a number of small concert producers operating in the Swedish market (e.g. United Stage and Nöjet AB).

To sum up, then, the primary products part of the Swedish popular music cluster displays some paradoxical tendencies. The global majors have to a large extent acquired Swedish record companies and music publishers. However, it seems as if companies like Stockholm Records (affiliated to Universal) have managed to use the global marketing organisation of their parent company to export music produced and recorded in Sweden. Furthermore, there is evidence of continuous new firm formation manifested by a growing number of independent record companies, publishing companies, production companies etc. Strong local dynamism seems, in this case, to go hand in hand with dominating foreign ownership.

Speciality inputs The artistic labour market in Sweden involves approximately 10,000 individuals. The actors that we regard as the localised specialised inputs to the Swedish music cluster, i.e. professional musicians, lyrics writers, composers, producers etc., account for some 3,000 of these (Forss, 1999). Along with a high number of amateur musicians, these professionals constitute the basis for the speciality inputs, or in other words, the creative backbone of the industry.

As outlined above, there has been a tendency towards an increase of project-based and freelance works in the music industry during recent decades. One well-known feature that the music industry shares with other cultural industries and sports etc., is that the distribution of income across the set of actors is extremely uneven, referred to sometimes as the 'superstar theory', meaning that in these type of sectors, the winner, as in the ABBA refrain, 'takes it all'. In other words, a few artists do extremely well, while most others have to struggle hard to make a living. Thus, in considering the workforce of artistic labour markets, Menger (1999) has identified a set of characteristics that appear to coincide with the Swedish music industry, e.g. high rates of self-employment, unemployment, constrained underemployment, multiple job holding (see also Hallencreutz and Lundequist, 2000b; Negus, 1992).

Whether the source of specialty input, in the form of talented creators of popular music is particularly rich in Sweden, such that this is a major explanation to the competitive success of the cluster, is a matter of debate. We will return to this issue in the final section of the chapter.

Machinery and equipment The core sector entitled 'machinery and equipment' embraces producers of CD-pressing technology, musical instruments, studio equipment etc. This core sector is relatively small in Sweden with the exception of CD-pressing plants. Most of these plants are relatively small and focus on the Swedish market. However, a few internationally competitive companies producing machinery for the pressing plant industry are located in Sweden (e.g. Toolex Alfa and M2 Engineering). In the case of the production of musical instruments, Sweden has a long tradition in the artisanal production of pianos, organs, accordions, strings, and hurdy-gurdies. Since the 1960s, however, most of the production units have been closed down or relocated to other countries. As for the production of more 'modern' musical instrument and studio equipment, Clavia DMI – founded in the beginning of the 1980s in Stockholm – is one of the few. According to our findings so far, this part of the cluster does not seem to be a major contributor to the overall success of the Swedish music industry.

Associated services Associated services are supporting all the different parts of the cluster. Firstly, as regards associated services supporting the *speciality inputs*, one tendency in Sweden during the last decade has been the growth of business services, particularly artist agencies and management companies. However, this growth is still in its infancy in Sweden compared to more 'mature' music-producing countries like the US and UK.

Secondly, associated services supporting the *producers of primary goods* embraces a great variety of sectors such as printing, video, advertising, marketing, photography, packaging, graphical design, festivals, venues, providers of stage equipment (spotlights, backdrops etc.), catering, security, transportation. In video production, for example, Swedish companies have been internationally competitive during recent years. Directors such as Jonas Åkerlund's and Bo Johan Renck's (Stakka Bo) are internationally renowned through productions for Madonna, Metallica, Iggy Pop, Prodigy, Suede, U2 etc.

Finally, the distribution of phonograms in Sweden is dominated by the Association of Gramophone Suppliers (GLF) which has ten members – the four majors, their subsidiaries and the MNW Records Group. In addition to these members, another dozen distributors/wholesalers are connected to this system.

All in all, when considering the Swedish music clusters four core sectors, one may identify three prominent features. Firstly, it appears that the cluster is highly competitive with respect to the specialty inputs. In this context, it is interesting to note that production companies seem to constitute the most competitive – and growing – part of the cluster. Secondly, there are indicative features suggesting that the competitiveness of many firms (record companies, music publishers etc.) is, at least partly, explained by a high number of skilled staff with international networks. Thirdly, it is interesting to note that the cluster consists of a number of internationally competitive associated services, most notably video producers.

Customers, Related Industries and Supporting Institutions

In addition to the four core sectors outlined above, *customers, related industries and supporting institutions* are central components of the Swedish music cluster.

When considering customers, one may distinguish between domestic and international consumers of records, concerts, music etc. Despite a small market in Sweden, there are two distinctive home-base features, namely, the presence of sophisticated customers and a stable level of home demand. The mechanisms contributing to these home-base features are anticipatory buyer needs created by the fact that Sweden has been regarded as a 'pilot market' for the majors. There exist a number of examples indicating that Swedish record consumers have been early adopters of new music. Hence, many international artists reached great success in Sweden on an early stage in their career, such as Jimmy Hendrix, Bruce Springsteen, Roxy Music, and David Bowie, well before they made it big in other countries. Moreover, Sweden has not only a stable but one of the highest per capita consumption rates in the world (Lilliestam, 1998).

As concerns *related industries*, the music cluster is, of course, more or less interrelated to a number of sectors of which media, fashion and consumer electronics are the most prominent. Thus, it may be argued that the music cluster is part of a greater 'evententertainment' cluster in Sweden. One prominent example of the music cluster's interrelatedness with the 'evententertainment' cluster is the recent growth of companies in the interface between the music industry and Internet companies (e.g. Mediacord.com, Volflow.com, Deo.com etc.).

Turning to supporting institutions, they can be divided into four main sub-groups, namely 1) public authorities, 2) third sector organisations, 3) public educational institutions and 4) industry and worker's organisations (Table 1.2).

Public authorities The main authority for cultural policy in Sweden is the National Council for Cultural Affairs. One may divide the financial support to musical activities from the National Council for Cultural Affairs into three different categories of grants. Firstly, the Council allocates government grants directly to national cultural institutions, e.g. Royal Swedish Opera and The Royal Dramatic Theatre of Sweden. Secondly, public bodies such as local authorities and county councils receive grants for financial support to musical activities (e.g. 'Länsmusiken'). Thirdly, there are a number of grants targeted towards independent music groups (e.g. audio recording) and concert arrangements. In relation to popular music, however, Swedish governments have traditionally passed it over and prioritised other genres (classical music, folk music, jazz etc.). This can be exemplified by the fact that the financial support to audio recording and independent pop and rock groups has accounted for no more than ten per cent of the Council for Cultural Affairs's total support to phonogram production/support to independent groups.

Third sector organisations There are a number of third sector organisations supporting musical activities in Sweden. In general terms, these organisations can be divided into two groups, namely providers of musical education and local culture associations.

Table 1.2 Supporting institutions

	National	Regional	Local
Public authorities	Ministry of Culture	County administrative board	
	Swedish National Council for Cultural Affairs		
	The Federation of Swedish County Councils	County Councils	
	The Swedish Association of Local Authorities		Local Authorities
Third sector organisations	Kontaktnätet (a national organisation for voluntary culture associations)		Local voluntary culture associations
	Swedish National Council of Adult Education		Educational associations
			Folkhögskolor 'Folk high-school'
Public educational institutions	College of music		Municipal school of music
	Departments of musicology		Musical education in primary school
	College/University programmes in music management		Aesthetic secondary school programmes
Industry and workers' organisations	E.g. STIM, ExMS and IFPI		

In terms of *providers of musical education* there exists a system of adult educational centres in Sweden called Folkhögskolor or 'folk high schools'. They offer musical education, ranging from short courses in, for example, afro-cuban percussion, to longer courses such as two-year cantorial programmes. There exist some 150 Folkhögskolor of which two thirds are run by various popular movements and associations (e.g. NGOs). County councils manage the remaining schools, thus making them a part of the public educational system (see below). Approximately 30 per cent of the folk high schools in Sweden offer different types of music courses. In addition to the 'folk high schools', there exist a dozen study associations in Sweden providing musical education. These study associations provide courses in their local affiliates. In total, 350,000 study circles are arranged annually. Approximately 50 per cent of these are related to cultural activates, e.g. music, art, and dance. The density of affiliates on a local level is high. There are at least a few study associations present in each of the 286 municipalities in Sweden. Thus, a rough estimation indicates that approximately 100,000 'amateur' musicians participate in popular music related study circles (Lilliestam, 1998).

Local culture associations are the second type of third sector organisations. It is difficult to estimate the actual number of such organisations since they span from short-term parties to formalised membership organisations. According to the national organisation of voluntary organisations ('Kontaktnätet') there are 155 voluntary associations in Sweden of which a great number are in music related activities, for example arranging music concerts.

In addition to these venues, there is a Swedish phenomenon called 'Folkpark' or 'Folkets park' – local amusement parks offering live music, theatre, dancing etc. – with its origin in the Swedish popular labour movement in the 19th century. Until the late 1980s, these parks played an important role as sites for concerts of both professional and non-established artists. However, the increased competition in the 1990s with festivals and 'event tours', in which a few popular artists share the bill have made it less attractive for established artists to perform in the 'parks'.

Public educational institutions There are three different kinds of musical education in Sweden, namely higher educational institutions, musical education in primary and secondary school, and municipal schools of music.

In terms of *higher education* there exist a dozen music related academic departments of which six are colleges of music. In addition to these departments, the late 1990s has witnessed the establishment of a number of music management programmes at the university level. One case in point is the three-year programme at the University of Kalmar (Table 1.3). The purpose of this programme is to educate students interested in pursuing careers as managers, agents, market managers etc.

Table 1.3 The course structure of the BA in music management programme at Kalmar University

Year one	Year two	Year three
Introduction to music business	Production of music	Business studies
Business studies	Business studies	
• Organization	• Online marketing and e-commerce	• Marketing and communications
• Marketing		• Managing and marketing of consumer services
• Finance	• Business relations	
• Accounting	• Organizational theory and management	• Dissertation
Music Production	Law	Individual course (e.g. a language)

A second component of the public educational system is *musical education in primary and secondary school*. Besides compulsory education in music, several schools offer aesthetic programmes specialised on music education. The third category of musical education is the *'Municipal schools of music'*. These schools provide subsidised musical education for students up to an age of 18 years. Taking courses at Municipal schools of music is common in Sweden. According to the Swedish Association of Local Authorities, some 340,000 children in primary school (more than 30 per cent of all children in the age group), participate in music education at the Municipal schools. In addition to these three kinds of musical education, there are local labour market programmes providing vocational education and training related to media, music and IT.

Industry and workers' organisations In Sweden, there exists a wide array of industry organisations and workers' organisations (i.e. unions and professional associations) supporting the music industry (Table 1.4). In addition to the organisations outlined in Table 1.4, there are also two bodies promoting Swedish music in general. Export Music Sweden (ExMS) encourages and co-ordinates Swedish participation in international trade fairs, seminars, festivals and other activities for the international promotion of Swedish music. ExMS was formed in 1993 by the major supporting bodies within the Swedish music industry, i.e. IFPI, SOM, SAMI, SMF and STIM (see Table 1.4). The Swedish Music Information Centre is funded by the Swedish performing rights society (STIM). The purpose of this organisation is to promote copyright-protected music in close collaboration with lyrics writers, composers and music publishers affiliated to STIM.

Table 1.4 Main industry and workers' organisations in Sweden

Core sector	Supporting organisations
Composers, artists etc. (i.e. speciality input)	The Swedish Society of Popular Music Composers (SKAP)* Swedish Performing Rights Society (STIM)* Swedish Musicians's Union (SFM) Swedish Artists' and Musicians' Interest Organisation (SAMI)* Society of Swedish Composers (FST)
Record companies, publishers etc. (i.e. producers of primary goods)	International Federation of the Phonographic Industry (IFPI)* Independent Swedish Record Producers' Association (SOM) The Swedish Music Publishers' Association (SMFF) Swedish Impresarios' Association (SVIMP) Swedish Music Festivals (SMF)
Distribution	The Association of Gramophone Suppliers (GLF)

* These organisations are also collecting societies.

All in all, production of popular music in Sweden is supported by a plethora of institutions. It is worthy to note in this context, however, that the rise of a competitive cluster has taken place without any deliberate public policy interventions. In terms of policy interventions, it has predominantly been a question of funding and subsidising cultural and educational institutions rather than supporting popular music production as an economic activity.

The Dynamics and Embeddedness of the Swedish Music Cluster

In this paper we have so far described the cluster characteristics of the Swedish music industry. Clearly, the empirical findings presented above confirm the geographical underpinnings that Porter (2000, p. 16) emphasizes as defining an industrial cluster, namely 'specialized suppliers, service providers, firms in related industries, and associated institutions'. However in order to explain the sources of competitive advantage it is necessary to identify the mechanisms that explain the origins, growth and sustainability a cluster.

Diamond Dynamics?

Table 1.5 outlines mechanisms that can explain the sources of competitive advantage in the Swedish music industry, drawing on the empirical findings presented in the paper. In addition to these findings the mechanisms identified are based on a survey of recurring statements by industry spokesmen, music journalists, researchers on popular music, and policy-makers concerning common explanations for the international success of the music industry in Sweden (see also Hallencreutz and Lundequist, 1998; Hallencreutz *et al.*, 2000).

The following provides a tentative discussion concerning various mechanisms that appear to have created and/or supported these home-base features. When considering *factor conditions*, the music cluster exhibits three prominent home-base features – a high level of human knowledge resources, appropriate infrastructure for musical production and capital resources. The Swedish music cluster also exhibits appropriate 'infrastructure' supporting potentially professional musicians and artists. There is a good access to rehearsal premises, a high level of instrument provision and accessible new technology mark this. *Demand conditions* refer to the characteristics of domestic demand for the core sectors composing an industrial cluster. In terms of demand conditions, there are two distinctive home-base features, namely, the presence of sophisticated customers and a stable level of home demand. Turning to *related and supporting industries*, they include firms supporting the producers of primary goods. As demonstrated, Sweden has numerous internationally competitive supporting activities ranging from CD-plants and packaging to studios and video producers. As concerns *firm strategy, structure and rivalry*, it refers to the conditions governing how firms are created, organised, and managed, as well as the nature of domestic rivalry. Regarding this key determinant there are a number of mechanisms, which seem to be crucial to consider in order to explain the home-base features contributing to the recent success of the Swedish music industry. Examples of such mechanisms are high levels of innovative tacit-knowledge exchange and new business formation.

Table 1.5 Dressing the Swedish music cluster for international success – the Porterian 'diamond' at work?

The four diamond determinants, government, and chance	Home base features	Mechanisms creating/supporting home base features
Factor conditions	High level of human knowledge recourses	• Educational institutions and non-profit associations (specialised schools, training establishments etc.) • High exposure to English (no subtitling, strong presence of Anglo-American entertainment etc.) • Role models ('the ABBA-effect') • A widespread musical interest (amateur bands, choirs etc.) • Popular labour movement ('folkörelserna'), i.e. tradition of community corporate practices
	Appropriate infra-structure for musical production	• High rehearsal premises density • High level of instrument provision amongst amateurs • High accessibility of new technology
Firm strategy, structure and domestic rivalry	Export capability	• Open labour market and dense social networks facilitating knowledge inter-exchange and other externalities amongst firms
	Learning propensity	• Lead firms (majors) proving distribution, finance, and knowledge pools
	Innovative tacit-knowledge exchange	• Combination of intense competition, collaborative practices, factor attraction, and a capability of adapting and transforming cultural expressions
	Design capabilities	• Tradition of commercially viable industrial design transferred into the music industry
	New business formation	• High levels of spin-offs, internal diversification and outsourcing
Demand conditions	Sophisticated customers	• Anticipatory buyer needs (mass market and business to business)
	Stable level of home demand	• High per capita consumption
Related and supporting industries	Internationally competitive related and supporting industries	• Anticipatory buyer needs (mass market and business to business) combined with stable demand and sophisticated customers
	Supportive workers' associations	• A plethora of industry and workers organisations encompassing the music industry
	Extensive music festival activity	• Tradition of 'folkparks', public subsidies, local music club activities
Government (multilevel)	Supportive state regulations and policies	• Long period of economic growth in tandem with the evolvement of the Swedish welfare state • Domestic rivalry and export success channelling government policies • Positive and changing view amongst politicians on cultural-products and design intensive industries as important for the economy
Change	'Ubiquitification' of music-related technology	• Transformation from analogue to digital technology. Increasing accessibility through lowering production costs
	New cultural impulses	• Migration
	New medias and channels, e.g. internet and MTV	• Cross-sectorial impulses

An Embedded Cluster?

Below we turn to the forms of embeddedness identified by Zukin and DiMaggio (1990) and examine what we consider to be the most prominent mechanisms that appear to explain the sources of competitive advantage of the Swedish music industry. The following discussion makes no difference between cultural and cognitive embeddedness, as there are great 'difficulties in drawing distinctions between [these] aspects of (...) embeddedness' (Dacin et al., 1999; see also DiMaggio, 1997).

Cultural and cognitive embeddedness One may identify four kinds of cultural and cognitive embeddedness that have contributed to the emergence and sustenance of an internationally competitive music cluster in Sweden. Firstly, there is a long tradition of 'organised' amateur music such as choirs, orchestras, musician's rallies etc. This tradition is of course by no means a unique Swedish phenomenon. It is interesting to note, however, that this tradition of playing music has survived into the 'era' of pop music. Playing music is a widespread hobby amongst youths (Lilliestam, 1998). This is demonstrated by the fact that since the 1980s, playing popular music is by far the most common choice in the local study circles that is provided by the Swedish study associations (Statistics Sweden, 1999).

Secondly, Sweden has since the 1950s been culturally orientated towards the US and UK. This has contributed to a relatively high knowledge of the English language through compulsory education in primary and secondary school, and a high exposure to spoken English, due to the tradition of not dubbing Anglo-American entertainment (Burnett, 1996). Moreover, this cultural orientation has manifested itself in a high market share for American and British entertainment in Sweden such as soap operas, movies, literature etc. In terms of literature, this is demonstrated by the fact that Anglo-American literature accounts for approximately 75 per cent of translations into Swedish (Statistics Sweden, 2000).

Thirdly, alongside domestic rivalry, a broad consensus seems to exist across the music cluster regarding the overall objective of marketing/promoting Swedish music and the music cluster as an internationally competitive brand. One example of this consensus is the establishment of *Export Music Sweden* (ExMS), the main organisation for promoting Swedish music internationally.

Finally, as a result of the export success, there has been a shift in policy-makers' attitudes to the relevance of cultural-products and design intensive industries for the economy. Traditionally, the popular music industry has been viewed as an 'ugly duckling' by policy-makers, venture capitalists, industrialists etc. since it has been regarded as non-serious and insignificant for the economy. However, this view appears to have shifted radically as a result of export success during the 1990s. This is, for example, marked by increased efforts to establish educational programmes ranging from music management to music engineering.

Structural embeddedness It is widely accepted (Scott, 1999b; Hirsch, 1972; Negus, 1992; Peterson, 1976) that the industrial organisation of cultural-product industries such as music, film, fashion etc. can be depicted as:

complex networks of workers within firms, linked together by tightly wrought networks of transactions between firms, in which many different hands are brought to bear on products as they go through the process of conception, fabrication and final embellishment (Scott, 1999b, p. 809).

The Swedish music industry confirms this depiction, since it is characterised by close inter- and intra-firm relationships boosted by dense social networks, stretching the boundaries of firms and organisations (Hallencreutz and Lundequist, 2000b).

Structural embeddedness is important to consider for explaining the competitive advantage of the Swedish music cluster. More specifically, the existence of dense interpersonal networks has facilitated knowledge inter-exchange amongst actors involved in the music cluster. Moreover, these networks have contributed to various collaborative practices such as joint projects at international fairs (e.g. Midem and Popkomm) and lobbying for standards in copyright law. The learning capability of the music industry has been further strengthened by a high staff turnover between various sub-sectors composing the music cluster. This cross-sectorial turnover has, for example, recently resulted in new business concepts in the interface between the music industry and Internet companies (e.g. Musicbay.com, Famestudios.com, and Popwire.com).

An interesting question in this context is, of course, how the evolvement and continuity of the structural embeddedness characterising the Swedish music industry can be explained. Drawing on empirical findings arising from our interview survey and a survey of professional journals, it appears that five features can be identified for explaining the evolvement and continuity of this structural embeddedness:

- Key people acting as 'industry mentors', network brokers, and role models,
- Intra- and cross-sectorial joint career trajectories as well as interlocking directorates boosting knowledge inter-exchange and shared conventions,
- A mutual desire for creating music and develop new business ideas and organisations rather than economic success *per se*,
- Lead firms acting as knowledge pools and nexuses of social networks,
- Meeting points (e.g. industry organisations, arrangements, clubs and fairs) that strengthen dynamic loose coupling and development of weak ties.

One way of visualising these five features is to examine individual career paths of key players in the music cluster. Examples of such key players are, to name a few, Per Gessle (Roxette/Tom Bone Music), Ola Håkansson (CEO, Stockholm Records), Sanji Tandan (CEO, Warner Music Sweden AB), Tomas Johansson (CEO, EMA Telstar), and Dag Häggqvist. In the following, we have chosen to focus on one of those players, namely Dag Häggqvist – today CEO of Gazell Records, and CEO of the Swedish branch of IFPI (International Federation of the Phonogram Industry). Häggqvist is also board member of a number of companies, most notably Deo.com – a music related Internet portal – and MNW Records Group; today the largest Swedish independent.

Career Paths and Social Networks of Key People: An Example

Dag Häggqvist launched his career at the age of 15 in the mid 1950s by setting up a company for importing jazz music. In 1957, he acquired the jazz label Gazell from the record company Sonet. In terms of Dag Häggqvist's career, it appears as the Gazell deal played an important role in a number of ways. Firstly, the acquisition of Gazell made it possible to move into the area of producing and releasing records. Secondly, one of Gazell's earliest record productions resulted in a lifelong business companionship with the pianist Rune Öfwerman, at present CEO of Gazell Music. Thirdly, it was the starting point for a business relationship with Sonet's founders Gunnar Bergström and Sven Lindholm. During the coming two decades, Häggqvist, Bergström and Lindholm together developed Sonet into one of the major independent Scandinavian record and publishing companies, an association that that continued until Polygram acquired Sonet in 1991 (Polygram, in turn, was acquired by Universal in the late 1990s). Moreover, Häggqvist played an important role in the late 1960s for the establishment of the Swedish branch of IFPI (International Federation of the Phonogram Industry) as well as the development of an annual music award called 'Grammisgalan'.

Too much of an independent spirit, Häggqvist left his position as chairman at Sonet and re-activated Gazell 1993, with the approval of Polygram. Or in the words of Häggqvist himself:

I decided to return to where I felt that I really belonged...to run an independent record company (Interview with Häggqvist, 1999).

During the years at Sonet, Häggqvist made a number of licensing and signing deals and developed himself as an internationally renowned name in the record industry.

Luckily, the label [Gazell] had a good reputation, and many of the publishers, such as the company Paul Simon Songs, wanted to continue to work with me when I left Sonet for reactivating Gazell. We also started to develop our own catalogue (Interview with Häggqvist, 1999).

In terms of Häggqvist's signing deals, one interesting example in the context of structural embeddedness is the deal in the mid 1960s with 'Ola & The Janglers', a pop group with a young singer named Ola Håkansson. Håkansson is today CEO of Stockholm Records and the most important player in – and spokesman for – the Swedish music industry according to a survey undertaken by the professional journal Musikindustrin.

When Ola & The Janglers broke up in the early 1970s, Ola Håkansson undertook university studies a couple of years. However, lack of money and a desire to return to the music business contributed to reunite Håkansson and Häggqvist. More specifically, Håkansson applied for a job at Sonet and was offered one at the publishing department. Häggqvist acted as a mentor for Håkansson over a number of years. Hence, in the 1980s, Håkansson gradually advanced in his career and ended up as member of the Sonet board as well as a co-owner. In parallel with his business career advancements at Sonet, Håkansson also pursued a second career as a 'pop star' with the internationally successful group Secret Service. When Polygram acquired Sonet in the early 1990s, Håkansson left his position and set up a new record company (Stockholm Records) in a joint venture with Polygram.

I told Polygram that I didn't want to work in one of those large [corporate] groups...that I wanted to set up a joint venture with them [Polygram]. My business idea at the time was of course viewed as completely insane...to find Swedish artists for international exploitation. I thought it was an exiting idea trying to export Swedish music. I needed that challenge...building a 'salmon ladder' out of Sweden. I mean, we have always imported almost everything, film, TV-shows, from UK and US (Interview with Håkansson, 1999).

Finally, when considering the structural embeddedness of the Swedish music cluster, a notable feature is that it shares a common denominator with the music industry in other countries (Negus, 1992) as well as with other 'creative industries' such as the British Motor Sport Industry. Pinch and Henry (1999, p. 826) have in this context pointed out that such industries generally are characterised by being 'male-dominated, seemingly fluid and chaotic in character, with elements of geographical agglomeration'.

Political embeddedness The political embeddedness of the Swedish music industry includes three dimensions: global intra-industry power relations, governmental policies and institutional support structure for music production. One may identify two dimensions of *global intra-industry power relations*. Firstly, the global media industry influences the Swedish music industry by acquiring Swedish independents and controlling affiliates. These power relations differ between various corporate groups depending on inter-personal networks, corporate culture etc. Secondly, the Swedish music industry has to adjust its operations in accordance with the international regulatory system in terms of copyrights, royalties etc.

The *Governmental policies* in Sweden have since the 1950s been characterised by the emergence of institutional arrangements in accordance with the welfare state ideology; these arrangements include, for example, relatively generous unemployment benefit funds. As concerns these funds, one may argue that they have been important for many artists, composers, musicians etc. in some phase of their career. This is, at least partly, a result of the fact that artistic labour markets generally are characterised by high 'rates of unemployment and several forms of constrained underemployment (nonvoluntary part-time work, intermittent work, fewer hours of work)' (Menger, 1999, p. 545). In addition to these general expenditures of the welfare state, local public bodies subsidise popular music activities such as rehearsal premises and festivals. Turning to *the institutional support structure*, finally, the tradition of community corporate practices in Sweden explains, at least partly, the presence of the plethora of industry organisations and workers' organisations supporting the Swedish music industry.

Concluding Remarks

The findings presented in this chapter resonate well with recent theoretical developments in economic geography on the socio-economics of industrial production (Barnes and Gertler, 1999; Lee and Wills, 1997; Yeung, 2000a), i.e. that industrial production is socially and institutionally embedded. Accounts in this context commonly depart from notions of untraded interdependencies (Storper, 1995) and institutional thickness (Amin and Thrift, 1994). Examples of such accounts are regional innovation systems (Brazyck et al., 1998), knowledge communities (Henry and Pinch, 2000), network paradigm (Cooke and Morgan, 1993), localised learning (Maskell and Malmberg, 1999), and learning regions (Morgan, 1997). Although these accounts differ, one common denominator is that they stress the socially and institutionally embedded character of firms and industries and the role of knowledge as the key determinant in creating and sustaining industrial competitiveness. Central to this work is also the recognition of the territorialised nature of knowledge (Malmberg 1996, 1997; Maskell et al., 1998; Maskell and Malmberg, 1999).

Despite the fact that this theoretical discourse partly focuses on the embedded nature of industries, empirical research in mainstream economic geography has tended to focus on 'macro-level patterns', e.g. research on agglomerations, clusters and industrial systems (Yeung, 2000b). Our analysis of the Swedish music industry suggests that macro-level approaches such as the Porterian diamond model can be used as a departure for identifying the sources of competitive advantage as identified in recent theoretical contributions on the socio-economics of industrial production (cf. Austrian, 2000). However, when extending the diamond's determinants with the notion of embeddedness, it appears that the diamond model partly fails to identify the underlying *mechanisms* that explain the origins and development of competitive advantage.

Thus, this chapter confirms Amin and Storper's critique of the inability of the cluster concept to identify the social and institutional arrangements that facilitate innovative knowledge inter-exchange and other determinants for the creation of industrial competitiveness. In this context, structural embeddedness is crucial for explaining sources of competitive advantage since dense social networks appear to boost organisational learning through collaborative practices and knowledge inter-exchange (Grabher, 1993). In this respect, Scott (1999b, p. 807) argues that social networks 'are decisive for understanding processes of creativity and innovation in the cultural economy'. All in all, this stresses the need to elucidate the origins and sustenance as well as the degree and nature of social networks when studying the sources of competitiveness in cultural-product industries such as the music industry.

Finally, it is worthy to remark that the Swedish music cluster traditionally has shown no overt signs of institutional thickness. This is manifested by the fact that the presence of institutions explicitly established for supporting the music industry is relatively weak. Thus, traditionally there has been a weak institutional presence of 'financial institutions; local chambers of commerce; training agencies; trade associations; local authorities; development agencies; innovation centers; clerical bodies; unions; government agencies; business service organizations; marketing boards and so on' (Amin and Thrift, 1994, p. 14). However, this chapter suggests that the music cluster shows clear signs of another type of thickness, namely high levels of 'inter-institutional interaction and synergy, collective representation by many bodies, a common industrial purpose, and shared cultural norms and values' (Amin and Thrift, 1994, p. 15). In conclusion, an issue for further research is to examine the potential of public policy to actively foster this form of thickness. In other words, what is the role of public policy in fostering home-base features – and their underlying mechanisms, nota bene – which appear to be crucial to consider when explaining the sources of the Swedish music cluster's competitive advantage.

Note

1 This chapter presents some preliminary findings from a newly started research project on the international competitiveness of the Swedish music cluster. The Bank of Sweden Tercentenary Foundation (Dnr. 98-0222) supports the research project. Comments on this paper by Dominic Power are gratefully acknowledged. We would also like to extend our thanks to Johan Jansson who has provided the project with research assistance.

References

Amin, A. (1999), 'An institutionalist perspective on regional economic development', *International journal of urban and regional research*, 23, pp. 365-378.
Amin, A. and Thrift, N. (1994), 'Living in the global', in A. Amin and N. Thrift (eds), *Globalization, institutions, and regional development in Europe*, 1-22, Oxford University Press, Oxford.
Austrian, Z. (2000), 'Cluster case studies: the marriage of quantitative and qualitative information for action', *Economic development quarterly*, 14, pp. 97-110.
Barnes, T. and Gertler, M.S. (1999), *The new industrial geography: regions, regulation and institutions*, Routledge, London.
Björkegren, D. (1996), *The culture business: management strategies for the arts-related business*, Routledge, London.
Braczyk, H-J., Cooke, P. and Heidenreich, M. (eds) (1998), *Regional innovation systems*, UCL Press, London.
Braczyk H-J., Fuchs, G. and Wolf, H-G. (eds) (2000), *Multimedia and regional economic restructuring*, Routledge, London.
Burnett, R. (1996), *The global jukebox*, Routledge, London.
Burnett, R. (1997), *Den svenska musikindustrins export 1994-95*, ExMS, Stockholm.
Cooke, P. and Morgan, K. (1993), 'The network paradigm: new departures in corporate and regional development', *Environment and Planning D*, 11, pp. 543-564.
Cunningham, M. (1998), *Good vibrations: a history of record production*, Sanctuary, London.
Dacin, M.T., Ventresca, M.J. and Beal, B.D. (1999), 'The embeddedness of organizations: Dialogue and directions', *Journal of Management*, 25, pp. 317-356.
DiMaggio, P. (1997), 'Culture and cognition', *Annual Review of Sociology*, 23, pp. 263-287.
Doeringer, P.B. and Terkla, D.G. (1996), 'Why do industries cluster?', in U. Staber, N. Schaefer and B. Sharma (eds), *Business networks: prospects for regional development*, Walter de Gruyter, New York.
Dosi, G., Teece, D. and Chytry J. (eds) (1988), *Technology, organization, and competitiveness: perspectives on industrial and corporate change*, Oxford University Press, Oxford.
Edquist, C. (ed.) (1997), *Systems of innovation: technologies, institutions and organizations*, Pinter, London.
Enright, M. (1993), 'The geographic scope of competitive advantage', in E. Dirven, J. Groenewegen, and S. van Hoof (eds), *Stuck in the region? Changing scales for regional identity*, Nederlands Geographical Studies, Utrecht.
Enright, M. (1996), 'Regional clusters and economic development: a research agenda', in U. Staber, N. Schaefer and B. Sharma (eds), *Business networks: prospects for regional development*, Walter de Gruyter, New York.

Feser, E.J. and Bergman, E.M. (2000), 'National industry cluster templates: a framework for applied regional cluster analysis', *Regional Studies*, 34, pp. 1-21.

Forss, K. (1999), *Att ta sig ton: om svensk musikexport 1974-1999*, Ds 1999, 28, Fritzes, Stockholm.

Gordon, I. and McCann, P. (2000), 'Industrial clusters: complexes, agglomeration and/or social networks', *Urban Studies*, 37, pp. 513-532.

Grabher, G. (ed.) (1993), *The embedded firm: on the socioeconomics of industrial networks*, Routledge, London.

Granovetter, M. (1985), 'Economic action and social structure: the problem of embededness', *American Journal of Sociology*, 91, pp. 481-510.

Håkansson, H. (1989), *Corporate technological behaviour: co-operation and networks*, Routledge, London.

Hallencreutz, D. and Lundequist, P. (1998), 'Populärmusik och produktionsmiljö: lokal miljö och internationell konkurrenskraft inom svensk musik industri', paper presented at the *The Second SPIET Workshop - On the micro foundations of institutional and evolutionary theory*, April 1998, Uppsala.

Hallencreutz, D. and Lundequist, P. (2000a), 'Popmusik och virtuella visioner', *www.Alba.nu*, 13.

Hallencreutz, D. and Lundequist, P. (2000b), 'Producing pop and competitive advantage – the problem of embeddedness and communities of knowledge', paper presented at the *Association of American Geographers Annual Conference*, New York City, 27 February - 3 March 2001.

Hallencreutz, D., Lundequist, P. and Malmberg, A. (2000), 'Production of popular music: on the industrial geography of the Swedish music cluster', *Nordisk Samhällsgeografisk Tidskrift*, 30, pp. 37-59.

Hesmondhalgh, D. (1996), 'Flexibility, post-fordism and the music industries', *Media, Culture and Society*, 18, pp. 469-488.

Hesmondhalgh, D. (1998), 'The British dance music industry: a case study of independent cultural production', *British Journal of Sociology*, 49, pp. 234-251.

Hirsch, P.M. (1972), 'Processing Fads and Fashions: an organization-set analysis of cultural industry systems', *American Journal of Sociology*, 77, pp. 639-659.

Jansson, J. (2000), 'Musikindustri I Hultsfred och Malmö. En studie av två lokala produktions miljöer', *Arbetsrapporter Kulturgeografiska Institutionen*, 395, Uppsala Universitet.

Lee, R. and Wills, J. (1997), *Geographies of Economies*, Arnold, London.

Lilliestam, L. (1998), *Svensk rock: musik, lyrik, historik*, Ejeby, Göteborg.

Lundvall, B-Å. (ed.) (1992), *National systems of innovation: towards a theory of innovation and interactive learning*, Pinter, London.

Malm, K. (1997), *Musik, makt och massmedier*, Rådet för mångfald inom massmedierna, 1997:1, Kulturdepartementet, Stockholm.

Malmberg, A. (1996), 'Industrial geography: agglomeration and local milieu', *Progress in Human Geography*, 20, pp. 392-403.

Malmberg, A. (1997), 'Industrial geography: location and learning', *Progress in Human Geography*, 21, 573-582.

Maskell, P., Eskelinen, H., Hannibalsson, I., Malmberg, A. and Vatne, E. (1998), *Competitiveness, Localised Learning and Regional Development. Specialisation and Prosperity in Small Open Economies*, Routledge, London.

Maskell, P. and Malmberg, A. (1999), 'Localised learning and industrial competitiveness', *Cambridge Journal of Economics*, 23, pp. 167-185.

Melin, A. (1999), *Musikbranschen i Sundsvall 1999 – En möjlighet till en 'hit'*, Sundsvall, Sundsvalls kommun (mimeo).
Menger, P.M. (1999), 'Artistic labor markets and careers', *Annual Review of Sociology*, 25, pp. 541-574.
Middleton, R. (1990), *Studying popular music*, Open University Press, Milton Keynes.
Morgan K. (1997), 'The learning region: institutions, innovation and regional renewal', *Regional Studies*, 31, pp. 491-503.
Negus, K. (1992), *Producing pop*, Edward Arnold, London.
Negus, K. (1999), *Music genres and corporate cultures*, Routledge, London.
Nelson, R. (ed.) (1993), *National Innovation Systems – A Comparative Analysis*, Oxford University Press, New York.
Nelson, R. and Winter S. (1982), *An Evolutionary Theory of Economic Change*, Harvard University Press, Cambridge.
Oinas, P. (1998), 'The embedded firm? Prelude for a revived geography of enterprise', *Acta Universitatis oeconomicae Helsingiensis*, 143, Helsinki.
Peterson, R. (1976), *The production of culture*, Sage, Beverly Hills.
Pinch, S. and Henry, N. (1999), 'Paul Krugman's geographical economics, industrial clustering and the British Motor Sport Valley', *Regional Studies*, 33, pp. 815-827.
Pinch, S. and Henry, N. (2000), 'Spatialising knowledge: placing the knowledge community of Motor Sport Valley', *Geoforum*, 31, pp. 1999-208.
Porter, M.E. (1990), *The competitive advantage of nations*, MacMillan, London and Basingstoke.
Porter, M. E. (1998), 'Clusters and the new economics of competition', *Harvard Business Review*, Nov-Dec, pp. 77-90.
Porter, M.E. (2000), 'Location, competition, and economic development: Local clusters in a global economy', *Economic Development Quarterly* 14, pp. 15-34.
Pratt, A.C. (1997), The cultural-industries production system: a case study of employment change in Britain 1984 – 91, *Environment and Planning A*, 29, pp. 1953-1975.
Rao, B. (1999), 'The Internet and the revolution in distribution: a cross-industry examination', *Technology in Society*, 21, pp. 287-306.
Sadler, D. (1997), 'The global music business as an information industry: reinterpreting economies of culture', *Environment and Planning A*, 29, pp. 1919-1936.
Saxenian, A-L. (1994), *Regional advantage: culture and competition in Silicon Valley and Route 128*, Harvard University Press, Cambridge MA.
Scott, A. (1997), 'The cultural economy of cities', *International Journal of Urban and Regional Research*, 21, pp. 323-339.
Scott, A. (1999a), 'The US recorded music industry: on the relations between organization, location and creativity in the cultural economy', *Environment and Planning A*, 31, pp. 1965-1984.
Scott, A. (1999b), 'The cultural economy: geography of the creative field', *Media, Culture and Society*, 21, pp. 801-817.
Scott, A.J. (2000), 'French cinema – Economy, policy and place in the making of a cultural-products industry', *Theory Culture & Society*, 17, pp. 1-38.
Sölvell, Ö., Zander, I. and Porter, M.E. (1991), *Advantage Sweden*, Nordstedts, Stockholm.
Statistics Sweden (2000), *Statistical Yearbook of Sweden*, Stockholm.
Statistics Sweden (1999), *Adult study associations 1999*, Stockholm.
Storper, M. (1995), 'The resurgence of regional economies, 10 years later: the region as a nexus of untraded interdependencies', *European Urban and Regional Studies*, 2, pp. 191-221.

Storper M. (1997), *The Regional World. Territorial Development in a Global Economy*, The Guilford Press, New York and London.

Whitley, R. (1992), *Business systems in East Asia: firms, markets, and societies*, Sage, London.

Yeung, H. (2000a), 'Organizing "the firm" in industrial geography: networks, institutions and regional development', *Progress in Human Geography*, 24, pp. 301-315.

Yeung, H. (2000b), 'Reconceptualising the "Firm" in new economic geography: an organisational perspective', paper presented at the Workshop on *"The Firm" in economic geography*, 9-11 March 2000, University of Portsmouth, UK.

Zukin, S. and DiMaggio, P. (ed.) (1990), *Structures of capital: the social organization of the economy*, Cambridge University Press, Cambridge.

Chapter 2

The Local Embeddedness of Ethnic Entrepreneurship – Over- and Under-Embeddedness in the Israeli Arab Economy

Michael Sofer and Izhak Schnell

Introduction

The current pattern of industrial production in Israeli Arab settlements may be viewed as a peculiar form of peripheral industrialisation. It is peripheral in a number of ways: it is located in what is perceived as the national periphery; it specialises in old industries; it shows high dependence on local markets; and it had been integrated into the national economy under subordinating conditions. Nevertheless, industrial entrepreneurship is highly appreciated as important means for economic mobility, and a significant share of Arab entrepreneurs managed to break ethnic barriers and to access Jewish market. About half of them even succeeded in expanding into markets in the national core (Schnell et al., 1999).

Arab industry in Israel has grown intensively during the 1970s and 1980s, more than doubling the number of operating enterprises, their average size and the form of production. In the same period, Arab industry experienced a restructuring process based on the transformation from mimicking strategies of operation to more competitive strategies based on entrepreneurs efforts to exploit any slight opportunity in the market (Sofer and Schnell, 2000). Nevertheless, Arab entrepreneurs were rarely able to translate these achievements into dynamic processes of capital accumulation based on scale economics and multipliers of economic growth. This discrepancy calls for a better explanation of the barriers that Arab entrepreneurs – as an example of a peripheral ethnic minority – are forced to overcome in their struggle for further integration into the state economy.

Relevant literature confirms the hypothesis that inter-firm linkages and networks are key factors for business growth with implications for industrial efficiency and industrial development (Hakansson and Johanson, 1993). Appropriate intensive linkages may generate, along other economic benefits, economic multipliers to the firm resulting in economic and social benefits to the local and the regional economy (Scott, 1991; Felsenstein, 1992; Staber and

Schaefer, 1996). A key issue in the study of local economic development is the degree to which firms and their networks are embedded in wider socially and politically structured milieus (Curran and Blackburn, 1994). In this context, particular attention should be devoted to minorities' need to insert themselves in two different separate milieus. Albeit the challenges and barriers that each milieu may cause, entrepreneurs success in being embedded in both milieus and developing wide business linkages and networks is crucial for their integration into the economy as well as society (Aldrich and Waldinger, 1990; Barrett et al., 1996). This form of mixed-embeddedness is a target to be reached by ethnic entrepreneurs, who alternatively may find themselves trapped within ethnic enclaves, not being able to overcome barriers that stem from their ethnic origin and/or location in the national, regional and urban periphery (Kloosterman et al., 1999).

Arab entrepreneurs in Israel may demonstrate a typical case, by facing both - the wider Israeli capitalist economy, largely dominated by the Jewish sector, and their own socio-economic system. This means that they have to face each sector's value and norm system, which underlies the business culture and power relations - the power of firms to determine exchange relations.

The aim of this article is to offer an analytical framework for the explication of the degree and form of embeddedness of a marginal minority group within the state economy. Based on the experience of Israeli Arab entrepreneurs, we discuss some of the difficulties that minority entrepreneurs encounter in their attempts to break barriers of peripherality and ethnicity and to participate in both minority and majority business cultures, politics and information networks. We thus offer the use of two new concepts concerning embeddedness. The first concept, 'over-embeddedness', characterises those entrepreneurs whose commitments to the local community and to kinship groups prevent them from exploiting opportunities in inter-ethnic markets. The second concept, 'under-embeddedness', characterises those entrepreneurs who fail to translate their existing wide and complex networks into an economic advantage in the markets. This is due to lack of understanding of the wider (Jewish in the Israeli context) business culture, or absence of capability to improve their positions in economic exchange networks.

The data presented in this paper were collected from three primary sources: open interviews with 70 Arab industrial entrepreneurs; a questionnaire addressed to the heads or secretaries of Arab local councils; and a questionnaire addressed to the owners and managers of 514 industrial plants in 35 Arab settlements. An industrial plant was defined as a production unit with at least three workers. The comprehensive questionnaire included items relating to all components of production, sources of labour and capital, marketing and purchasing of inputs. These sources enabled to gather information on industrial networks, strategies of survival, estimated barriers for growth and views regarding the future of their enterprises.

Our discussion develops along five stages starting with a description of Arab industry in Israel. This is followed by a short review of the theoretical issues concerning the analysis of mixed-embeddedness within the framework of ethnic relations. The third section focuses on the evaluation of the structure and features of Arab enterprises' embeddedness in the Israeli economy, followed by a demonstration of both situations: over-embeddedness and under-embeddedness.

Arab Industry in Israel

It took fifty years and three stages for Arab industry to achieve its current state of development. Three major mechanisms influenced these restructuring phases: majority-minority relations, core-periphery relations, and selective government policies (Sofer and Schnell, 2000). The majority-minority relations, supported by the government's selective policy, have since been overlapped by the relations established between the Jewish dominant core and the Arab subordinate periphery. The result of the integrated operation of these mechanisms has affected the form of Arab industrialisation, including branch selection, plant formation and entrepreneurial style.

The relative neglect and the enforcement of martial law during the 1950s had created the preconditions for reintegrating the Arab sector as a subordinated periphery during later periods. Under conditions of exclusion, Arab industry was restructured into an ethnic enclave-type of economy with very limited external economic links. The government, aiming at nation building but facing limited resources, invested in housing and industrial infrastructure in the Jewish periphery, leaving the Arab labour force to commute to the second labour markets in the evolving Jewish urban concentrations.

Starting in the late 1960s, the conditions for economic development and entrepreneurial initiatives in the Arab sector changed significantly. The combined effect of the establishment of basic infrastructure in the settlements, the rise in educational level, the entrance of women into the labour market and the gained professional experience by the Arab labour force paved the way to industrial entrepreneurship. Accordingly, during the 1970s, the evolution of Israeli large industrial corporations exerting monopoly power affected the spatial pattern of industrial production, thus signifying the beginning of a second stage. Arab settlements gained from the shift of industrial enterprises to the periphery by the emergence of sewing shops as subcontractors to textile corporations. A strategy of growth from below was adopted (Khamaisi, 1984; Falah, 1993), expressed by a rapid rate of growth in the number of new plants in the food and construction sectors, coupled with the adoption of new style of entrepreneurship. Most plants doubled their size to an average of 15 workers per plant, managers began to use more formal management techniques, and divided production into specialised lines. Thus in the early 1990s, although continuing to operate in the same branches, entrepreneurs proved their ability to compete on Jewish markets. A new perception of the market and advanced marketing methods have led to increased penetration into Jewish markets including core metropolitan areas (Schnell et al., 1999).

During the 1990s, the Israeli economy has hesitantly started to experience globalisation. A shift of industrial interests towards Middle Eastern labour markets, brought about the establishment of around 30 projects (especially sewing shops) in

Jordan, Egypt and the Palestinian territories (Sofer and Schnell, 2000). Most of these projects resulted from the relocation of standardised production processes formerly based in Arab settlements. The current (third) restructuring process has had a destructive impact on Arab entrepreneurs in Israel due to the lack of their participation in (some may say exclusion from) the new opportunities offered by the peace process and globalisation. Cautious estimates suggest that between 50 to 60 per cent of the medium- and large-sized textile plants and sweatshops in Arab settlements have been closed since 1995, and a much larger share of the labour force employed in this industry has been laid down. Despite the visible signs of its growth potential as of the early 1960s, Israeli Arab industry has not shown any clear signs of shifting towards hi-tech or sophisticated industrial branches in the last decade of the 20th century. The same branches persist, responding to the changing economic milieu from their marginal position.

The data gathered in the early 1990s has shown that industry is spread among the 60 settlements that represent the majority of those Arab settlements boasting a population of over 5,000. Compared with the 1980s, plants employing three or more workers doubled in number, reaching more than 900 (Schnell et al., 1995), with the size of the industrial workforce employed in Arab settlements growing to about 12,000 (Atrash, 1992). National figures indicate that in the 1990s, Arab-owned enterprises represented nearly six per cent of all Israeli plants employing five or more workers (Central Bureau of Statistics, 1992).

Table 2.1 Branch specialisation index of the labour force in plants with three employees or more, 1992

Specialised branches		Marginal branches	
Textiles & clothing	4.2	Food & beverages	0.4
Construction materials	3.7	Metal products	0.2
Woodworking	1.5	Paper & printing	0.2
		Rubber & plastics	0.2
		Electronics & electricity	0.002

Notes:
1) The figures for Israeli industry are from 1989, those for Arab industry from 1992.
2) Specialisation Index is the rate of employee distribution by branch in the Arab sector, as compared with the branch distribution in Israeli industry as a whole.

Source: Schnell et al. (1995).

Typically, small household production and informal subcontracting activities, which constitute 43 per cent of enterprises in this sector, exist side by side with an increasing number of workshops and factories. In the late 1980s even a very small number of large-scale enterprises (about one per cent which employ more than 50 workers each) has emerged. The pattern of branch specialisation by labour force appears in Table 2.1 and some major characteristics appear in Table 2.2.

Table 2.2 Selected characteristics of industrial plants by main branches, 1992

Branch	Plants (%)	Employees			Plants with Sales volume below US$200,000 (%)	Plants located in dwelling (%)
		Number	Average per plant	Ave. no. females per plant		
Textiles & clothing	26	5,101	36.7	31.7	63	84.1
Food & beverages	19	563	5.8	0.3	92	79.8
Construction materials	17	898	10.2	0.5	65	33.0
Woodworking	17	479	5.5	0.1	85	78.7
Metals & metalworking	8	260	6.2	0.4	89	67.3
Rubber & plastic	5	186	6.0	0.2	91	75.7
Others	8	299	8.3	0.7	92	67.5
Total	100	7,786	15.1	8.8	81	69.0

Source: Adapted from Schnell *et al.* (1995).

A shown by the figures, a significant proportion of plants (above two thirds in most branches) are located in residential areas, especially on the ground floor of the owner's home or in rented residential buildings. Where an industrial area is available, it is of inferior quality, lacking an appropriate physical infrastructure (Sofer *et al.*, 1996). In 1992, the average number of employees per plant was about 15, a high percentage of whom were women, employed primarily in sewing shops. Despite the increase in their mobility, most women work in the settlement in which they reside (Atrash, 1992). The formal training of the labour force is limited, with less than two per cent having any formal academic or technical education. Most of the training of the professional workers is done on the shop floor. For most entrepreneurs, personal savings are the most common source of initial capital investment, while other family members are also an important source. Only 14 per cent sought bank loans as a major source of investment. The most common type of ownership is individual or family (83 per cent), where several brothers own and manage a plant.

Firms, Networks and Embeddedness

A significant amount of empirical and theoretical contribution has been published in recent years on the complex relations between firms and their embedded ties and networks. The synthesis of that material shows that the study of industrial geography is increasingly concerned with the socio-spatial organisation of industrial firms and their networks (Yeung, 2000). To wit, firms competitiveness and growth, and the resulting regional growth, requires firms' embeddedness in concrete ongoing (local, regiand/or national) systems of social relations (Granovetter, 1985). Networks may be seen as both a governance mode and a process of socialisation through which different actors and institutions are performing exchange relations, which are connected in a coherent manner for mutual benefits (Hakansson and Johanson, 1993; Yeung, 2000). In this context there exists a variety of networks of which the major ones are marketing and suppliers, information and innovations networks, and production networks based on labour and capital recruitment. These networks can be formal as well as informal (Malecki and Tootle, 1996), based on resource sharing (Perry and Goldfinch, 1996), as well as on decentralised learning and knowledge (Maskell and Malmberg, 1999). These networks are, however, often embedded in communities and localities with strong (formal and informal) institutional legacies and linkages (Portes and Sensenbrenner, 1993; Waldinger, 1995; Grabher and Stark, 1997).

In several studies the intensity and the dynamic of inter-firm linkages and networks are treated as indicators for economic growth (Scott, 1991; Grabher, 1993; Taylor, 1995; Oinas, 1999), while external networks have a particularly decisive impact on small plants' growth chances (Kay, 1993; Hardill et al., 1995). The key issue in these investigations is the degree to which firms are embedded in various markets through their relationships with competitors, suppliers, business organisations and public decision making forums, as well as with members of their community (Best, 1990; Harrison, 1992; Markusen, 1994; Lakshmanan and Okumura, 1995).

Generally speaking embeddedness tends to refer to the three perspectives: cultural, socially structured and institutional milieus in which entrepreneurs perform as economic agents. From the cultural perspective, embeddedness may be viewed as processes in which agents acquire customs, habits, or norms in an unerring way that unintentionally determine their decisions and behaviours, and structure of awareness to their relevant milieus. From the structural perspective, embedded networks may be characterised by agents' connectedness, reciprocity, interdependence, autonomy, and power relations in terms of control over both economic and social relations (Grabher, 1993; Portes and Sensenbrenner, 1993; Oinas, 1999). From the institutional perspective, embeddedness relates to agents' accessibility to education and training institutions, incubation and innovation centres, market organisations, business associations, and business practices which regulate particular markets (Tödtling, 1994; Kloosterman et al., 1999).

Looking at the networks of small firms, Curran and Blackburn (1994) gave attention to economic and non-economic linkages largely divided into two main types. Firstly, those related to the firm such as membership of local chambers of commerce, trade associations etc. Secondly, those linkages not related to the business directly but reflect embedded relations such as owners' social relations, political party membership, leisure activities and friendship and family relations. The latter may nevertheless have some relevance to economic activities. Business owners are epitomised as strong 'networkers' by participating in and sustaining a web of economic and social links for information, customers and suppliers. These linkages are seen as indicators of the level of integration into the economy and of the small firm's embeddedness including participation of owners in local community groups, in political parties, sports and social clubs. These latter connections are seen as underpinning a vibrant local economy and a prerequisite for a successful local economy of the 'industrial district' type (Curran and Blackburn, 1994). Looking from another angle, Uzzi suggests that 'the network acts as a social boundary of demarcation around opportunities that are assembled from the embedded ties that define membership and enrich the network' (1996, pp. 693-694). In this context the type of ties used by the entrepreneur to link his activities and operation to his network's partners are dictating the firm level of embeddedness.

Talmud and Yanovitzky (1998) offer a specific model for the analysis of firm's embeddedness. In line with Grabher (1993) and Oinas (1999) they analyse networks within cultural and power fields. Networks, according to them, should be analysed less in terms of number of links and intersections and more in terms of power relations and horizons of the players' awareness. Moreover, embeddedness is related to different sectors of society such as political and economic elite and institutions, and structure of market networks. Politically, evidence shows that firms closely attached to political centres better succeed to appropriate benefits for their operation and to develop greater autonomy in their relations with governments (Han, 1992; Talmud and Mesch, 1997). Market autonomy may be also achieved by maximising the flow of information about market opportunities and conditions, as well as by developing reciprocal relations rather than relations of dependency (Burt, 1992).

A specific case of embeddedness is that of ethnic minorities, since they are forced to operate in more than one milieu. Ethnic entrepreneurs frequently tend to concentrate their economic activities within their ethnic milieu as it is implied by the ethnic enclave hypothesis, but even in these cases they are not able to escape the majority institutional milieu of the region in which they operate (Aldrich and Waldinger, 1995). When entrepreneurs try to escape their limited ethnic enclave economy, they are forced to keep their links with their ethnic milieu and at the same time to establish links with the majority milieu. Only by understanding entrepreneurs' need to operate in and out of their own milieu, embeddedness may encompass its original meaning concerning the interplay among economic, social and institutional contexts of ethnic entrepreneurship (Kloosterman *et al*, 1999).

Applying the embeddedness concept to the case of Israeli Arab ethnic minority requires the recognition that there are deep cultural, economic and political gaps between the Jewish and the Arab milieus. Arabs are economically, politically and culturally marginalised (Gradus, Razin and Krakover, 1993; Falah, 1993; Haidar, 1993) in an economy that is highly politicised. Entrepreneurs, particularly those who have escaped the mimicking behaviour strategy, act as the Yanus goddess while turning their faces toward the two different milieus. This form of mix-embeddedness means that in each milieu they are required to link themselves to the market players as well as to the economic and political elite and institutions (Figure 2.1). As shown by the figure, entrepreneurs operating in the Arab milieu are highly dependent on kinship relations in recruiting resources and developing markets. They use personal contacts with local political and economic elite to support their operations. Encapsulation in intra-ethnic markets is used as a survival mechanism resulting in a situation where a large number of small enterprises compete on the limited local markets. Regarding the Jewish milieu, the challenge of overcoming political, social and cultural barriers is crucial for Arab entrepreneurs. Breaking these barriers may enable them to penetrate the larger markets, to get a long-standing grasp on these markets and to avoid dependency relations. The most severe barrier is the power exerted by large corporations who dominate the markets.

Entrepreneurs' embeddedness within such milieus, as shown in Figure 2.1, may be measured in terms of the complexity and intensity of networks, power relations and horizons of awareness (or the ability to accommodate themselves) to the codes of the two business cultures, opportunities and risks. This system has experienced a number of restructuring processes, by which types of entrepreneurship and institutions were transformed. Within such a process the Arab entrepreneur has been required to counterbalance his embeddedness in each milieu in order to achieve higher economic (and even social) returns. It is basic to our argument that well-balanced embeddedness means mutual and integrated co-ordination of the three dimensions (networks complexity and intensity, power relations and horizons of awareness), while lagging behind in one of them may lead to an unbalanced embeddedness. This argument raises a major dilemma: what is the embeddedness level required by any firm in order to survive. A question that was raised also by others, although implicitly (Granovetter, 1985; Uzzi, 1996). Too little embeddedness may expose networks to erosion of their supportive tissue of social practices and institutions. Too much embeddedness, however, may promote a petrifaction of this supportive tissue and, hence, may pervert networks into cohesive coalitions against more radical innovations, and even major change.

We thus offer here to consider two concepts that may identify imbalances in entrepreneurs' embeddedness. First, 'over-embeddedness' defined here as a situation in which entrepreneurs manoeuvred their kinship and community systems to support their entrepreneurship, and the resulting commitment, which impedes on them from participating in inter-ethnic markets. Second, we define 'under-embeddedness' as entrepreneurs' success in developing intensive and complex inter-ethnic networks, while failing to gain adequate evaluation capabilities of relevant business opportunities and/or to gain enough power to translate the complex networks into economic growth and development. Not being able to find the proper balance, entrepreneurs may be entangled and locked in the local ethnic networks, thus being pushed to a state of over-embeddedness. Likewise, they can be forced to compete in the inter-ethnic markets where they may face an uneven status and trapped in dependency relations, which means operating in an environment of under-embeddedness.

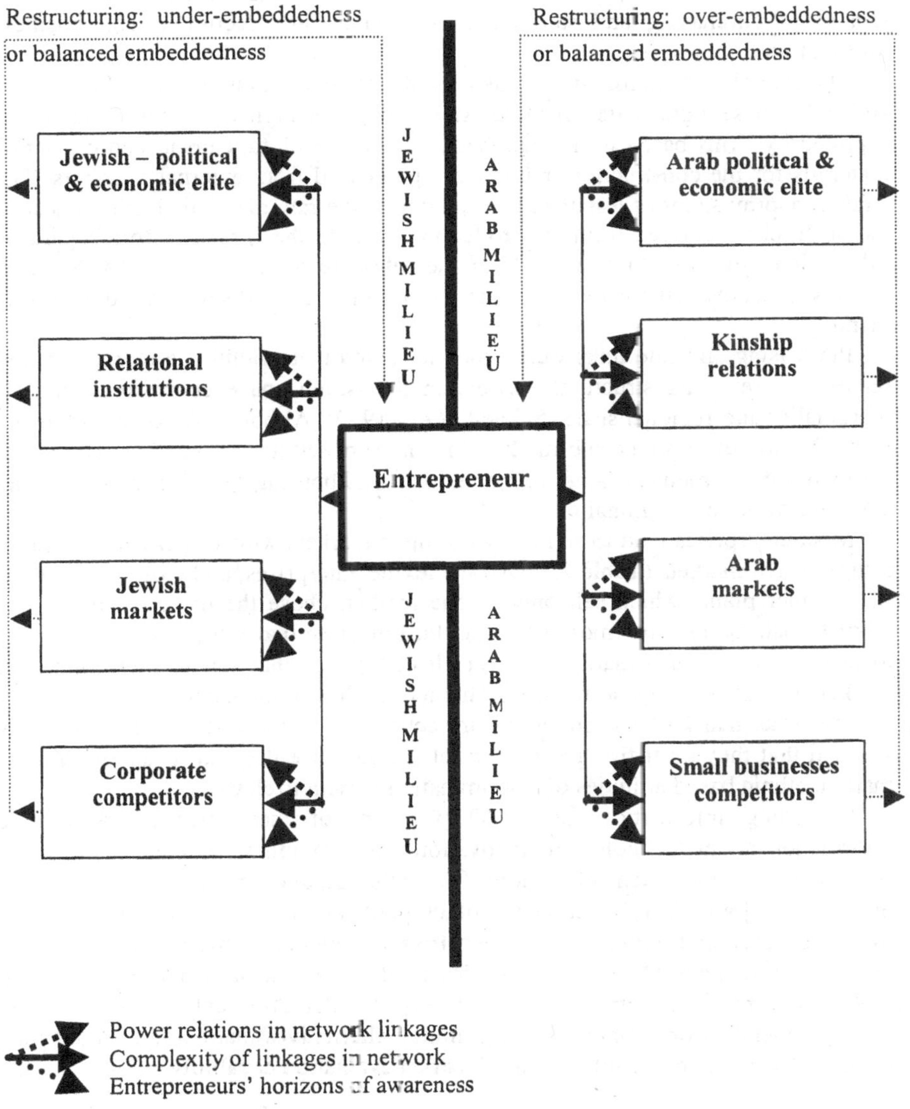

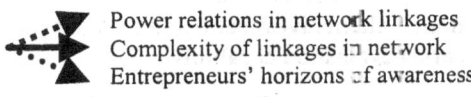

Figure 2.1 A general model of mixed embeddedness

Firms and Networks in the Arab Sector

The pattern of embeddedness of Arab enterprises is studied here through the analysis of firms' business networks, leaving the analysis of the other two dimensions of embeddedness (power and awareness) to the following sections. Empirical evidence may shed light on the intensity and structure of networks related to purchasing and sale linkages, labour force recruiting and business information.

The spatial distribution of purchasing and sales linkages is shown in Figures 2.2 and 2.3. These figures demonstrate Arab industry's high dependency on inputs supplied by firms based in the national core. Textile cloth, cement and other raw materials for the construction industry are purchased from external suppliers. The Arab economy supplies less than one quarter of the raw materials leaving most of the profit chain derived from the production cycle to the Jewish sector. Regarding sales, although close to two thirds of the sales are directed mainly to the Arab regions, it seems that for most regions 30 to 40 per cent of sales aimed at Jewish markets.

Purchasing and sale links were subdivided into meaningful sub-markets, based on major prevailing structural barriers in the Israeli space economy: ethnicity, marginality and regional scale (Schnell et al., 1999). Although Arab entrepreneurs were able to develop nine sub-markets they have penetrated in practice mainly five of them: intra-settlement, Arab home region, neighbouring Jewish region, national core and Arab inter-regional markets.

Most enterprises tend to sell to two or three markets with 13 per cent selling to four and five markets (Table 2.3). All the textile enterprises, and close to one third of all other plants which sell only to one market, chose the more rewarding but risky Jewish market, and more than one third of those that sell to two markets sell to at least one Jewish market. Almost all enterprises that sell to more than two markets sell also to Jewish markets. This means that ethnic barriers are frequently overcome as many of the entrepreneurs confirmed in the open interviews. They stressed that they must first prove themselves, but once they succeeded to win the market, ethnic based attitudes of discrimination remain irrelevant.

Regarding information, about 60 per cent of the entrepreneurs receive information about technological innovations from suppliers, while about 28 per cent of them gather such information from other sources. Such sources could be professional journals (27 per cent), other publications and television programs (nine per cent), and only seven per cent from competitors – mainly small firms in the same settlement. Other sources of information remain marginal (Abo Sharkia, 1996). As a result it seems reasonable to suppose that Arab entrepreneurs remain largely dependent on suppliers, facing limited alternatives that could have enabled them to develop a reasonably unbiased market evaluation capability.

Local Embeddedness of Ethnic Entrepreneurship in the Israeli Arab Economy   39

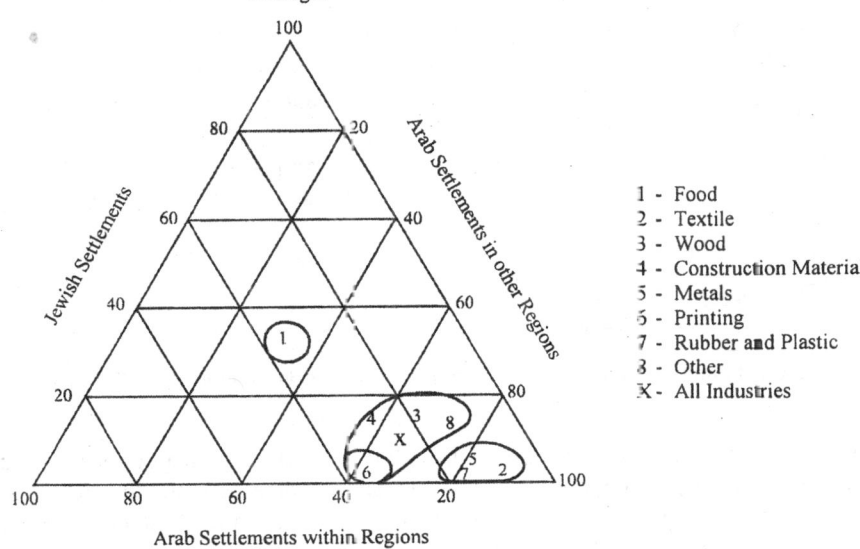

Figure 2.2 The spatial distribution of purchasing linkages

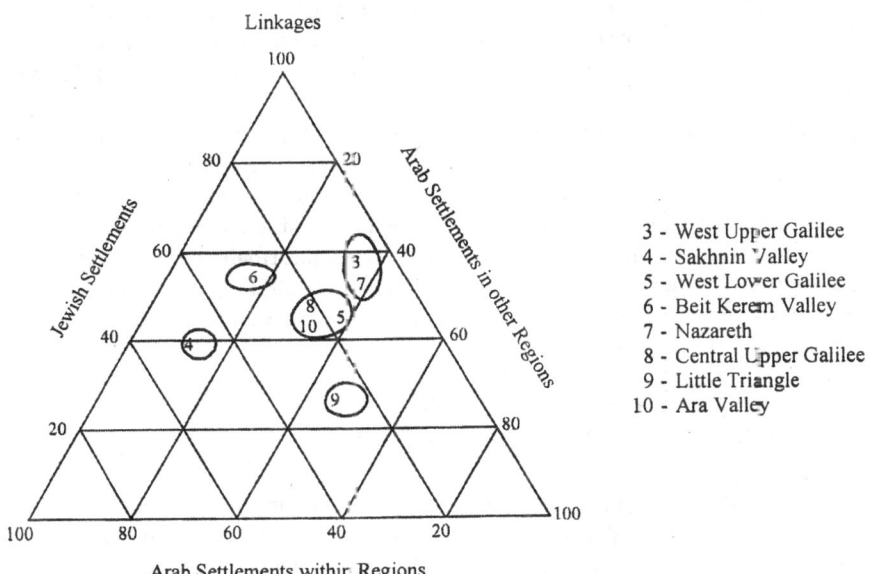

Figure 2.3 The spatial distribution of sales linkages

Table 2.3 Enterprises by number of markets and per cent overcoming barriers

No. of markets	% plants	% overcoming barrier of	
		Ethnicity	Peripherality
1	17	33 (98)*	0 (93)*
2	35	34	24
3	35	92	48
4+	13	100	48
All markets	100	71	48

* Note: The first number is for non textile enterprises and the second one for textile ones.

With regard to recruiting employees the local network is the major source. The home settlement provides three-quarters of the labour force with one third of them coming from the employer's clan (*hamula*). Employers from the extended family, and in some cases from the *hamula*, serve as managers and clerks, while the majority of manual workers are from other local families of the plant settlement. The latter are employed in under privileged jobs that pay low salaries, frequently below the allowed minimum wage level. This is mainly due to the low profitability of most Arab enterprises. Consequently, Arab skilled labourers prefer to commute to the Jewish hubs of industry where better opportunities are offered. Jewish employees are less than one per cent of the labour force in Arab enterprises, mainly in specific jobs such as engineers and sales managers, especially when the Jewish market is targeted.

Altogether, Arab entrepreneurs in Israel have developed wide and complex sale linkages, compared with relatively limited linkages with other aspects of the networking process. A question to be asked here is whether they managed to achieve reciprocal power relations in the business milieu they operate in, and whether they succeed in obtaining better access to information flows, evaluation capabilities and other aspects of the two business cultures they operate in. In discussing these issues we turn to discuss entrepreneurs possible position within the networks: over- and under-embeddedness.

The Arab Milieu and the Over-embedded Firm

Over-embeddedness characterises some Arab firms that are highly embedded in the local milieu, operate under the influence of kinship structures and a petrified supportive tissue that downgrades networks into cohesive coalitions opposing radical innovations and even minor changes. The business culture adopted by firms' owners impedes possibilities for integration in the larger market economy.

Many Arab entrepreneurs have experienced the condition of over-embeddedness within the Arab milieu. Since most of them opened their businesses with intensive support of the extended family and the home community, they feel indebted to their supporters once they have succeeded. The story of the owner of a concrete block factory, who complained about his two brothers, may demonstrate the dilemma:

> It's bad because I can't give instructions to brothers freely. I have to consult with them and accept all their crazy ideas. I also can't fire a brother or reprimand him. It's a serious problem for the work in the factory. I'd rather work with managers from outside the family. I could demand from them what I think should be done and could fire them if they weren't good.

It seems that this example describes the situation of many Arab entrepreneurs. Due to the intensive support from the extended family the entrepreneur is obliged to support his/her relatives. Typical forms of support are contribution to the initial capital investment, allocating space (usually at the ground floor of the extended family house), paying for the entrepreneur's everyday life expenses, and moral support. In most cases wider kinship units also provide support. For example, entrepreneurs can rely on the clan as a guaranteed market. In some cases they may obtain release from paying municipal taxes, particularly when the mayor belongs to their *hamula*, and to operate a business from the owner dwellings without a permit.

The warm hug of the family and the community, which means he is less free to change his plant location, may prohibit further development. An entrepreneur who is located in the residential area and who wants to expand his business frequently finds it impossible. Roads are too narrow, infrastructures are inadequate and tracks cannot reach most houses. He is forced to move out to industrial zones, which rarely exist in the Arab towns. The dilemma of an entrepreneur who was thinking to locate his plant in a Jewish town may demonstrate the problem of over-embeddedness:

> In order to expand I had to move to an industrial area. My place was too small for the plant. We have an industrial area, but with no infrastructure. There is no sewage, road, and electricity, not mentioning a building. To build all of it on my own is too expensive for me. So I decided to check the possibility to leave to the industrial zone of the Jewish neighbouring town. The extra-expenses for renting the place, the permit etc. were so high that paying them would have forced me to sell at higher prices. This experience made me afraid that another small enterprise could be established in the entrepreneur's family home in our town, stealing from me my local clients, before I would gain even one new client outside my home town.

The obligation and indebtedness to extended family and clan matters, on the expense of recruiting professional skilled labour is a sort of limitation on the firm efficiency and demonstrates the form of links within the network. We may claim that it is also a form of restriction on the horizons of awareness of the entrepreneur and its economic potential. The next example emphasises the role of the extended family in managing the enterprise and in limiting access to other labour sources:

I am the eldest. Two brothers work with me and three sisters sew. I am the manager but much of my time I search for customers. One brother manages the production line and the other the books. My sister learns now to use the computer. Each of us can cover the responsibility of the other brothers, a situation that gives us a lot of flexibility. As you see the factory is a family project and its success is the success of the whole family.

To emphasise, the limitation on the horizons of awareness is also related to the absence of risk reducing mechanisms, which prompted the extended family to become the main source of entrepreneurial support. At the same time the family conveyed on successful entrepreneurs' demands that prohibit them from further economic growth. The same complaints may be heard also by an owner of an enterprise:

It turned to be a big obstacle to work with my brothers. I have to consult them, to accept ideas that I know are harmful for the business and I cannot fire them. I owe them so much and any problem at work becomes immediately a family issue. From time to time one of my brothers needs some money urgently for a wedding, school or any other purpose and it force us to hold further development. I feel that the partnership with my brothers enabled the establishment of the enterprise in the beginning, but it prohibits further development today when we are in a new era in which each family looks for itself.

Another aspect of over-embeddedness, which is related to entrepreneurs' horizons of awareness, is concerned with the situation of a mixed milieu - operating in both the Arab and the Jewish milieus. An older entrepreneur told us:

Jews refuse to buy concrete blocks from me because I am an Arab. They discriminate against me because they prefer to provide work for Jews. My blocks are significantly cheaper and their quality is higher than the regular standard. Still I don't get any Jewish customers. (Question: We do not see any quality control signature on your product, don't you think that this is necessary in order to attract Jewish customers?) Answer: Everybody in the town knows me and knows the quality of my product. I don't have to pay 10,000 Shekel for the quality control approval seal and Jews will never trust me anyway because I am an Arab.

Entrepreneurs are establishing themselves as an Arab economic elite that gains the support of the community at large, which capture the imagination of many frustrated youngsters who view entrepreneurship as a major route for mobility within Israeli society. Even the Moslem fundamentalists develop symbiotic relations with entrepreneurs by asking them to donate for Mosques and community services. Entrepreneurs succeeded in transforming this support to an economic advantage, gaining privilege standing within the family and the local political elite. Over-embeddedness than is articulated in the dominance of intra-ethnic pattern of business networks, the power that entrepreneurs gain in their intra-ethnic milieu in respect to their weakness in inter-ethnic milieus (as will be demonstrated in the next section), and barriers on entrepreneurs' horizons of awareness. The advantages that Arab entrepreneurs gain in their intra-ethnic milieu encourage them to play according to the informal norms of conduct required in this specific reality, and to enjoy entrepreneurs' independence even when channelled to a state of low profitability, typical to local markets. The persistence of this pattern reduces their chances to compete in the more rewarding markets of the Jewish milieu, where they should play according to different rules. Many entrepreneurs refuse to take the risks and retain only intra-ethnic networks. Others, mainly younger generation entrepreneurs, are highly motivated to make any effort and to take personal sacrifices and risks in breaking ethnic barriers (Schnell *et al.*, 1995).

To sum up, the over-embedded entrepreneur tends to remain contained in the safe and supporting milieu of his intra-ethnic stronghold. The use of over-embedded strategy may be initiated voluntarily by Arab entrepreneurs as a result of various entrepreneurial motivations, like political motivation to develop an autonomous economy. On the other hand the use of over-embedded strategy may be viewed as a survival strategy adopted when barriers of ethnicity and peripherality are turned to be unbreakable. It seems that the small local market and intense competition compel entrepreneurs to cut down costs, even by exploiting kinship relations and paying reduced wages, which typify informal economic activities. The persistence of such strategy may strengthen traditional institutions, and may result in the enlargement of the gap, in terms of economic behaviour, between both milieus. The consequence of which is the entrepreneur's decreasing prospect to integrate into the inter-ethnic market.

Under-Embeddedness within the Larger Israeli Economy

Under-embeddedness characterises some firms located in the periphery that manage to develop and maintain a wide though externally dependent set of networks. The owners of these firms are open to the erosion of the local supportive tissue of social practices and institutions, but did not manage to penetrate the highly rewarding markets. When they manage to get access into the wider markets they locate themselves within the network under conditions of dependency, where the firms and entreon the other side of the network dictate the terms of exchange relations.

Arab entrepreneurs' conditions of under-embeddedness surface explicitly in the context of inter-ethnic networks. As we have shown, a significant number of Arab enterprises have a certain degree of access (in many cases only limited access) to Jewish markets, including the national core, through their sale linkages. These findings may lead to the conclusion that some Arab enterprises have developed intensive and complex networks with various segments of the national economy, including the relatively more privileged sectors. Nevertheless, Arab entrepreneurs fail to overcome their marginal position within the Israeli economic space. What thus can explain the discrepancy between relatively complex networks and the lack of economic growth? Our argument is that this failure is the result of the subordinate position Arab entrepreneurs have experienced in the markets. They are cut off from valuable information flows and evaluation sources as well as power positions within the business networks. This discrepancy is the setting for the formation of conditions for under-embedded entrepreneurship.

The type of linkages formed between Arab entrepreneurs and Jewish markets can be illustrated by the food industry. This industry combines modern technology with traditional methods of production. Traditional know how learnt from the 'grand mother' is transformed into a modern production line. Such entrepreneurs, as shown below, base themselves on local networks and markets, but they search also inter-ethnic (relatively random and simple) networks without taking great risks.

> The idea to open a cheese factory crossed my mind when my grand father told me how grand ma had made great cheese from the sheep milk. I used her recipe and I started to sell to people in the town. After a wile I bought machines and I bought milk from other farmers in the village in order to increase production. We sell in most of the Arab settlements in the region and we have even Jewish customers. They come on Saturdays to buy in the shops in our town and we sell them directly from the plant. Once a week I go to Tel Aviv to buy some raw materials so I sell cheese to some stores at the market. On my way home I sell also to a store in Nataniya.

The issue of power relations inside the networks is exemplified by some construction enterprises, which were able to take advantage of changes in the Jewish market, but they are very much dependent on Jewish expertise and know-how concerning access to markets. In the late 1970s and during the 1980s, the government promoted a self-construction housing policy, hoping to enable the able segments of the 'new towns' and rural population to build new private houses and to remain in the peripheral regions of the country. Builders were ready to hire Arab construction contractors and to purchase construction material from Arab plants in their regions. Moreover, in the 1990s, the large expansion of the construction industry as a result of the massive immigration from the former Soviet Union created shortages in construction materials. These events opened a niche for Arab construction plants in the Jewish sector, which have been efficiently used until the economic recession of the mid-1990s. The dependency conditions are illustrated here:

> Take the Sa'ida family from Peqi'in. They were small-scale producers of concrete blocks and building materials. When they started to grow, they hired a Jewish economist. He helped them, and today they deal in millions. All the settlements in the area work with them, even to Jewish ones. You have no choice. If you want to grow, you have to be modern. Small family businesses are okay, but you can't drive Mercedes 300 based on them. Among us there still aren't many with expertise in financing and banks, and we really feel the lack. So meanwhile, anyone who starts to grow has to hire a Jew.

The dependency relations are mostly emphasised in the case of entrepreneurs operating in the textiles industry as subcontractors for Jewish mother corporations. Their high level of dependency on mother corporations and/or customers in the Jewish sector means lack of power to create for them a degree of autonomy in the market. The following example may demonstrate some of the problems that such enterprises confront:

> When our plant gained the trust of our mother corporation we have received a loan from them to buy sewing machines and we grew fast. I sent one brother to study machine engineering, my other brother study management. The rest of the family accumulated 50,000 Shekel to help me. We received the support of workers from my extended family that manages women from the occupied territories. We are highly reliable producers and we gained very good reputation every where. Now I plan to produce on my own and to sell to stores. I have to do it because I have only extremely marginal profit as a sub-contractor. I need more income to be able to help back my family who have helped me.

So far no entrepreneur operating in the textiles and clothing branch was able to make it. These entrepreneurs have faced the dilemma of focusing their efforts. Locating in Tel Aviv, searching for customers, attempting to follow leading enterprises and new trends in fashion, meant losing control over their production lines and even facing sanctions from their mother corporations. Yet, they remain in their home settlements, they continue to be cut off from necessary information that could assist in the evaluation of financial and market possibilities. This dilemma stresses difficulties in expanding Arab entrepreneurs' horizons of awareness into the Jewish milieu, which makes it extremely hard (to a certain degree) for them to develop evaluation capabilities.

Earlier findings suggest that lack of developed industrial areas, investment capital and government subsidies, equivalent to those given to neighbouring development towns, are the three major barriers for enterprises development (Schnell *et al.*, 1995). Yet, the in-depth interviews with a sample group of entrepreneurs shed light on the fact that Arab entrepreneurs have failed to embed themselves in the inter-ethnic milieu. While there are over-embedded entrepreneurs who avoid any attempt to break the safe intra-ethnic market, others are willing to make any necessary effort to break these barriers. They even succeed in exploiting marginal niches in Jewish markets, but they fail to expand into the more rewarding markets by virtue of their conditions of under-embeddedness. Failure to determine sale conditions, inferior position in the networks, dependency on mother plants and limited horizons of awareness leave them with low profitability and low rate of growth. As a consequence they cannot afford to take bank loans, and to pay the necessary expenses to operate as an officially registered enterprise in developed industrial zones.

Conclusions

Our study demonstrates several examples of discrepancies among the three complementary dimensions of ethnic entrepreneurs' networks: intensity and complexity of networks; power relations and entrepreneur's horizons of awareness. We realised that vertical links are kept under dependency relations. Moreover, entrepreneurs are cutting down on the number of links as a compromise with the larger corporations with whom they want to trade. The most prominent examples show that inter-ethnic networks do not give ethnic entrepreneurs instantaneous advantage unless they learn to operate outside their business culture, and unless they develop some business autonomy that may enable them to improve their bargaining position in the market. The fact that Arab entrepreneurs are rarely members of business organisations like the industrialists association, bureau of commerce and other small business national organisations, does not assist them to secure better access to the national economic and political elite. Arab entrepreneurs only rarely make use of support programs offered by the ministry of industry and commerce since they do not believe in their ability to adapt to their prerequisites. These features emphasise the absence of links with the Jewish and the national economy and political elite, as well as with Jewish competitors. In this context it is understandable why Arab entrepreneurs fail to translate into profits their efforts and ability to expand into Jewish markets.

Competition with the corporations has been identified as the hardest obstacle for embeddedness in the inter-ethnic milieu. Entrepreneurs are willing to take risks and to expand markets, but they find it difficult to translate entrepreneurship into high profit and multipliers of growth. The following example of a bakery from Daburya shows a form of compromise achieved between this bakery and a larger Jewish owned bakery. This compromise may offer a form of an acceptable mixed-embeddedness thus presenting a more even form of embeddedness.

> In an attempt to grow I started to convince Jewish food stores in the region to buy from me the Arab bread (pitta). I promised storeowners to bring them twice a day fresh pittas and I sent them little bit cheaper. For a while my business grew rapidly and it was a great success. I even started to plan the expansion of the bakery in an industrial zone, but than the problems started. The bread bakery, which has a monopoly standing on standard bread, put pressure on the stores not to buy from me the pitta. It was hard to compete with Oranim (owned by a kibbutz near Nazareth) because the bakery forced its customers to buy its pitta if they wanted to buy its bread. Since our pitta is better, we had to buy bread in Haifa and supply our customers with both pitta and bread in order to fight Oranim's monopoly. Then Oranim proposed an agreement: They would supply the bread and we would supply the pitta. There's still competition and some hitting below the belt. Oranim gets tax exemptions and subsidies so they can give the buyers discounts. Here we don't get subsidies: it's not a development area. I managed to compete because of my personal approach to the customers and because my product is better than the others are. I supply on time, in the amount required, and on credit. However I was forced to compromise with them and to distribute the pitta through them sharing with them part of my profit.

This is an example of which it is hard to find many other genuine examples due to the fact that these are rare. This bakery succeeded to overcome barriers of ethnicity and peripherality and managed to find the proper tactic by which it has succeeded to find the appropriate conditions for mixed-embeddedness.

Our last remark is related to policies. It could be said that Arab entrepreneurs may somewhat improve their awareness to opportunities in the Jewish markets by adapting to Jewish business culture, but they have little chance to improve their power relations with national corporations without public support. Since the restructuring of an intra-ethnic informal business culture is a response to powerlessness in inter-ethnic networks, it seems that Arab entrepreneurs are caught in a vicious circle of marginalisation. Interviews with managers of Jewish corporations who tried to initiate partnerships with Arab entrepreneurs show that almost all of them have failed because of their inability to get used to informal forms of management. Therefore, there is an urgent need to initiate special programs for the integration of Arab enterprises into the national economy, an integration that may also serve as an appropriate mechanism for socio-political integration. Lack of such programs may halt Arab entrepreneurs from a proper and balanced integration into the wider Israeli economic milieu, and may lead them to a retreat and entrenched over-embeddedness within their Arab intra-ethnic milieu.

References

Abo Sharika, N. (1998), *Small Businesses and Their Networks among the Arab Minority in Israel*, Master Thesis, Department of Architecture and Town Planning, Technion, Haifa.

Aldrich, H.E. and Waldinger, R. (1990), 'Ethnicity and Entrepreneurship', *Annual Review of Sociology*, 16, pp. 111-135.

Atrash, A. (1992), 'The Arab Industry in Israel: Branch Structure, Employment and Plant Formation', *Economics Quarterly*, 152, pp. 112-120 (Hebrew).

Barrett, G.A., Jones, T.V. and McEvoy, D. (1996), 'Ethnic Minority Business: Theoretical Discourse in Britain and North America', *Urban Studies*, 33, 4-5, pp. 783-809.

Best, M. (1990), *The New Competition: Institutions of Industrial Restructuring*, Harvard University Press, Cambridge, Ma.

Burt, R.S. (1992), *Structural Holes: The Social Structure of Competition*, Harvard University Press, Cambridge, Ma.

Central Bureau of Statistics (1992), *Statistical Abstracts of Israel*, Jerusalem.

Curran, J. and Blackburn, R. (1994), *Small Firms and Local Economic Networks*, Paul Chapman, London.

Falah, G. (1993), 'Trends in the Urbanization of Arab Settlements in Galilee', *Urban Geography*, 14, 2, pp. 145-164.

Felsenstein, D. (1992), 'Assessing the Effectiveness of Small Business Financing Schemes: Some Evidence from Israel', *Small Business Economics*, 4, pp 273-285.

Grabher, G. (1993), 'Rediscovering the Social in the Economics of Interfirm Relations', in G. Grabher (ed.), *The Embedded Firm*, Routledge, London, pp. 1-31.

Grabher, G. and Stark, D. (1997), 'Organizing Diversity: Evolutionary Theory, Network Analysis and Postsocialism', *Regional Studies*, 31, pp. 533-544.

Gradus, Y., Razin, E. and Krakover, S. (1993), *The Industrial Geography of Israel*, Routledge, London.

Granovetter, M. (1985), 'Economic and Social Structure: the Problem of Embeddedness', *American Journal of Sociology*, 91, 3, pp. 481-510.

Haidar, A. (1993), *Obstacles to Economic Development in the Arab Sector in Israel*, The Israeli Arab Centre for Economic Development, Tel-Aviv (Hebrew).

Hakansson, H. and Johanson, J. (1993), 'The Network as a Governance Structure: Interfirm

Cooperation Beyond Markets and Hierarchies', in G. Grabher (ed.), *The Embedded Firm*, Routledge, London, pp. 35-51.

Han, S.K. (1992), 'Curning Firms in Stable Markets', *Social Science Research*, 21, pp. 406-418.

Hardill, I., Fletcher, D. and Montagne-Villette, S. (1995), '"Small Firms" Distinctive Capabilities and the Socioeconomic Milieu: Findings from Case studies in Le Choletais (France) and the East Midlands (UK)', *Entrepreneurship and Regional Development*, 7, pp. 167-186.

Harrison, B. (1992), 'Industrial Districts: Old Wine in a New Bottle?', *Regional Studies*, 26, pp. 469-483.

Kay, J. (1993), *Foundations of Corporate Success*, Oxford University Press, Oxford.

Khamaisi, R. (1984), *Arab Industry in Israel*, Unpublished Magister Thesis, Technion, Haifa (Hebrew).

Kloosterman, R., Van Der Leun, J. and Rath, J. (1999), 'Mixed Embeddedness: In Formal Economic Activities and Immigrant Businesses in the Netherlands', *International Journal of Urban and Regional Research*, 23, 2, pp. 252-266.

Lakshmanan, T.R. and Okumura, M. (1995), 'The Nature and Evolution of Knowledge Networks in Japanese Manufacturing', *Papers in Regional Science*, 74, pp. 63-86.

Malecki, E.J. and Tootle, D.M. (1996), 'The Role of Networks in Small Firms Competitiveness', *International Journal of Technology Management*, 11, pp. 43-57.

Markusen, A. (1994), 'Studying Regions by Studying Firms', *Professional Geographer*, 46, 4, pp. 477-490.

Maskell, P. and Malmberg, A. (1999), 'Localised Learning and Industrial Competitiveness', *Cambridge Journal of Economics*, 23, pp. 167-185.

Oinas, P. (1999), 'Voices and Silences: the Problem of Access to Embeddedness', *Geoforum*, 30, pp. 351-361.

Perry, M. and Goldfinch, S. (1996), 'Business Networks Outside an Industrial District', *Tijdschrift voor Economische en Sociale Geografie*, 87, pp. 222-236.

Portes, A. and Sensenbrenner, J. (1993), 'Embeddedness and Immigration: Notes on the Social Determinants of Economic Action', *American Journal of Sociology*, 98, 6, pp. 1320-1350.

Schnell, I., Benenson, I. and Sofer, M. (1999), 'The Spatial Pattern of Arab Industrial Markets in Israel', *Annals of the Association of American Geographers*, 89, 2, 311-336.

Schnell, I., Sofer, M. and Drori, I. (1995), *Arab Industrialization in Israel*, Praeger, Westport.

Scott, A.J. (1991), 'The Aerospace-Electronics Industrial Complex of Southern California: The Formative Years 1940-1960', *Research Policy*, 20, pp. 439-456.

Sofer, M. and Schnell, I. (2000), 'The Restructuring Stages of Israeli Arab Industrial Entrepreneurship', *Environment and Planning A*, 32, pp. 2231-2250.

Sofer, M., Schnell, I. and Drori, I. (1996), 'Industrial Zones and Arab Industrialization in Israel', *Human Organization*, 55, 4, pp. 465-474.

Staber, U. and Schaefer, N. (eds.) (1996), *Business Networks: Prospects for Regional Development*, Walter de Gruyter, Berlin.

Talmud, I. and Mesh, G.S. (1997), 'Market Organization and Corporate Instability: The Ecology of Inter-Industrial Networks', *Social Science Research*, 26, pp. 419-441.

Talmud, I. and Yanovitzki, I. (1998), 'The Contradictory Demand Paradox: Social Embeddedness and Organizational Performances', *Israeli Sociology*, 1, 1, pp. 55-90 (Hebrew).

Taylor, M. (1995), 'The Business Enterprise, Power and Patterns of Geographical Industrialization', in S. Conti, E.J. Malecki and P. Oinas (eds), *The Industrial Organisation and its Environment: Spatial Perspectives*, Avebury, Aldershot, pp. 99-122.

Tödtling, F. (1994), 'The Uneven Landscape of Innovation Poles: Local Embeddedness and

Global Networks', in A. Amin and N. Thrift (eds), *Globalization, Institutions, and Regional Development in Europe*, Oxford University Press, Oxford, pp. 68-90.

Uzzi, B. (1996), 'The Sources and Consequences of Embeddedness for the Economic Performance of Organizations: The Network Effect'. *American Sociological Review,* 61, pp. 674-698.

Waldinger, R. (1995), 'The Other-Side of Embeddedness: a Case-Study of the Interplay of Economy and Ethnicity', *Ethnic and Racial Studies,* 18, 3, pp. 555-580.

Yeung, H. (2000), 'Organizing "the firm" in industrial geography: Networks, institutions and regional development', *Progress in Human Geography,* 24, pp. 301-315.

Chapter 3

High-Technology Clustering in Cambridge (UK)

Philip Cooke and Robert Huggins

Introduction

High-technology clusters are one of the most visible manifestations of what Michael Storper and Allen Scott (1995) term the construction of place-specific economic culture and order. This is often based on gaining an early start within the development of infant industries for which product frameworks have not yet matured into a specific identifiable technological trajectory. This results in an innate requirement for business *networks*, since:

> (T)he high levels of openness in these cases has to do with the need for additional technological developments before products can be fully commercialised. Considerable risk and uncertainty exist for potential producers in these nascent sectors (Storper and Scott, 1995, p. 513).

This openness within a potentially highly competitive marketplace is an important indicator of the link between high-technology activity and cluster formation.

Clusters have become a key mode of economic co-ordination and focus of government policies across the world, incorporating a wide variety of industries. In particular, they have rapidly gained prominence as the hierarchical firm, a pronounced feature of the mid-twentieth century corporate landscape, no longer acts as the dominant model of economic co-ordination. The rise of global competition, the mobilisation of innovation as a leading competitive weapon, and the subsequent growth of knowledge-based firms have all contributed to the emergence of new forms of territorial development and competition. In the UK since 1997 and the arrival of New Labour in government, there has been some policy-leapfrogging over parts Europe, the USA and Japan, with government enthusiasm and special funding for cluster development in both 'new' and 'old' economies but with an emphasis on high-technology product or process solutions for both (see DTI, 2001).

This paper presents an analysis of the economy of Cambridge in the UK, exploring the means by which two sectors of high-technology activity – biotechnology and Information & Communication Technology (ICT) – are forming distinct clustered organisational structures based on informal and formal, hard and soft forms of networking between firms and their agencies. By means of an analysis of existing quantitative data and a series of twenty-five in-depth interviews, representing a broad cross-section of the relevant sectors, including both firms and agencies, the paper enters the 'black box' of cluster activity within the Cambridge high-tech sector. In part of the ICT cluster, specifically, it traces in detail the nature and variety of intra-cluster network linkages. The sequence of the paper involves a theoretical outline of the cluster concept, reference to some developments in the UK, followed by an empirical analysis of the Cambridge biotechnology and ICT clusters. The paper concludes by highlighting some of the positive capabilities but also growth barrier factors connected to clusters as a particular form of business development and economic growth.

The Concept of High-Technology Clusters

As a point of conceptual departure it is perhaps pertinent to highlight Michael Porter's (1998) definition of clusters as: 'a geographically proximate group of interconnected companies and associated institutions in a particular field, linked by commonalities and complementarities'. There is nothing conceptually wrong with this definition except that it is static whereas the key feature of clusters is that they are *dynamic*. Hence we prefer the following factors to be taken into account:

- A cluster displays a shared identity and future vision.
- It is characterised by 'turbulence' as firms spin-off, spin-out and start-up from other firms or institutions.
- A cluster is an arena of dense and changing vertical input-output linkages, supply chains and horizontal inter-firm networks.
- It is likely to have developed localised, third-party representative governance associations that provide common services but also lobby government for change.
- A cluster may have caused governments to develop policies to assist cluster development, especially where market-failures are present.
- Over time, clusters can reveal features of emergence, dominance and decline.

This is a much more rigorous lead-in to a definition of clusters than Porter's because of its sensitivity to *process*, and it is more meaningful than the objects catalogued in DTI (2001) which consist of regional sub-sectors with marginally above-average location quotients. The latter lack spatial identity, even in terms of localisation economies, or agglomeration, and they absolutely lack a sense of human agency supplied by the concept of *governance*. So we prefer to define clusters as: *geographically proximate firms in vertical and horizontal relationships, involving a localised enterprise support infrastructure with a shared developmental vision for business growth, based on competition and co-operation in a specific market field.*

Furthermore, we agree with findings expressed at the British Association for the Advancement of Science reported by Cookson (1999) that states:

- Looser groupings of firms in clusters have better, more efficient knowledge transfer than stand-alone hierarchical corporations.
- Clusters (e.g. Silicon Valley) combine higher turnover of scientists and engineers with extraordinary openness about technical information.
- Clusters kill-off unproductive projects through insolvencies while large firms have weak mechanisms for ceasing them.

Returning to Porter (1998), we are in agreement that a number of advantages are derived from clusters. In particular, productivity gains arise from access to early use of better quality and lower cost specialised inputs from components or services suppliers in the cluster. Local sourcing can be cheaper because of minimal inventory requirements and transaction costs generally can be lower because of the existence of high trust relations and the importance of reputation-based trading. Common purchasing can lower costs where external sourcing is necessary. Serendipitous information trading is more likely in contexts where formal or informal face-to-face contact is possible. Complementarities between firms can help joint-bidding and scale benefits on contract tenders, or joint marketing of products and services. Access to public goods from research or standards bodies located in proximity can be advantageous.

Also, innovation gains come from proximity between customers and suppliers where the interaction between the two may lead to innovative specifications and responses. User-led innovation impulses are recognised as crucial to the innovation process and their discovery has led to a better understanding of the interactive rather than linear processes of innovation. Proximity to knowledge centres makes the interaction processes concerning design, testing and prototype development physically easier, especially where much of the necessary knowledge is partly or wholly tacit rather than codified. Localised benchmarking among firms on organisational as well as product and process innovation is facilitated in clusters. Qualified personnel are more easily recruited and are of key importance to knowledge-transfer. Furthermore, informal know-how trading is easier in clusters than through more distant relationships.

Finally, new businesses are more readily formed where better information about innovative potential and market opportunities are locally available. Barriers to entry for new firms can be lower because of a clearer perception of unfulfilled needs, product or service gaps, or anticipated demand. Locally available inputs and skills further reduce barriers to entry. A cluster in itself can be an important initial market. Familiarity with local public, venture capital or business angel funding sources may speed up the investment process and minimise risk premiums for new start-ups and growing businesses. Clusters attract outside firms and foreign direct investors who perceive benefits from being in a specialised, leading-edge business location. These may also be a further source of corporate spin-off businesses.

Clusters work through networks between a variety of businesses and other appropriate actors who are familiar with each other's expertise, trustworthiness, reliability and willingness both to share relevant assets (e.g. information or lending a machine or employee if needed) and engage in normal business relationships based on market or arm's length exchange. Networks can be formal or informal, soft (e.g. reputational) or hard (i.e. contractual, with an agreed project and business plan). In high technology industry, such linkages are likely to involve research organisations such as universities both for knowledge, but also indirectly through spin-out firms.

Clusters operate through acting as an 'economic community' based on informal and formal, hard and soft forms of networking between firms and agencies. Consciousness of cluster existence and a formalised, membership-based association able to keep all in touch as needed is often key to successful clustering. Finally, public efforts to create clusters, as distinct from mere agglomerations of similar activity (e.g. R&D) have not been entirely successful, or as the recent experiences of such spaces as Sophia-Antipolis or North Carolina's Research Triangle Park demonstrate, extraordinarily slow to bear fruit in terms of interactive innovation (see, for instance, Longhi, 1999). Where a 'seed crystal', such as a key outsourcing firm or research laboratories seeking to commercialise knowledge and intellectual property (IPR) exist, public intervention can be important in further activating and enhancing cluster development. This explains, for example, high technology clustering in Munich in relation to Siemens (after Sternberg and Tamásy, 1999) or the Xerox Palo Alto Research Centre (PARC) in Silicon Valley (Saxenian, 1994).

In other words, simple geographical concentration is not enough if there is insufficient synergy to create an innovative surplus of value from planned or serendipitous interactions on a recurring basis between the key actors in different parts of the cluster. This is what differentiates a mere agglomeration of similar firms from a cluster. A cluster is a geographically focused concentration of complementary firms capable of collaborating and competing, supported by necessary, external organisations supplying research, intelligence, financial resources and networking capabilities. In knowledge-driven or knowledge-intensive sectors research outputs of universities and specialised institutes are the core elements and, because such industries are new, they have a greater role than normal in stimulating the formation of commercial enterprises, such as start-up firms and the incubator premises such new businesses need.

Of equivalent practical importance are sources of start-up or seed-corn funding, leading eventually to sources of venture capital and the chances of forming long-term business partnerships with multinational firms for production and marketing. In these financial dimensions, biotechnology is unique because of the extremely long lead-time from initial 'proof of concept' that a discovery has exploitation value, to the transformation of the concept into a product. Thus, high technology clusters rely, especially at 'proof of concept' stage, on proximity to leading knowledge centres such as universities and research institutes. Also, because such fledgling firms rely on a supportive and entrepreneurial culture for start-up, incubation and early financing activities, a proximate innovation and enterprise support market is essential (as shown by Crevoisier, 1997). Good links with large customer firms as well as good networking between start-ups and public support agencies are also necessary. Thus sources of venture capital, business angels and seed-corn funding should ideally be located in proximity to, if not at the heart of, the cluster. Appropriate human capital is required from the education and training system, and staff must be able to be attracted with appropriate housing and environmental qualities.

The key competitive advantages of cluster formation, particularly in biotechnology and ICT, have been neatly summarised in a report for the Organisation for Economic Co-operation and Development (Roelandt and den Hertog, 1998) where they render business more effective, efficient and competitive by enabling firms to:

- Lower transaction costs.
- Gain access to new and complementary technology.
- Capture economies of synergy and interdependent activities.
- Spread risks.
- Promote joint R&D efforts with suppliers and users.
- Act as a defensive strategy to reduce harmful competition.
- Obtain reciprocal benefits from the combined use of complementary assets and knowledge.
- Speed up learning processes.
- Overcome (or create) entry barriers to markets.

A weakness of evolutionary economic theorising, shared with the 'regulationist' approach is a reliance on chance as the explanation for events when causality cannot be tracked down (Arthur. 1994; Leborgne and Lipietz, 1988). As Elizabeth Garnsey (1998) has argued, analysing the genesis of high-tech clusters is a study in complexity. For instance, the economists' favoured 'accident theory' for understanding the location of economic development does not sufficiently explore the complexity of evolutionary systems, in particular the vital, yet often impossible to measure, human and social components. These human and social components are key variables in facilitating a selection regime – as proposed by evolutionary economists – based on availability and access to resources, many of which are best gathered through networked collaboration as opposed to market competition. It is precisely this mode of business development that is able to protect clusters against external forces such as recession and consumer product sentiment.

Paul Krugman (1994) has argued that 'given a slightly different sequence of events, Silicon Valley might have been in Los Angeles, Massachusetts, or even Oxfordshire' (p. 416). This appears to be a massive exaggeration, almost completely ignoring the complex forces at work at both the cluster inception and growth stages. The social infrastructure differential within these regions is such that even if the same sequence of events were to take place in each, an entirely different form of business evolution, that may or may not involve cluster development, is most probable.

To assume a stance based on historical accident is to ignore the influence of existing culture within a location. For instance, although there is obvious empirical evidence to suggest that the creation of high-tech clusters can be associated with the existence of university and research institutions, this is clearly an insufficient explanation given the majority of such institutions around the world have not acted as cluster catalysts. The initial, and ensuing, conditions are necessarily complex and interrelated, making the deconstruction and isolation of core variables an intricate task. For instance, the location of the Motor Sport Valley cluster, centred around Oxfordshire in the UK, is not accidental but the outcome of a mix of variables, including an abundance of racing tracks, the coalescence of mass car production and aerospace activity, specialised labour, and cheap land availability (Pinch and Henry, 1999).

The weakness of the 'chance' explanation is closer to being captured in the way Michael Storper (1995) expresses it: 'In evolutionary economics, what we do is path-dependent, that is truly historical; it is not the result of a series of actions on spot markets, where the long-term can be disconnected instants' (p. 204). This is due to technological development being the product of interdependent choices that are predicated by the existing network systems. It is the system of networks within high-tech clusters upon which the technological 'spillovers' and 'untraded interdependencies' – or the linkage reliance between cluster members beyond the market – portrayed by Storper are channelled and communicated, facilitating cluster actors to travel along what he refers to as 'superior technological trajectories'. However, the weakness in Storper's argument is to give insufficient attention to the extent of 'arm's length exchange' present in 'spillovers' as disclosed in research on biotechnology by Zucker et al. (1998). An as yet unanswered research question concerns the extent to which 'trade' actually goes on when what appear to be 'untraded' interdependencies are activated. In biotechnology even tacit knowledge exchange is often hemmed-in by confidentiality clauses and the cash nexus.

Hierarchical firms are becoming rapidly deconstructed, and replaced or replacing themselves by networks of small and medium-sized companies. In biotechnology and ICT, otherwise distinctive sectors, out-sourcing of key assets, including R&D by large corporations is a largely completed act by firms assailed by global competition and injunctions to adopt 'lean' management and production. At the lower end of the value chain this entails formation of global production networks (Gereffi, 1996). For high value-added services like research they are often strategically aware of the importance of proximity as a pivotal factor in their portfolio of capital assets. The apotheosis of this is Cisco Systems whose strategy is to 'innovate by acquisition', mainly in its Silicon Valley home-base, something practised for longer, through its 'look-out' facility there, by Microsoft. Venture capital *keiretsu* firms like KPCB create their own equity-based clusters, also mainly in Silicon Valley, and Intel do the same through their Corporate Venturing investment arm. Such new business practices and forms of marketised networking activity are catalysing cluster building as a virtuous cycle for managing both growth and risk (Cooke, 2001).

The dynamism of these clusters is such that there is an ever-changing balance in the relative importance of the conditions leading to the genesis of a cluster or of its growth and sustainability. In particular, there is a shift away from cost factors, physical infrastructure and regulatory policies to the strength of the softer and social infrastructure, focused on the long-term socio-economic business culture. It is this business culture that provides the social infrastructure with feedback loops that are sufficiently rapid to ensure the cluster as a whole maintains a position at the head of its global innovation chain. Also, it is the prevailing business culture that acts as the key magnet attracting other high-value companies into the cluster.

There is growing evidence to suggest that who innovates and how much innovation takes place is closely connected to a phase of the industry life cycle of sector, product, or process. The important question of where this innovation takes place is often strangely ignored. Therefore, a simple yet fundamental question must be asked do firms in clusters actually innovate more? Evidence from the UK shows that firms are considerably more likely to innovate if own-sector employment in its home sector is strong (Baptista and Swann, 1998). In other words, the higher the level of geographic concentration of production, the greater is the propensity towards catalysing innovative activity. Furthermore, strong clusters are more likely to attract newly formed firms, resulting in strong clusters growing faster than non-clustered industrial locations (Feldman and Audretsch, 1999). These processes, therefore, have very important implications for the economic and industrial development policies of national, regional and local governments.

Perhaps the most important variable affecting the sustainability of strong clusters is social attachment to a particular location in terms of residency and lifestyle and its influence on both non-work and economic decision-making. This attachment to a location increases the likelihood of further network development that will have a positive bearing on economic forces. This is shown to be particularly the case in the emergence of important software clusters in three less-expected urban locales in India, Israel and Ireland. Bangalore, Tel Aviv and Dublin each displays variants of 'café society' and 'ambience' that, according to Balasubramanyam & Balasubramanyam (2000) have allure for highly-paid young software engineers. These are examples of 'node coalescence' where social relationships may iteratively, or perhaps suddenly, present a particular business opportunity due to a change in selection regime for one of more nodal elements (Cooke, Davies and Wilson, 2001). As Castells and Hall (1994) have shown, the development of high-tech clusters involves the close integration of the 'usual' factors of production – capital, labour, and raw material, brought together by some kind of institutional entrepreneur, and constituted by a particular form of social organisation.

According to David Audretsch (1998, p. 23) 'the role of tacit knowledge in generating innovative activity is presumably the greatest during the early stages the industry life cycle, before product standards have been established and a dominant design has emerged'. This indicates the high potentiality for the overlap of cluster evolution with industrial and product life-cycles and trajectories. This argument is clearly proven by the clusterisation and declusterisation that has occurred within traditional industries as a direct result of product and technological change. However, the crucial distinction of high-tech clusters is their seeming ability to renew themselves beyond the limits of normal industrial life-cycles, due to the particular socio-economic forces at work. It is the difference between firms that merely co-located with an area, as opposed to those possessing the features of clusters. However, the requirement for specialised technological research, supply, and servicing means that high-technology industries are bound by very specific knowledge base, limiting the number of locations within which high-technology development across the globe has so far occurred. This in itself has been a pre-conditioning factor consistent with emergence of high-tech concentrations and clusters.

High-Technology Clusters in the UK

In the UK cluster development in Cambridge is far more progressed than it is in Oxford (and the associated M4 Corridor zone), with network development and usage being almost 50 per cent higher in Cambridge (Garnsey and Lawton Smith, 1999). Within Cambridge it is very much informal channels and personal relationships that have shaped the formation of the high-tech cluster, in particular the links between the University and its spin-off companies (Lawson, 1999). Also, while Oxford University has a policy of claiming Intellectual Property Rights generated by staff and students, Cambridge University has adopted a more entrepreneurial policy of endowing originators with Intellectual Property Rights. Furthermore, Cambridge University has sought to stimulate network development through the provision of innovation support initiatives. This is further sustained by the formation by entrepreneurs of the private Cambridge Network Ltd. organisation to enhance local and global *associativeness*. Oxford University, on the other hand, has taken the more insular route of seeking to achieve competitive advantage through the maintenance of legally-binding in-house intellectual capital.

As Elizabeth Garnsey and Helen Lawton Smith (1998) find, it is the better network endowed region of Cambridge, through its role as a centre of both computer hardware and software, that is continuing a create the localised multiplier effects associated with clusterisation – the so-called 'Cambridge Phenomenon'. David Keeble and others at the University of Cambridge (1999) have further found evidence that although the University provides an important socio-cultural precondition for learning, it is firm spin-offs, inter-firm and organisational networks, and local scientific and managerial recruitment practices that significantly act as dynamic collective learning processes.

Clusters elsewhere in the UK generally do not have this consciousness of clustering translated into marketised organisational forms. It is a learned rather than self-generated form even in Cambridge. The role-model is California, specifically Silicon Valley and the San Diego 'Connect' network that formalised the informal networking activities that were claimed to differentiate the former from Route 128 Boston (Saxenian, 1994). That such networking and cluster-building activity can be learned and the knowledge transferred is testified to in the 'resurgence of Route 128' which Best (2000) shows to be directly caused by the adoption by Massachusetts policy advisers and Route 128 entrepreneurs of a Californian 'open systems architecture' and the cluster-promotion mentality during the 1990s. The task for policy elsewhere is to understand the key mechanisms at the cognitive and learning levels and adapt them to different circumstances. One of the reasons why old economy clusters in the UK and elsewhere atrophied was because once 'community' was no longer enough to ensure systemic information flow, firms themselves acted as though they required only protection from competition rather than exposure to co-operation in order to prosper. Thus the Macclesfield silk and Stoke-on-Trent silk industries were weakened by attempts to keep labour market competitors out of the district by controlling or influencing spatial planning decisions. They then sought to compete on low-wages, hence price-competition, often to protected markets like the military or government, rather than innovation. A key cultural feature of their absolute decline, in the case of Macclesfield silk, and relative decline in Stoke ceramics, was the absence of local associationalism and predominance of predatory acquisition practices towards local competitors (Cooke, 2001).

When ICT firms in Cambridge were questioned as to the regional advantages most important to business development the most important variables all related to social infrastructure developments: (1) attractive local living environment for staff and directors; (2) credibility, reputation and prestige of a Cambridge address; and (3) informal local access to innovative people, ideas, technologies. More than three-quarters of such firms in the Cambridge cluster possess close links and networks with other local companies, with almost all of these firms rating such networks as important business development assets, in particular through a high level of informal contact between the management and research staff of cluster companies (Keeble et al., 1999).

With respect to biotechnology, the UK is Europe's leading location for biotechnology and ranks second in the world, some way behind the USA. Cambridge is the leading location for biotechnology businesses in Europe. The Ernst and Young Sixth Annual Report on European Life Sciences reported 273 biotechnology companies in the UK in 1999, up from 250 in 1998. Germany is the UK's closest European rival with some 220 firms, a 50 per cent increase since 1997, largely caused by investment of £50 million by the federal government in commercialisation grants through its BioRegio programme 1997-2001. Some 24,500 are employed in UK bioscience firms with less than 50 employees according to UK Bioindustry Association statistics, compared with perhaps 5,000 in Entrepreneurial Life Sciences Companies (ELISCOs) in Germany according to Ernst and Young (1998). American equivalents number 1,274 firms and some 140,000 employees. The industry has grown rapidly and world markets are estimated at $70 billion in 2000. As will be shown, as many as 200 firms in and around Cambridge are in touch with biotechnology, with a core of some half or less than that being active in the key fields of diagnostics and drug-development. The Human Genome project was co-hosted by the Sanger Institute, located near to and an offshoot of Cambridge University.

High-Technology Cambridge

Cambridge is well known for possessing significant clusterisation in high technology, particularly around University sites such as the Cambridge Science Park and the St John's Innovation Centre, with total employment in the high-tech sector of approximately 38,000 (1998 estimate). The sector is growing rapidly, and expanded by 20 per cent since the mid-1990s (approximately 5,000 new jobs created since 1995). Overall, the high-tech sector accounts for 11 per cent of employment in Cambridgeshire, with approximately 70 per cent of high-tech firms situated either in Cambridge City or South Cambridgeshire. Cambridge is the home of academic research at Cambridge University, Cambridge Science Park (founded in 1969 by Trinity College and housing approximately 70 firms) and St John's Innovation Centre (founded in 1987 by St John's College, also housing approximately 70 firms). Cambridge also has a very strong cluster of R&D establishments, including the following major independent and company research organisations:

- Babraham Institute
- Cambridge Consultants Ltd
- Medical Research Council
- National Institute of Agricultural Botany
- PA Technology
- PBI (Plant Breeding Institute)
- Sanger Centre
- Scientific Generics
- Technology Partnership
- TWI (The Welding Institute)
- Agrevo
- Hitachi
- Microsoft
- AT&T
- Schlumberger
- Toshiba.

A recent trend is that of high-tech re-locations from city-edge positions back into the city (for example: Acorn Computers and Tadpole). However, South Cambridgeshire remains an important area for high-tech activity, with an increasing number of science parks and research institutes. South Cambridgeshire also accounts for 45 per cent of all high-tech manufacturing sector jobs in Cambridgeshire. Almost three-quarters (74 per cent) of firms are small in size, with less than 25 employees with the main sub-sector representation consisting of R&D (24 per cent of high-tech employment); electronic engineering (17 per cent); and computer services (13 per cent).

However, there has been little research that has attempted to 'unpack' the make-up of these rather generic sub-sectors, in order to look at the linkages and inter-linkages between firms and their activities. Also, we consider that to some extent the figures may be misleading with regard to what high-tech actually entails. For example, the figures indicate that five per cent of high-tech employment consists of aero-engineering, which on further analysis consists almost entirely of Marshall's Aerospace facility. However, the majority of employment at Marshall's cannot be considered to be high-tech in its nature, although it is nevertheless a vitally important high-performance engineering establishment.

The issue of proximity to Cambridge University is clearly of importance to certain companies. However, it has been estimated by Garnsey (1995) that firms growing directly out of Cambridge University probably account for only some 20 per cent of the total of high-tech firms in the area. Nevertheless, such spin-out firms themselves do have major influence on resulting enterprise activity. In particular, Garnsey (1995) suggests that the 'demonstration effect' of successful enterprise is a major stimulus to further company formation by employees of 'first generation' firms, and clear that 'more extensive business networks are needed to encourage innovative interaction on a wider basis'. Hence, serial entrepreneurship exists, involving spin-off from academic entrepreneurship. If networking were as pronounced as in Silicon Valley more entrepreneurship should ensue. A key question for policy, of course, is what are the obstacles to such further networking. We show below that Cambridge elitism is the proximate cause and that the privatisation of networks acts as an exclusionary mechanism. Paraphrasing, we can suggest with reasonable confidence that, culturally, despite adoption of learned practices such as formalised networking, Cambridge is a long way from California.

The Cambridge Biotechnology Cluster

Cambridge is the UK's leading centre for biotechnology research and commercialisation, closely followed by Oxfordshire, Surrey and central Scotland, all of which have more than fifty firms. Cambridgeshire's core biotechnology industry consists of approximately 90 firms and the broader cluster (venture capitalists, patent lawyers etc.) consists of approximately 200 firms, with the core biotechnology firms employing 2,500-3,000 people. Table 3.1 shows the distribution of biotechnology companies and support services in Cambridge.

Cambridge has a rather diverse biotechnology processing and development as well as services support structure, even though the industry is relatively young and small. Some of the service infrastructure and perhaps the equipment sector benefits from the earlier development of Information Technology businesses, many also spinning out from university research in Cambridge. The infrastructure support for biotechnology in and around Cambridge is impressive, much of it deriving from the university and hospital research facilities. The Laboratory of Molecular Biology at Addenbrookes Hospital, funded by the Medical Research Council; Cambridge University's Institute of Biotechnology, Department of Genetics and Centre for Protein Engineering; the Babraham Institute and Sanger Institute with their emphasis on functional genomics research and the Babraham and St. John's incubators for biotechnology start-ups and commercialisation, are all globally-recognised facilities, particularly in biopharmaceuticals. However, in the region are also located important research institutes in the field of agricultural and food biotechnology, such as the Institute for Food Research, John Innes Centre, Institute of Arable Crop Research and National Institute of Arable Botany.

Table 3.1 Shares of biotechnology and services functions

3.1a Biotechnology Firm Distribution (%)		3.1b Biotechnology Services Distribution (%)	
Biopharmaceuticals	41	Sales & Marketing	29
Instrumentation	20	Management Consulting	23
Ag-food Bio	17	Corporate Accounting	15
Diagnostics	11	Venture Capital	15
Reagents/Chemicals	7	Legal & Patents	8
Energy	4	Business Incubation	10

Source: ERBI (1999).

Within a 25-mile radius of Cambridge are found many of the 'big pharma' or specialist biopharmaceutical firms with which commercialisation development by smaller start-ups and R&D by research institutes must be co-financed. Firms like Glaxo Wellcome, SmithKline Beecham, Merck, Rhone-Poulenc Rorer, Hoechst Pharmaceuticals in this category are represented, and in the specialist biopharmaceutical sector: Amgen, Napp, Genzyme and Bioglan *inter alia*. Thus on another of the criteria for successful cluster development, namely access within reasonable proximity to large customer and funding partner firms, Cambridge is, again, nodally positioned. Finally, with respect to agro-food biotechnology, Rhone-Poulenc, Agrevo, Dupont, Unilever and Ciba are situated in proximity to Cambridge. Hence the prospects for linkage, though more occluded by public concerns about Genetically Modified Organisms than in the case of health-related biotechnology, are nevertheless propitious in locational terms.

Cambridge is relatively well supplied with science and technology parks, though the demand for further space is pressing. At least eight biopharmaceuticals and vaccines firms are located on Cambridge Science Park itself. St. John's Innovation Centre, Babraham Bioincubator, Granta Park, the Bioscience Innovation Centre and Hinxton Science Park are all recently completed, under construction, or beyond spatial planning review. Most of the newer developments are taking place within short commuting distance of Cambridge itself, on or near main road axes. This is evidence of the importance of *access* for research-applications firms to centres of basic research, reinforcing also the point that not everything concerning biotechnology must occur 'on the head of a pin' in Cambridge city itself.

The final, important, feature of the biotechnology landscape in Cambridge and the surrounding region is the presence of both informal and formal networking between firms and research or service organisations and amongst firms themselves. Cambridge Network Ltd was set up in March 1998 to formalise linkages between business and the research community, connecting both from local to global networks in a systematic way. It is mostly IT-focused, though some of this spills over into biotechnology, given its demand for IT equipment and opportunities for IT delivered patient and clinician services through, for example, bioassay equipment. Of more direct relevance to the biotechnology community are the activities of ERBI. This biotechnology association is the main regional network with formal responsibilities for: newsletters, organising network meetings; running an international conference; website; sourcebook and database on the bioscience industry; providing aftercare services for bio-businesses; making intra- and international links (e.g. Oxford, Boston, San Diego); organising common purchasing; business planning seminars; and government and grant-related interactions for firms.

Thus it is clear that the Cambridge biotechnology sector operates as a cluster. Indeed, it could be said to be a paradigm case of the clustering phenomenon, which though presently small, has major growth potential. This is because it is Europe's leading biotechnology cluster in a business that had a predicted global turnover of $70 billion in 2000. Because of the sunk costs associated with co-location by venture capitalists, specialist patenting, legal, accountancy and insurance services, the immobility of the key knowledge-driving resource, the University, and the presence of a critical mass of biotechnology firms and entrepreneurs, Cambridgeshire is likely to remain the focus it has become. However, there are several barriers as well as opportunities on the horizon.

One leading, successful biopharmaceutical firm interviewed – with 50-100 employees in sites in Cambridge UK and Cambridge USA – spoke positively of Cambridge as a centre of excellence from which the firm will not be moving, not least because its entrepreneurial culture and infrastructure are highly suitable, human capital is readily available and it is a desirable location. However, there was perceived to be danger of Cambridge becoming a victim of its success due to congestion (especially traffic immobility) and highly expensive industrial and residential costs. The firm is highly networked locally and globally, had just moved into new premises but was anxious about anticipated space requirements. In terms of business organisation and development, the firm spoke of the need for the biotechnology-funding gap to be addressed from the stage of proof of concept to making a partnership deal with pharmaceuticals firms. Currently, the normal situation where a pharmaceuticals firm takes an eventual equity position does little to lessen the difficulty in raising finance in the first five to ten years of the firm's existence.

A smaller firm spun out of the MRC Laboratory of Molecular Biology perceived the advantages of Cambridge, and its present incubator site, as very positive because of cost-effective infrastructure (including DNA library and sampling facilities), attractiveness to skilled personnel, and access to leading inventions. But space for future expansion in the context of a need to stay in Cambridge was a major concern. Specialised 'wet' laboratory space, with no necessity to spend on expensive fitting-out was hard to find and there was evidence that the property-development industry had been slow to recognise this. Two other smaller firms, one a recent start-up, complained of the funding gap, explaining it as caused by a relative absence of public funding, and private deals of interest to venture capital being set at too high a level and with too many conditions. Hence, for firms, premises, congestion and pre-venture capital development funding are of common concern. But each sees this as the price of success in a location that they value extremely highly.

Three major research institutes in Cambridge, each highly-networked to pharmaceuticals firms, other international institutes and with local start-up firms, all commented on planning regulation being a big barrier to the growth of the biotechnology sector in Cambridge and public transport being poor. However, two of them spoke of human resource anxieties, one in respect of the very limited pool of good CEOs available to run biotech start-up or growth firms, the other about both a lack of entrepreneurship and appropriately skilled scientific researchers in biotechnology. The high cost of re-training traditionally trained scientists is hard to bear, occasioning international recruitment from less developed countries where biotechnology degrees are established, notably in Asia. Attachment to tradition meant such degrees were not available in the University, though biotechnology technicians' qualifications were available in limited numbers from new courses established at Polytechnic-University level.

Thus, in addition to diseconomies of agglomeration associated with successful clusters, such as congestion, lack of affordable industrial space, and high costs of housing, all of which needed addressing, there are two further problems. The first is endemic to the biotechnology industry and refers to the development 'funding gap'. This is particularly pronounced in biotechnology, since the gap may last over a ten-year period. Any localised pre-venture funding that could be pooled with the support and on the initiative of local agencies would find ready takers. Secondly, there is an obvious gap in the skills increasingly required as the biotechnology industry expands. Moreover, such skills are yet to be satisfactorily provided by the elite higher education institution at the heart of the cluster.

The Cambridge Information Technology Cluster

The Information and Communication Technology (ICT) sector, including both hardware and software activities, has been at the core of the growth in high-technology employment in Cambridge, being the most dynamic and turbulent, in terms of the proportion of new and 'merging' companies. For instance, between

1995-1997 computer service companies alone accounted for 27 per cent of all high-tech businesses and contributed 42 per cent of all new high-tech starts. These figures undoubtedly reflected the vibrancy and increasing importance of the Internet within the sector, and the high level of mergers and buy-outs that are also a characteristic of this fast growing industry.

Our analysis of the Cambridgeshire County Council database indicated the growing importance and size of the ICT sector in Cambridge. The analysis identified 245 firms in Cambridge, employing 3,913 involved in ICT software and hardware. The average number of employees per firm is 16, highlighting the dominance of small companies. Of the 245 firms identified 98 had been established in the 1990s, confirming the expansion that was then taking place in Cambridge, as well as probably under-estimating ICT start-ups that were not currently covered by the local authority's database. Software development was the key activity of 112 of firms, employing 1,966, while there were 18 specialist Internet and Web companies employing 200 (undoubtedly now an out-of-date estimate); 23 hardware manufacturers and research companies employing 606, with the majority of other companies being involved in computer consultancy and computer aided design. The spatial concentration of the sector involved also the development of a strong (far stronger than the biotechnology sector) 'hub-and-spoke' ICT cluster in and around Cambridge.

Networks were discovered to consist of a range of temporary, contract-based (hard networks) inter-firm collaborations, and longer-lasting informal relationships among firms in common business areas (soft networks). The cluster was revealed as sets of direct network linkages of the hard or soft variety connected also to non-firm or non-industrial organisations such as Cambridge University, the Cambridge Network Ltd. or Business Angel networks. One interviewed firm – Hypereality Systems, an Internet Games company – through membership of the Chamber of Commerce accessed the Cartesia Business Angel network, accessing some £500,000 to build and advertise Hypereality's services. Cambridge University's Wolfson Centre for technology liaison had played a useful signposting role in linking the firm to Cartesia. However, in this sub-cluster of Internet games and related services, informal networking among friends and colleagues with other Internet firms – in a non-negative competition environment – was the key source of 'enterprise education'. However this firm-owner spoke negatively of an insider culture within the Cambridge Network, that was unwelcoming to the likes of he and his somewhat 'counter-cultural' leisure software associates. Whether the sense of such exclusion was real or imagined was confirmed to be the former in interviewing a founder-member who agreed that its 'club-like' atmosphere was highly likely to be unappealing to the newer generation of, especially, Internet games entrepreneurs.

Despite this, an example of the network-like character of relationships between ICT firms in Cambridge is that Hypereality provided basic systems development work for Fontel – an interviewed Internet company that provides on-line 'grey literature' and related business information – ranging from website to system design. Fontel's service is sold to subscribers in the fields of education, government and business-to-business relations, including on-line texts, directories and other sources. It employed eight people in-house, all advanced ICT-literate information scientists and technicians, and a further eight consultants as contractors outside the firm. This firm emphasised the relatively low intensity of competition and the advantages involved in conducting business through informal networks.

A software company, Sunrise Systems, producer of Pipenet software, had a more 'captive' network relationship to its customers. Specialised in producing a complete software tool for network flow analysis Sunrise's product enabled large clients to design their pipework systems by pipe size and pump selection, and compute hydraulic forces needed for pipe stress analysis. Pipenet began as a Ph.D. thesis at Cambridge University. The firm operates a 'small company culture' aiming to grow in turnover rather than personnel. The client base and market reach of Sunrise is global, 54 per cent of revenue coming from overseas, including Japan, Korea, Australia and the US as well as Europe. The company has few formal supplier links, though has formal links to CAD Centre in Cambridge with its complementary customer base. Rather, informal networks and a recognition that many of the most useful meetings can even take place informally or even accidentally, underline the background in Cambridge of a stimulating environment with critical mass in ICT.

The St John's Innovation Centre is a paradigmatic case of an incubator (i.e. high-tech managed workspace) acting as a strong informal network clustering facilitator. The Centre is home to a range of small high-tech companies, particularly within the ICT software sector. The strength of the Centre is precisely that there is no need to prescribe networking as it is carried out organically and informally, due to the close proximity and common focus of the firms. Also, the 'St John's' badge acts as a strong branding image, with the intermediaries, in the case the staff of the Centre, playing an almost invisible role.

In general, Cambridge's ICT is far more clustered in its activities than even the biotechnology sector, with a large number of inter-linked businesses involved in technical consultancy that have spun-out of the University. It became clear that ICT, and software in particular, are 'relational' businesses, where the requirement for a high level of inter-personal interaction is a necessity. However, such sharing experiences tend be confined to such sectors. Others, like aerospace, are differently structured, being focused on a local monopoly that, until recently, had not appreciated the importance of 'knowledge spillovers'. This is changing as the lead firm has forged strong relationships with local human capital providers and engaged in research co-funding in aerospace engineering at Cambridge University. This is illustrative of a certain 'contagion effect' of clustering and networking locally, and evidence of the lessons to be learned about developing the 'knack of networking' being adopted within other sectors. Further evidence that this is already occurring within Cambridge comes with the growth of significant and intimate links between ICT firms and firms within the localised high-performance engineering sector. Briefly, three interviewed engineering firms of relevance here are Cambridge Advanced Electronic, Hansatech and Mega. Here we will simply discuss their links to other parts of the cluster, then move on to discuss the aspects of the cluster discernible from the responses to our interviews.

- Cambridge Advanced Electronic is a company involved in advanced design of scientific instrumentation. The company supplies global firms such as Shell, Unilever and Glaxo but also worked recently on a contract for Epson and Sony, which involved Hansatech in system design development work. The CEO is well integrated with the Cambridge Network, was formerly employed by Cambridge University and currently sits on numerous DTI and other committees tasked with developing Cambridge's high technology sector. CAE is a quite important node in the Cambridge cluster as can be seen in Figure 3.1.

- Hansatech is downstream in the chain from software services firms like CAE, but performs a vital function as prototype developer of advanced printed circuit boards (PCBs). In addition to having worked with CAE, Hansatech is currently working on Formula 1 on-board computer PCB design for a Grand Prix motor racing client and, amongst other contracts, through Symbionics, another software engineering design firm, on Ericssson's 'Bluetooth' communication system which enables home appliances to communicate with mobile phones and laptop computers or PCs. Hansatech developers have close personal (former career) links to PA Consulting and Cambridge Consultants, who in turn have origins in the research scene associated with Cambridge University and with the Cambridge Network. Hansatech also works with its neighbour Pixelpower on graphics for TV studios. So Hansatech is also something of a node in the cluster, its main competitors being SCI in the US, Celestica (ICL) and Caltec in Malden and Kelso (UK).

- Mega supplies Hansatech and other firms with PCB substrate material in small batches and also distributes a wide range of PCB cutting, safety and other equipment. The PCBs supplied are for research purposes, both in university and private laboratories (UV sensitive substrates). Substantial clients include aerospace firms such as Marshall's of Cambridge, Virgin Airline, BA and American Airlines. Suppliers are mostly outside Cambridge, but given the research focus within Cambridge some customers are local as well as global.

As can be seen from Figure 3.1, which illustrates only a small segment, there are many connections between firms in the Cambridge ICT cluster. There are numerous sub-nodes and network relationships in evidence. At the high end and interacting with the University and Cambridge Network are the high value-adding software and systems design services firms like CAE and Symbionics. These can be intimately linked with large, expert consulting houses such as PA and Cambridge Consultants. In the case of CAE, it animates networks of complementary firms and in 1999 established itself as a *virtual firm*, totally dependent on local and global networks. In a different corner, and with more tenuous links to the overall cluster, but at the heart of a distinctive, new sub-cluster or network of Internet services, and especially games suppliers is a firm like Hypereality, operating partly as a kind of 'counter-culture' to the former sub-cluster, but dependent on access to local Business Angel funding sources, and doing contract systems work for the likes of

Fontel. Third, and lower down the 'cluster-chain', but extremely important, is a firm such as Hansatech, transforming advanced system designs into prototype PCB products of high sophistication. Hansatech is a link between the higher-value systems design part of the Cambridge cluster through to final ICT customers for very advanced products such as Ericsson, and suppliers of specialist materials and equipment such as Mega, who also link into the University, selling to research departments and the aerospace industry, partly locally but also globally. To repeat, this is just a segment of the overall ICT cluster in Cambridge, but it illustrates the nature and extent of the network relationships, both in terms of business transactions but also of other kinds of inter-linkage to enhance business competitiveness that can be found in the Cambridge cluster as whole.

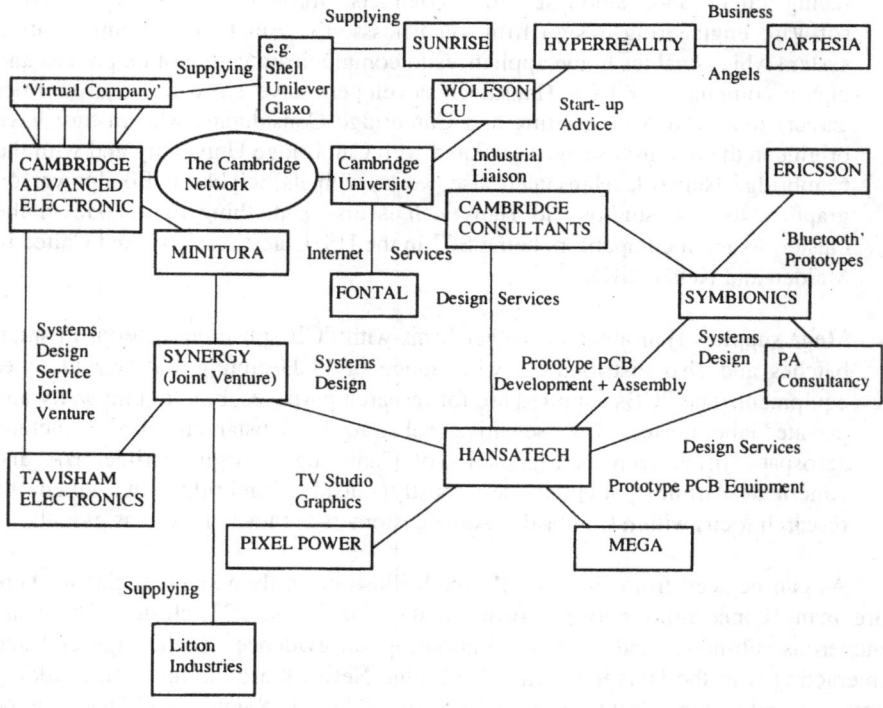

Figure 3.1 Aspects of the Cambridge IT cluster

Of key importance are market-exchange or *traded* interdependencies linkages that predominate and drive the cluster forward economically. But underpinning these are relationships of *familiarity* from being past colleagues in the engineering and systems design consultancies or university departments and production or services firms (Lawson and Lorenz, 1999). The involvement of the public innovation support infrastructure is mostly in the background and responsive to animation from firm networks, or specific lead firms or organisations, seeking solutions to problems of market failure, skills provision being the most obvious case in point.

Concluding Remarks: Alleviating Cluster Congestion

This paper has found modest but convincing evidence of a high degree of clustering, networking and collaboration within Cambridge's biotechnology and information technology sectors, although there is a high degree of variation in terms of institutional processes, and market exchange through the cash nexus is pronounced in both. In particular, ICT in Cambridge is the UK's best example of a growth cluster, where there is a high degree of inter-linkage and interaction between firms, as well as intermediaries and support organisations, especially in the private sector. Biotechnology is a smaller, yet fully functional example of a high-tech cluster, which will require further support and intervention if it is to continue to grow in cohesive manner. In particular, it needs to produce advanced therapeutic products or genetically-derived drugs on the market if it is to prove itself a potential challenger to US hegemony. Scale may have to be increased through merger and acquisition activity for this to happen in ways that can induce large sums of venture and other equity capital to fund high-risk and long-term drug-development processes.

It is clear that there is continued pressure for business development in and around Cambridge, and that whilst small technical service firms and computer software/systems companies may be accommodated fairly easily, the requirement of biotechnology companies seeking 'wet lab' space, for example, will restrict the area of search. On the other hand, the expectations of the local and regional policy community suggest that companies involved in distribution, marketing and support activities may have site demands which are more about the labels – name, address and postcode – as well as road access – than about University links, the skills of the local labour force or networking.

If high-tech clusters are to continue to grow and disperse in the Cambridge area, as we have seen signs they may tend to do because of local 'learning spillovers' then agglomeration diseconomies will prove problematic. In particular, there is a requirement for an adequate property infrastructure to ensure the cluster can grow naturally. Due to the nature of the sector, these requirements go beyond simple 'managed workspace' but are directly linked to technological needs. Also, careful planning for expansion needs to take account of congestion in the city and rationally consider good-access locations away from Cambridge for expansion.

A particular kind of duality within the cluster derives from the cultures of inclusiveness and exclusiveness that operate, apparently inter-generationally and between popular and elite software applications. Although the outsider group showed itself to be highly capable of becoming well-networked, there is a sense of resentment which may rebound negatively upon cluster linkages as new and less exclusive, more 'democratic' technologies and applications become part of the ICT cluster. Cambridge does not yet have the characteristics sometimes caricatured in observations of Silicon Valley as the 'High-tech and Homelessness' model of cluster development. However it does possess an economic development problem in that the success of the high-tech sector is also having the long-term effect of creating a 'dual economy' in the locality.

This other duality involves the marginalisation and polarisation of those employed or seeking employment in more 'traditional' sectors, resulting in an accelerating prevalence of unskilled workers in companies which are not fulfilling their potential in terms of upgrading and creating value-added activities. Also, such duality is visible in terms of its mixed urban and rural geography, involving both 'over-heating' and 'underdevelopment'. However, it should be noted that the architect of modern cluster theory, Michael Porter, has always asserted that competitive advantage can be gained through strength in traditional industries as well as new sectors, providing there is sufficient innovation taking place. Clusters offer a means for upgrading and producing higher value-added by tapping into and distributing the potential of local sectors as a whole, rather than as a series of fragmented companies.

Acknowledgements

We are grateful to Cambridge Training and Enterprise Council/Business Link for funding this project, and to Geoff Plummer and Stuart Ellis of the above for their co-ordinating and logistical skills during the research process. Some of the information on biotechnology arose when the first author was a member of UK Minister of Science, Lord Sainsbury's 'Biotechnology Clusters' Task Force in 1999. All opinions expressed in the chapter are those of the authors alone.

References

Arthur, B. (1994), *Increasing Returns and Path Dependence in the Economy*, Michigan University Press, Ann Arbor.

Audretsch D.B. (1998), 'Agglomeration and the Location of Innovative Activity', *Oxford Review of Economic Policy*, 14, pp. 18-29.

Balasubramanyam, V. and Balasubramanyam, A. (2000), 'The Software Cluster in Bangalore', in J. Dunning (ed.), *Regions, Globalization, and the Knowledge-based Economy*, Oxford University Press, Oxford.

Baptista, R. and Swann P. (1998), 'Do Firms in Clusters Innovate?', *Research Policy*, 27, pp. 525-540.

Best, M. (2000), 'Silicon Valley and the Resurgence of Route 128: Systems Integration and Regional Innovation', in J. Dunning (ed.), *Regions, Globalization, and the Knowledge-Based Economy*, Oxford University Press, Oxford.

Castells, M. and Hall, P. (1994), *Technopoles of the World: The Making of the Twenty-first-Century Industrial Complexes*, Routledge, London.

Cooke, P. (2001), *Knowledge Economies: Clusters, Learning, and Co-operative Advantage*, Routledge, London.

Cooke, P., Davies, C. and Wilson, R. (2001), 'Innovative Advantages of Cities: From Knowledge to Equity in Five Basic Steps, paper to ESRC *'Cities'* Programme Research Workshop', *Innovation and Competitive Cities in the Global Economy*, Worcester College, Oxford, March 28-31.

Cookson, C. (1999), 'Cloning Silicon Valley May Be Key To Success', *Financial Times*, September 14, p. 10.

Crevoisier, O. (1997), 'Financing Regional Endogenous Development: the Role of Proximity Capital in the Age of Globalization', *European Planning Studies*, 5, pp. 407-416.

DTI (2001), *Business Clusters in the UK: A First Assessment* (3 Vols.), Department of Trade & Industry, London.

ERBI (1999), *Background Information for Cambridge and Eastern Region Biotechnology Cluster*, Eastern Region Biotechnology Initiative, Cambridge.

Ernst & Young (1998), *European Life Sciences 1998*, Ernst & Young International, London.

Feldman, M. and Audretsch, D. (1999), 'Innovation in Cities: Science-based Diversity, Specialization and Localized Competition', *European Economic Review*, 43, pp. 409-429.

Garnsey, E. (1995), 'Cambridge Tech Success: Growing High Technology Industry From the Science Base', *New Economy* pp. 262-265.

Garnsey, E. (1998), 'The Genesis of the High Technology Milieu: A Study in Complexity', *International Journal of Urban and Regional Research*, 22, pp 361-377.

Garnsey, E. and Smith, H.L. (1998), 'Proximity and Complexity in the Emergence of High Technology Industry: The Oxbridge Comparison', *Geoforum*, 29, pp. 433-450.

Gereffi, G. (1996), 'Commodity Chains and Regional Divisions of Labour in East Asia', *Journal of Asian Business*, 12, pp 75-112.

Keeble, D., Lawson, C., Moore, B. and Wilkinson, F. (1999), 'Collective Learning Processes, Networking and "Institutional Thickness" in the Cambridge Region', *Regional Studies*, 33, pp. 319-332.

Krugman, P. (1994), 'Complex Landscapes in Economic Geography', *American Economic Review*, 84.

Lawson, C. (1999), 'Towards a Competence Theory of the Region', *Cambridge Journal of Economics*, 23, pp. 151-166.

Lawson, C. and Lorenz, E. (1999), Collective Learning, Tacit Knowledge and Regional Innovative Capacity', *Regional Studies*, 33, pp. 305-317.

Leborgne, D. and Lipietz, A. (1988), 'New Technologies, New Modes of Regulation: Some Spatial Implications', *Society & Space*, 6, pp. 263-280.

Longhi, C. (1999), 'Networks, Collective Learning and Technology Development in Innovative High Technology Regions: the Case of Sophia-Antipolis', *Regional Studies*, 33, pp. 333-342.

Pinch, S. and Henry, N. (1999), 'Paul Krugman's Geographical Economics, Industrial Clustering and the British Motor Sport Industry', *Regional Studies*, 33, pp. 815-827.

Porter, M. (1998), *On Competition*, Harvard Business School Press, Boston.

Roelandt, T. and den Hertog P. (1998), *Cluster Analysis and Cluster-Based Policy in OECD-Countries*, paper presented at OECD Workshop on Cluster analysis and cluster-based policy, Vienna, May.

Saxenian, A. (1994), *Regional Advantage*, Harvard University Press, Cambridge.
Sternberg, R. and Tamásy, C. (1999), 'Munich as Germany's No.1 High Technology Region: Empirical Evidence, Theoretical Explanations and the Role of Small Firm/Large firm relationships', *Regional Studies*, 33, pp. 367-377.
Storper, M. (1995) 'The Resurgence of Regional Economics, Ten Years Later: The Region as a Nexus of Untraded Interdependencies', *European Urban and Regional Studies*, 2, pp. 191-221.
Storper, M. and Scott, A. (1995), 'The Wealth of Regions: Market Forces and Policy Imperatives in Local and Global Context', *Futures*, 27, pp. 505-526.
Zucker, L., Darby, M. and Armstrong, J. (1998), 'Geographically Localised Knowledge: Spillovers or Markets?', *Economic Inquiry*, 36, pp. 65-86.

PART II

TRUST SHAPING COLLECTIVE ACTION

Chapter 4

The Relations of Co-operation in Group Enterprises and Associations in Ghana – Exploration of Issues of Trust and Power

Fergus Lyon[1]

Introduction

This chapter aims to examine how groups can sustain collective action. The analysis is based on rich empirical cases that feed into the theoretical literature on the nature of co-operation and will attempt to understand the reasons behind the success of group activities by exploring how their actions are embedded in social relations (Granovetter, 1985). The survey will concentrate on the 'how' questions as well as the 'why' (Granovetter, 1994).

The analysis will go beyond the functionalist arguments that suggest that motives for forming these institutions can explain the occurrence in terms of reducing transaction costs, or the non financial benefits such as prestige, recognition and other psychological rewards. Considerable incentives for group activities can be seen in a wide range of activities, although groups operate in only a limited number of these. The analysis will ask what allows or makes people co-operate, and how such institutions emerge.

Powerful hypothetical models such as the Tragedy of the Commons (Hardin, 1968), as well as the influential work of Mancur Olson (1965) on the 'Logic of Collective Action', have been used to argue that co-operation depends on individual self interest because of the premise that human behaviour is dominated by short term self maximisation. Empirical work has shown that people can cooperate through establishing rules and not acting in their own short term interest all the time.[2] Self interest is a major factor in both promoting free riding or loss of co-operation (Olson, 1965), and in leading to co-operation when certain conditions are established (Axelrod, 1984).

In contrast to these approaches that are based on simplified models of social life, I want to argue that the evidence from actual community groups suggest that the dynamics of group formation are more complex. This chapter challenges approaches to co-operation based on simplified models as they do not allow for a discussion of co-operation based on trust, power and social norms or sanctions for norm breakers that may be external and prior constraints of culture on individual rational choice. Such assumptions also limit any examination of power relations that influence the choice of individuals (Mulberg, 1995).

The types of collective action taken in the Ghanaian case studies include micro-saving groups, palm oil processing groups and transport associations. These have differing social relations of co-operation and therefore very different organisational forms. Definition of what is a benefit has to be examined closely as several of the groups investigated are highly successful at supporting the interests of their members while restricting the opportunities and economic activities of others, especially the rural poor. The analysis will therefore explore what is defined as a successful group and how some groups can have potential negative consequences through reducing competition by excluding others.

Collective action and issues of co-operation have become an increasingly important aspect of economic policies around the world. There is a long history of the co-operative movement in the provision of services, marketing and finance, although in the 1970s and 1980s these were largely discredited. Major problems were faced because of the unquestioning replication of western models and they became increasingly politicised and seen as a way of exerting political control especially in many Southern countries (Attwood and Baviskar, 1988).

In the 1990s co-operative activities came back to the fore of economic policies in three forms. Firstly, there has been increased interest in community based organisation and 'social enterprises'. These are seen as useful tools to improve livelihoods, provide services and empower people. A large range of different forms of co-operative groups has emerged although they use a different language than the co-operative model. These include alternative financing systems such as micro-credit, local exchange and trading systems (LETS), and community enterprises. The second form of collective action is attention to cluster development policies and inter-firm networking. The link between concentrations of inter-linked firms and economic development in particular regions has fuelled interest of regional policy in attempts to replicate these successes elsewhere (Porter, 1990 and 1998; Enwright, 2000). The process and causes of inter-firm networks have also raised considerable interest (Huggins, 2000; Lane, 1998). Finally, the concept of social capital has captured the attention of policy makers as the networks, trust and norms from which it is formed are linked to economic development (Putnam, 1993; Woolcock, 1998).

This chapter starts with a background to formal group activities in southern Ghana, before exploring in detail several types of group activities and the factors behind their organisation and sustainability. These include saving groups, palm oil processing groups and transport associations. The data presented is based on a survey that involved group and individual in-depth semi structured interviews with members of existing groups in two districts of Ghana's Central Region (Lyon, 1999). The cases were selected following discussions with district officials and other key informants. The interviewees included 17 processors, 12 traders, 11 transport union members, and 23 farmers' groups. There were also 22 interviews with NGO and government officials at the district and regional level. In-depth interviews were carried out with leaders and members of each case study group. The number of interviews depended on the size of the group. Questions centred around what happened at key particular moments, such as disputes, in order to differentiate what people actually do from what they say they would want to do.

Conceptualising Trust and Power

The analysis of the case studies will examine the extent to which the co-operation is based on trust and on coercion. Attention will be given to the interplay of trust formation and the exercising of power that ensures that group members do co-operate. It is hypothesised that all group activities involve the interplay of trust and power although to different degrees. The balance of power and the extent of trust will shape the organisational structure and leadership. Other research has shown that successful groups are based on self identified goals and rules (Coulter et al., 1996; Ostrom, 1998). The process of negotiating the goals and the rules will be analysed as it is hypothesised that the process of negotiation leads to the building of a group identity and 'acceptable levels of inequality' (Ostrom, 1998). The ability to sustain the group activities will depend on the extent of trust between members that ensures that rules are not broken as well as the extent of power that can be used to enforce the rules and sanction those who violate them.

Trust comes about through an expectation that those being trusted will co-operate. A dictionary definition of trust is 'a firm belief in the reliability, truth or strength of a person; a confident expectation; and a reliance on the truth of a statement without examination'. Trust operates when there is confidence in other agents, despite uncertainty, risk and the possibility for them to act opportunistically (Misztal, 1996, p. 18; Gambetta, 1988, pp. 218-219). The varied definitions of the word 'trust' create difficulties in applying it. This chapter uses a definition of trust that fits the Twi word *gyedi*. This can also mean confidence, knowledge of a person's ability, belief and faith.

Previous research in rural Ghana has shown that trust based on social relations can be built on existing networks, working relations, friendships and through guarantors and intermediaries (Lyon, 2000). These relations allow each party information on others' reputations and also allow sanctioning through ending the relationship or applying social pressure and shaming. These social relations can be developed both consciously through intentional activities, as well as intuitively through the assimilation of tacit information, implicit actions and habits of thought (Hodgson, 1988). Each party also draws on accepted common ethics, values and norms of behaviour (Platteau, 1994). Norms define what actions are deemed to be right or wrong, and include customs of co-operation, reciprocity and interaction. They can be applied consciously or part of habitual behaviour that allows agents to assume away some of the risks (Hodgson, 1988; Levi, 1996).

Power is a term that has had considerable discussion in the social sciences although, like trust, the ability to use it as an analytical category is highly problematic because of the varied definitions and interpretations. Complications in the use of the term power arise because of the differences between 'power *from*', 'power *to*', 'power *with*', and 'power *over*' (Rowlands, 1997). In this chapter, I am most interested in understanding how actors are able to affect others or secure outcomes *over* others and thereby ensure that individuals act in accordance with the group's objectives rather than their own interest. In this way they have power *over* others, and power is seen as part of a zero-sum game where one side gains at the others' expense (Allen, 1997). The power *over* is based on three other forms of power: social structures or power *from* position and control of resources; agency or power *to* affect outcomes; and collective power or power *with* others.

There has been much attention paid to the structural bases of power, most notably those related to the issues of class and control of capital over the means of production, gender, ethnicity and age. This base of power is seen as something that is an inscribed capacity, or a position that is held or possessed. It should also be recognised that individuals, whatever their position can affect the outcome by creating some room for manoeuvring. (The exception to this is some forms of slavery.) Agency of power can be through individual and collective action and is produced or generated through mobilising resources rather than being inscribed (Allen, 1997).

Other ways of building power over others is through what Latour (1986) refers to as enrolment. Each actor has their networks of interest in which they attempt to get others to follow. In this way power can be seen to have a negotiated character of competing definitions and is built up by being reproduced both consciously and unwittingly (Clegg, 1989). Power is also produced through resistance. The simplest form of this is the threat to create delays, work slowly and pilfer and in this way even the weakest parties can build up power over dominating agents (Scott, 1985). An understanding of agency involves analysis of how the processes work, both consciously and through habits of thought.

The power *over* other agents is *exerted* through tangible threats or action, surveillance and/or norms of behaviour. The threats and actions used to exert power over others are more visible and easier to identify through empirical research. I have divided them into three means, strength, authority and peer pressure, which lead to a range of possible sanctions; violence, exclusion, penalising, shame and reputation loss. Surveillance in organisations comes in the form of supervision, routinisation and legislation to control members' behaviour (Clegg, 1989, p. 190). In this way the methods of surveillance are a form of gaining power as well as allowing trust to build up. Surveillance can have an effect through the watched being aware of the gaze or it can be internalised and they assume that they are always being watched (Crang, 1994).

The norms include moral obligations and routinised, habitual or unquestioning compliance. These may result in agents accepting power over them and also shape the nature of the threats and actions that can be undertaken. The moral obligations are internalised and can be seen as a form of moral economy (Thompson, 1971; Scott, 1976). Those with power are able to set the rules of the moral economy through processes of socialisation and acculturation, what Lukes (1974) refers to as the third dimension of power where the values of the dominant become internalised. Norms shape the power relations by restricting the scope for complaints, what Lukes (1974) refers to as the ability to avoid decisions and leave issues off the agenda. These issues are closely related to the ability of the more powerful to exert authority.

Cases of Group Enterprises and Associations

Susu Groups

There are a range of non formal financial institutions in Ghana the most common being the *susu* groups. These consist of groups of individuals who save together. It is found throughout the country and is especially common amongst traders (Bortei-Doku and Aryeetey, 1996; Chamlee-Wright, 1997).

There are a range of types of *susu*, although this chapter is concentrating on rotational *susu*s that operate as groups.[3] The groups range in size from five to 30 people and members save a fixed sum either weekly or daily. Each week or fortnight one member is selected to receive all the money contributed. The group members have to decide on the amount contributed, the frequency of payments and the process of selecting the order receiving the money. With very few exceptions, the *susu* groups are led by one person who co-ordinates the collection and payments. They may also be responsible for covering the losses when someone leaves the group before the end of the rotation but after receiving her money. This person may know how to find the members and know who has contributed. There is flexibility built into the system as members can delay payment by promising to pay the person receiving money the following week.

One complex part of the organisation is the fixing of the order for receiving. This can lead to conflict especially if members fear that the group will collapse. There is therefore a greater risk for the person toward the end of the rotation as there are more people who may try to stop contributing after receiving their lump sum. Some groups have no fixed order and each week they decide who should receive. The leader is responsible for deciding who gets it in these circumstances. Traders are keener to get money at the beginning of the rotation as that allows them more time to trade with the money and raise money for other contributions. When there is a risk of conflict then members can decide to ballot to decide the order. Those that want to change position can then negotiate with other individuals. One group did not like the ballot system as all the members would know the order and so know who had to receive money; this was seen to increase the chance of them dropping out when they knew that all their friends had received money.

To participate the individual has to have regular income. This can restrict some because they cannot afford to save as money earned is spent immediately. Richer traders will either set up their own group with others who can afford a larger contribution or contribute and receive more than once in each rotation. There tends to be more women in these groups as they dominate the retail trade. Traders may be a member of more than one *susu* especially if they sell in more than one market.

Some of the *susu* groups also include an element of credit supply. This is carried out by the leader using his or her own money to lend to members based on the trust they have and the ease in collecting money from them. This can create risks for the *susu* leaders so they ensure that the money lent is clearly separated from the money saved. This system is close to the credit unions that operate in Ghana.

Manual Palm Oil Processing Groups

The objectives of the oil palm manual processing groups are to share small amounts of equipment and use co-operative labour in order to increase incomes, especially for women. They also had a secondary benefit of training individuals. The palm nuts are boiled in large pans, pounded in mortars and then pressed. The oil is taken off and stored in plastic or metal containers. The equipment is owned by the group. It is available to members when the group is not working and is rented to non members. In both case studies examined some equipment was bought using small loans. The amount of group processing varies with the season. All members work together although there may be a division of labour according to age with younger women doing the pounding and older women squeezing the chaff. The Breku group consists of 15 women and the Koforidua group has 23 women and 4 men.[4]

In both cases, the groups were set up by men who play a leading role in their management. They also fixed the rules of the group and the leadership structures, which follow the co-operative model with chair-ladies, secretaries, treasurers and other committee members. One group leader had the benefit of having training and experience in setting up income generating projects. The cohesion of both groups is supported by the choice of a viable income generating activity and their continued profitability. Another factor are the strict rules on the disbursement of money. One group has decided not to have any disbursement for those in need or for funerals contributions. This is fully accepted by all members of the group which demonstrates their belief and trust in the long term viability of the group.

Mechanised Palm Oil Processing Co-operative Groups

Since 1993 an American NGO with a long history of involvement in Ghanaian post harvest development, has been supporting the promotion of palm oil processing groups. Groups were deemed to be necessary as part of the development goals and because there was a need to have machines that were larger than those suitable for individual farmers. The main objectives are to reduce the workload of women and allow them to generate more income.

The beneficiaries of the project include the shareholders (men and women) and the women who use the plant. The shareholders are mainly women processors although the groups include men who own oil palm farms. A few of the women also have oil palm plantations although women's access to land for plantations is often limited. Men rarely participate in the processing itself although male shareholders may work with their wives and children. In the case studies examined, the number of share holders has been increasing although the number of women processing was reported to have declined as many had made losses in previous years and so did not have the capital to buy the nuts or were scared of taking risks again. The women who use the processing as a major part of their livelihood require capital or close customer links to plantation owners that build up over several years of buying large quantities. This restricts many poorer members of the community, although the plant does create a small amount of casual employment for labourers. Non-members can use the plant but they pay slightly more for using it.

The supporting NGO has played a major role since the beginning by advising on the organisation of the groups, negotiating for the machines and putting them on site. The NGO has also taken on the responsibility of training operators, managers and mechanics, monitoring every few weeks for the past four years, and assisting the groups to get loans for the machinery from the state owned Agricultural Development Bank.

Both plants are still in operation after four years although only one has been able to pay off its loan for the equipment and could be said to be working as expected. The differing success depends two interconnected factors: financial viability of the enterprise and secondly, the ability of the groups to co-operate.

The financial viability of the enterprises is dependent on the processors being able to process large quantities of palm nuts. The success of one plant was attributed to the bigger farms in the area, and the processing women. These women have more capital to buy nuts and have closer customer relations with the plantation owners who allow them to take produce on credit.[5] This may be partly due to the wider share ownership in this community and the sense of obligation that palm plantation owners have to sell to women in their community rather than buyers from the large scale processing plants.

The groups were not formed before the NGO arrived, although there were loose affiliations of interested people led by a key individual in each case, who approached the NGO for the assistance. Before the groups got the machines they were told that they had to raise money through selling shares, to build the housing for the machine.

Successful operation is also based on the behaviour and commitment of the operators and managers. They are responsible for collecting fees and making the accounts. One of the case studies has had trouble with their original operator who was eventually sacked for misappropriation of funds. The members of the other group have faith in their operator as they have been working with him for some time. He is also at the same church as some of the leading members which may add further moral pressure.

Co-operation in the more successful case has come about because of the commitment given to the enterprise by the leaders, especially one highly committed woman. This is based on their long term confidence in its success and their willingness to sacrifice their time. This commitment is evident in the ability to maintain the machine, mend it quickly when broken, raise more money for new projects such as a palm kernel cracker and pay off the debts. This suggests that success is dependent to a certain extent on the leadership of the group.

Transport Associations and Unions

Commercial transport is highly organised in Ghana. There are a number of transport associations, although the transport system is dominated by one, the Ghana Private Road Transport Union (GPRTU) of the Trades Union Congress. The other major associations include Progressive Transport Owners Association (PROTOA) and the Co-operative Transport Owners Association. This chapter will concentrate on the role of the GPRTU.

The union branches have wide ranging objectives that cover members' welfare, dispute settlement, price setting, building stations, and lobbying on behalf of its members. The welfare roles are similar to other Ghanaian associations and centre around gifts and visits to the sick, funeral donations to members who are bereaved, as well as donations for other ceremonies such as weddings and 'out dooring' of babies. The associations give bonuses to members at the end of the year if there is a profit.

Association branches aim to buy vehicles as a way of generating revenue. Another aim of each branch is to give loans to the individual members to allow them to purchase vehicles or repair cars. The branches can also act as a guarantee for drivers so that they can pay for repairs over time.

The associations also act as arenas for settling disputes. This can be done at the branch level although those issues not resolved there can be taken to the regional level or national level. Common disputes concern the organisation of the stations. The associations institute a queuing system that reduces the conflicts. They also reduce the risk of disputes through enforcing the government set prices and fixing prices for the minor routes. They can also mediate in disputes between owners of vehicle and the employed drivers, especially if there has been an accident. Other aims include training drivers, improving the stations, checking the drivers and collecting income tax.

The GPRTU is organised in a clear hierarchy ranging from the national offices, to regional offices to branches. Each branch organises the transport in a single town or route, depending on the amount of traffic. Drivers found to be breaking the rules are 'arrested' by union guards and fined.

The members of the associations are the owners of the vehicles and drivers. Each car is only allowed to ply certain routes. All the drivers and fee collectors are men although some branches have women traders who are members. Members register by paying an entrance fee dependent on the size of vehicle, and pay monthly dues. For each journey vehicles have to pay a booking fee which is approximately 10-20 per cent of the total amount collected from the passengers. These fees are collected and held at the branches, who make contributions to the regional and national offices for their upkeep. The regional office trains branch secretaries, settles disputes and monitors the branch level elections. These are hotly contested and frequently result in conflicts because of the large amounts of money at stake.

While the associations can support the members and enable them to improve their standards of living, there are also negative externalities. GPRTU controls almost all the stations and they restrict other individuals and associations from using them. This limits competition and it was claimed that it affects the prices charged to customers. The drivers and car owners are therefore forced to join GPRTU or face the risk of physical attacks. Threats to this monopolistic position are challenged through lobbying local and national government, and intimidating competitors.

Sustaining Collective Action

A common theme running through this chapter is the question of what factors allow groups to survive. This question attempts to go beyond the functionalist assumptions prevalent in many development programmes that suggest occurrence is based on how much a group is needed or in terms of its potential benefit (Granovetter, 1994). Incentives are important for sustaining co-operation but in many cases co-operation breaks down despite the economic benefits. It is therefore necessary to explore the reasons *how* people manage to co-operate rather than acting in their immediate self interest, and avoid the 'Tragedy of the Commons' or the repeated defection in 'Prisoner's Dilemma'. The ability to co-operate depends on the trust that has built up between group members, altruism, and the power relations that restrict individuals from acting against the interests of the group. An understanding of the processes that result in successful group activities therefore requires a detailed exploration into how people or groups build up trust and exert power.

Building Trust

Collective action through trust is based on both norms of altruism and self interest. The latter comes from incentives and benefit from long term interaction or the experience of participation. To a certain extent, co-operation from interaction is universal although how the interaction takes place is based on norms, shared values and habits of thought, which in turn are created and shaped by the interaction. Members have to have access to information that would allow them to monitor the other group members. Transparency of operation also allows trust to be built up and monitoring or surveillance measures can be used to ensure rules are not broken. Where this does occur it is usually based on the leadership skills of individuals. Examples of these measures found in the case studies include regular meetings of group executives and auditing of processing groups by the supporting NGO. This restricts the opportunity for misappropriation. The ability to monitor is greater in some economic activities especially in marketing systems with highly uncertain price fluctuations.

Trust can also be built up when there is transparency that allows members to understand what others are doing and not feel cheated. On the one hand this takes place when members can watch activities taking place. *Susu* groups often insist on all financial dealings being carried out in front of other people, and the joint processing enterprises work if members are there to witness the amount produced and the selling price, and participate in the decision making of how much to plough back into the business and how much to distribute. This is usually done by the executives and the survival of one of the palm oil processing groups is attributed to this trust: 'Others fail because there is no truth (*nokare*) in them. ... The leaders say they sold for less than the actual amount ... So less interest by the members and they do not show up' (Charity, P10).

Norms can come in the form of habits.[6] Habits are articulated by practice and are hard to identify in empirical research. In this study they often became apparent by the reaction of respondents to questions that they considered to be ridiculous. When asked the question 'how do you know this person will pay you back?', many respondents laughed and had to think for some time before answering.

Many of the groups identified have been based on existing networks as the members knew each other well before they formed a group. The simplest form of such existing networks are the kinship links that are the basis of many forms of co-operation, the most common being the 'household unit'. Wider networks are also drawn on but the strength of the ties becomes weaker, the information on others becomes less rich and the moral obligations diminish. These ties create moral obligations at a range of scales. An example of community level moral obligations is the oil palm growers in one of the villages with a processing machine who sold to women in the group rather than buyers from outside the village. Trust among group members can be present from the start as they have information on people's reputation and character and they can vet potential members. However, this basis of trust is restricted in that the number of individuals a person may trust in an existing community is limited.

The second form of trust building opens up many more opportunities as it is based on trust being built up through working relationships. In this way trust grows the more it is used. This in turn leads to the development of common behaviour, values and ethics based on informal conventions and sense of shame based on moral obligations. In this way trust is self reproducing as each time it is used, informal social obligations are incurred. However, this does need trust to start with. Many groups form but collapse before they are able to build up enough trust to allow them to enter into a venture that requires a high degree of co-operation. The trust in the future of the group enterprise is based on the trust between members and the ability to get all members working together: 'We all understand each other ... whenever we meet to decide on the work, we all agree and do it wholeheartedly' (Charity, P10). While trust builds up through continued interaction, lack of trust results in the groups collapsing and the end of the group interaction. Successful groups start with activities that allow them to minimise misunderstanding and confrontations. The *susu* savers and transport association members have individual economic activities under the umbrella of the group and so avoid many of the conflicts over shared money.

Through working together and repeated interaction, groups can build up what Granovetter (1994, p. 463) refers to as a 'cognitive hook which actors may hold onto in order to construct trust relations at a higher intensity than with those outside the category'. Activities that bring people together include market trading for those in *susu* groups: 'We are all traders and have been here a long time and come here regularly, (...) So we know that the others come here regularly; all the people allowed to join are good, no one has run away'. This is also demonstrated by the two small scale palm oil manual processing groups who find co-operation easier than other groups because they have had previous experience of working together and negotiating rules (Ostrom, 1998). This trust has been built up over time through the members participating in other activities before moving into processing, such as farming, literacy classes, tree planting and health care training.

Trust is also built up through regular meetings, both formal and informal. These meetings may be part of other activities such as literacy classes or Christian prayer sessions. This allows them to make decisions together and may also act as a limitation on those shirking the work as they have to meet the other members and want to avoid shame.

The obligations in these working relationships can be strengthened by members supporting each other outside of their work and building up friendships. The most common form of this is through financial support in times of difficulty and most importantly in Ghana, the attendance at each other's funerals. This was found to be especially important amongst the transport associations.

Trust can also come about through working with intermediaries or by trusting a leading individual who is trusted by the other members. *Susu* groups often rely on having a strong leader in whom they can trust rather than having to trust the others in the group. In this way trust is based on intermediaries between members of the group. This individual will build up his or her reputation over time and draw respect and trust because of their other positions in the community such as being a leader in a church or a school teacher. Strong leaders can act to strengthen the trust by settling disputes quickly and simply based on their authority. Most of these individuals were men and were also school teachers or church leaders.

Coercing Co-operation and Exerting Power in Groups

Co-operation is not based only on trust, existing commonly held moral norms and on the information on others' reputations but also on potential sanctions that can be used on another individual. By considering the use of sanctions in analysing co-operation, there needs to be an analysis of the power relations involved. Each case of co-operation can therefore be seen as combinations of trust based on moral norms and information, and the power of sanctions.

The importance of power in group activities shifts as the size of groups increase. Co-operation in groups works if all members trust each other or there is trust in certain individuals who act as intermediaries. The larger the groups, the higher the transaction costs of building trust in the group because it is harder to establish interpersonal relationships based on moral norms and information about others' reputations. As numbers increase, groups appear to be more reliant on power relations to coerce people into co-operation. In this way the larger groups, such as transport associations, operate in hierarchies that are closer to the model of the firm or the military than co-operatives.

As mentioned in the introduction, the bases of power over others come from social structure, agency and collective action. Social structure or inscribed power is in the form of class, gender or ethnicity relations and these relate to norms of behaviour and routinised compliance. This was demonstrated by the interviewees who could not conceive of any occasion when someone might disobey the chief or leaders of transport associations; their reaction was often similar to the cases of non-calculative trust and norms when respondents laughed at my questions. Agency refers to the ability to build up power either individually or collectively. It is used to have power over others through setting organisational forms, surveillance, and enrolling or convincing others to join networks led by a trusted individual with power based on having information on others.

Surveillance can be done by members being able to observe others carrying out group activities. This is especially important when buying or selling as there is an opportunity for leaders of the group to cheat others. External agencies can play a role in surveillance that can stop cheating and as discussed in the previous section, builds up trust. This can be in the form of setting up routines, 'western' accounting procedures and supervision of decision making as was done by the NGO supervising the palm oil processing group.

These 'bases of power' lead to the ability to have power *over* others through threats and actions and through norms of behaviour. The norms of behaviour include moral obligations, both acknowledged explicitly and internalised such as routinised, unquestioning compliance to chiefs or group leaders. Power can be used to set the rules of the 'moral economy' allowing the values of certain groups to become internalised in the society (Lukes, 1974). In such cases the concepts of trust and power are closely intertwined as generalised trust is based on the power exerted over people that denies them the ability to reflect.

The strength can be either physical or in numbers and allows groups to inflict violence and/or exclude others from economic activities. The transport associations are all based to a large degree on the powers that they have to exclude non co-operators from certain spaces or economic activities. The basis of GPRTU's power lies in its control of the stations. In villages where there is not a clear station area, their powers are limited and cars can pick up passengers without paying a fee. Struggles by competing associations for access to stations and the right to operate have ended in physical violence and bloodshed in many instances. The control of the stations is based on official or tacit support from central and local government. This is also the case for distillers groups and the traders' associations (Lyon, 1999). Other groups also have the power to expel non co-operators from the group. The ability to exclude is only a threat if there is a risk of losing future benefits. This will only be the case when members believe that there are long term benefits to receive and the group will not collapse.

The second of the means of exerting power over others is the reference to authority. The strength of authority is based on common beliefs, values, traditions and practice that result in the recognition of the authority's right to command. This is shaped by the norms of behaviour and issues of organisational virtue and obedience (Clegg, 1989). The ability to exert power through leadership is shaped by the leadership patterns within groups and the external authorities that groups can call on to. In this case the most common external authorities are the police or chief. Chiefs have the ability to fine people and continued disobedience is restricted by the ability to refuse a person a burial in the community which is seen as a matter of greatest shame. Traders in market places can draw on the market leaders, who are often involved in the *susu* themselves, to put pressure on traders who stop paying by threatening to throw them out of the market.

Within the groups there are a range of styles of leadership. There is also a key supervisory role to be played by internal executives. This requires dedicated leaders to devote much of their time and remain largely unpaid. The skills required for good leadership are not something that can be expected to arise automatically. The key player in the Asamankese plant is a woman who has had much prior experience of group organisation.

The gender of the leaders raises interesting questions over the different leadership models. In the mechanised palm oil processing groups men are in most of the executive positions although women do most of the work. Recently Asamankese has changed the executive committee and brought in more women as committee members. The reason given for having men on the committee is that they were needed at the start to mobilise people as they had the plantations and there were few women who were processing oil for sale, having plantations or having the required literacy. The women also stated that they wanted men with oil palm farms on the committee so that they feel part of the group and will support the women processors by selling on credit to them. It appears that the groups are using the leadership titles of the co-operative movement to allow men to have prestigious positions while still having the power to manage the group as they want.

The Asamankese group of processors appeared to have their own leadership model that was closer to the indigenous market associations with a market queen leader and her deputy. The leader of the women processors, Auntie Mary has the official position of assistant secretary on the committee. However, her role appears to be much greater; she brought the original idea to the community, she has done much of the monitoring from the start, she has recently been made the manager since the previous person has left, and she was the person who the other leaders wanted us to talk to first.

The third of the means of exerting power over others is that of peer pressure and sanctioned through shame. This can be linked to the exertion of authority as they both use the sanction of shaming. Shame occurs when someone is seen to have broken a norm and for the other members of the group to ridicule and undermine the person's position in the community and their prestige (Bleek, 1981). This pressure can be exerted because they see each other frequently in other group activities and through knowing where the person lived so that moral and other pressure could be used. This is the central concept for group micro credit schemes[7] and manual processing groups discussed earlier because there are no other ways of putting on pressure except excluding the person. Peer pressure may not be explicit as it can be internalised by group members as a form of understood obligation and a form of moral economy. In this sense is it closely linked to the issues of trust.

Peer pressure can also be exerted by the threat to group's or individual's reputation. One issue that was not fully explored is the value that the members put on the reputation of being a successful model. Subtle pressure may be put on some groups as they are concerned about losing this prestige. The Asamankese members are very proud of its operation and the prestige of this is buttressed by the visits of numerous researchers as well as having considerable press coverage when some of them were presented to President Clinton during his recent visit to Ghana.

Conclusion

This chapter has attempted to look at the functioning of groups. Empirical studies have shown that common assumptions about how groups work have led to a weak conceptualisation of collective action. The assumption that groups will inevitably occur when there are the correct incentives and the minimisation of transition costs is rejected as there are many cases where co-operation does not take place where it might be expected. At the same time the evidence does not support the assumption of short term individual self maximisation (Olson, 1965); evidence shows that groups do occur when there are not immediate benefits as people act on trust and norms.

It is therefore necessary to move away from the reasons *why* groups should appear based on incentives and motives to understand *how* they are sustained in cases and people continue not to act in their own self interest (Granovetter, 1994). The cases presented here support the findings of Ostrom (1990 and 1998) that show the importance of having self identified and enforced rules, although the particular area of interest here is how these institutions are sustained. Such an understanding requires an examination of issues of trust and power. The analysis of the cases show that the structures and organisation of each case of co-operation are shaped by a balance of trust and power. Without such an understanding, conceptualisations of collective action and the policy recommendations that follow may continue to be shaped by the assumptions of individual self-maximisation or co-operation arising inevitably because of potential incentives.

This chapter also shows the importance of detailed empirical studies in different contexts. There is a temptation by policy makers to replicate models of best practice from other cultural contexts. The way that trust and power are articulated differs form place to place and attempts to facilitate and support co-operative activities have to build on the existing co-operative structures which are embedded in the local social relations. There are wider lessons from this study of collective action in remote rural parts of West Africa. The theoretical issues raise important questions that can be asked in studies elsewhere and present a framework for understanding co-operative relations in different contexts.

Notes

1. This chapter is based on work carried out for a PhD on 'Trust and Power in Farmer Trader Relations' and on research carried out for British Department for International Development on 'Cooperation and Group Formation: Its Potential for Poverty Alleviation in Off Road Communities'. Many thanks for the comments from Gina Porter, David Uhlir, Geof Hodgson, Angus Cameron. The author accepts responsibility for all views expressed.
2. The limitations of the short term self maximisation approach has been discussed at length in research on the process of organising systems of sharing irrigation water (Uphoff, 1996; Ostrom, 1990), managing common property resources (Acheson, 1989; Ostrom, 1990) and in the development of bilateral trading agreements based on trust (Lyon, 2000).
3. There are susu groups that are run by individuals as personal enterprises where the members may not know each other. Members make contributions every day and collect a lump sum at the end of the month. The money is often saved at a bank and so this form of susu is restricted in communities with no bank. The person collecting takes a commission of one day's contribution from each member every month. These groups will usually collapse when the person (usually a man) stops doing the collection. It is based on the trust customers have in that individual so others cannot take his place without building up the trust of his customers.
4. The Non Formal Education Division aims to increase literacy amongst adults who have not fully benefited from formal schooling. Groups are established with trained facilitators from the community who lead weekly classes. The facilitators are also trained in group mobilisation and encourage the members to establish income generating activities in addition to their education. Revolving loans are available to groups. The men are members of the education group and so are involved in other activities although it is not clear what role they play in the processing. The membership of the processing group is limited to those who participate in the education classes. There is pressure on the Breku group to expand as there are others who want to join. However, the existing members do not want to accept them until they can get more loans to expand the business.
5. The ability to get nuts on credit is based on trust that can be built up over time or is pre-existing amongst the individuals concerned. Lyon (2000) gives more details on the role of trust in bilateral trade and credit agreements.
6. Hodgson (1998, p. 178) defines habits as 'a largely deliberate and self actuating propensity to engage in a previously adopted pattern of behaviour'.
7. Peer pressure can be exerted explicitly if a member is forced to repay a loan when he or she does not have the resources to do so. The extent of this and the impact on those in debt is rarely questioned in the debates on micro credit (Lyon, 1999).

References

Acheson, J.M. (1989), 'Management of common property resources', in S. Plattner (ed.), *Economic Anthropology*, Stanford University Press, Stanford, California, pp. 351-378.
Allen, J. (1997), 'Economies of power and space', in R. Lee and J. Wills (eds), *Geographies of Economies*, Arnold, London.

Attwood, D.W. and Baviskar, B.S. (eds) (1988), *Who Shares? Co-operatives and Rural Development*, Oxford University Press, Delhi.
Axelrod, R.A. (1984), *The Evolution of Cooperation*, Basic Books, New York.
Bortei-Doku, E. and Aryeetey E. (1995), 'Mobilizing cash for business: Women in rotating susu clubs in Ghana', in S. Ardener and S. Burman (eds), *Money-Go-Rounds: The Importance of Rotating Savings Associations for Women*, Berg, Oxford, pp. 77-94.
Chamlee-Wright, E. (1997), *The Cultural Foundations of Economic Development: Urban Female Entrepreneurship in Ghana*, Routledge, London.
Clegg, S. (1989), *Frameworks of Power*, Sage, London.
Coulter, J., Stringfellow, R. and Asante, E.O. (1996), 'The provision of agricultural services through self-help in Sub-Saharan Africa: Ghana case study', Report prepared for Overseas Development Administration Policy Research Programme, by Natural Resources Institute and Plunkett Foundation.
Crang, P. (1994), 'It's showtime: on the workplace geographies of display in a restaurant in southeast England', *Environment and Planning D: Society and Space*, 12, pp. 675-704.
Enwright, M. (2000), 'The globalization of competition and the localization of competitive advantage: Policies towards regional clustering', in N. Hood and S. Young (eds), *The globalization of multinational enterprise activity and economic development*.
Foucault, M. (1977), *Discipline and Punish: The Birth of the Prison*, Allen Lane, London.
Gambetta, D. (1988), 'Can we trust trust?', in D. Gambetta (ed.), *Trust: Making and Breaking Co-operative Relations*, Blackwells, Oxford, pp. 213-237.
Granovetter, M. (1985), 'Economic action and social structure: the problem of embeddedness', *American Journal of Sociology*, 91, 3, pp. 481-510.
Granovetter, M. (1994), 'Business Groups', in N.J. Smelser and R. Swedburg (eds), *The Handbook of Economic Sociology*, Princetown University Press, Princetown, New Jersey, pp. 454-475.
Hardin, G. (1968), 'The tragedy of the commons', *Science*, 162, pp. 1243-1248.
Hodgson, G.M. (1988), *Economics and Institutions: A Manifesto for a Modern Institutional Economics*, Polity Press, Cambridge.
Huggins, R. (2000), 'The success and failure of policy-implanted inter-firm network initiatives: Motivations, processes and structure', *Entrepreneurship and Regional Development*, 12, pp. 111-135.
Lane, C. (1998), 'Theories and issues in the study of trust', in *Trust within and between organizations: Conceptual issues and empirical applications*, Oxford University Press, Oxford.
Latour, B. (1986), 'Powers of association', in J. Law (ed.), *Power, Action and Belief*, Routledge and Kegan Paul, London, pp. 246-280.
Levi, M. (1996) 'Social and unsocial capital: a review essay of Robert Putnam's Making Democracy Work', *Politics and Society*, 24, 1, pp. 45-55.
Lukes, S. (1974), *Power: A Radical Review*, Macmillan, London.
Lyon, F. (1999), 'Group Enterprises, Co-operatives and Associations. Their Functioning and Sustainability in Rural Ghana', Report prepared for Department for International Development, Crop Post Harvest Programme.
Lyon, F. (2000), 'Trust networks and norms: the creation of social capital in agricultural economies in Ghana', *World Development*, 28, 4, pp. 663-682.
Misztal, B.A. (1996), *Trust*, Polity Press, Cambridge.
Mulberg, J. (1995), *Social Limits to Economic Theory*, Routledge, London.
Olson, M. (1965), *The Logic of Collective Action*, Cambridge University Press, Cambridge.
Ostrom, E. (1990), *Governing the Commons: The Evolution of Institutions for Collective Action*, Cambridge University Press, Cambridge.

Ostrom, E. (1998), 'Social Capital: A Fad or Fundamental Concept?', Center for the Study of Institutions, Population and Environmental Change, Indiana University.

Platteau, J. (1994), 'Behind the market stage where real societies exist - Part II The role of moral norms', *Journal of Development Studies*, 30, 4, pp. 753-817.

Porter, M.E. (1990), *The Competitive Advantage of Nation*, Macmillan, London.

Porter, M.E. (1998), 'Clusters and the New Economics of Competition', *Harvard Business Review*, Nov-Dec 77-1.

Putnam, R. (1993), *Making Democracy Work: Civil Traditions in Modern Italy*, Princeton University Press, Princeton.

Rowlands, J. (1997), *Questioning Empowerment: Working with Women in Honduras*, Oxfam, Oxford.

Scott, J.C. (1976), *The Moral Economy of the Peasant*, Yale University Press, New Haven.

Scott, J.C. (1985), *Weapons of the Weak: Everyday forms of Peasant Resistance*, Yale University Press, New Haven.

Thompson, E. P. (1971) 'The moral economy of the English crowd in the eighteenth century', *Past and Present*, 50, pp. 76-136.

Uphoff, N. (1996), *Learning from Gal Oya: Possibilities for Participatory Development and Post-Newtonian Social Science*, 2nd ed., IT Publications, London.

Woolcock, M. (1998) 'Social capital and economic development: Towards a theoretical synthesis and policy framework', *Theory and Society*, 27, pp. 151-208.

Chapter 5

Social Capital and Development – Issues of Institutional Design and Trust in Mexican Group-Based Microfinance

Marina Della Giusta

Introduction

This chapter reports findings from a research project on social capital and group-based microfinance schemes. These constitute an example of institutions developing on the basis of social connections among individuals with the potential to contrast financial exclusion taking place due to financial markets and government failure. By using such social connections these institutions enable access to markets (in this case the credit market), and simultaneously foster the connections on which they are built.

The structure is developed on the basis of theoretical and empirical evidence on both social capital and group-based microfinance, which constitutes a widely studied social connections-based means for delivering financial services (on social capital see Putnam, 1993; World Bank, 2000; on group-based microfinance see Geertz, 1962; Stiglitz, 1990; Hulme and Mosley, 1996; Van Bastelaer, 1997; Matin et al., 1999). Social capital is here defined as an irreducibly social good (Gore, 1997), i.e. one that possesses both intrinsic and instrumental value. The intrinsic value comes from the fact that individuals are believed to be naturally social and concerned not just with the material gains, but also with the reputation effects stemming from their actions. The instrumental value derives from the fact that social connections enlarge individuals' entitlements, i.e. can be used to access markets (capital, labour, and product) (Della Giusta, 1999). Within the aforementioned structure, therefore, social capital is identified at the micro-level with social networks formed by households and intermediaries in accessing markets. The macro-level involves also local government institutions that can both directly invest in enhancing their own reputation (tangibly through policy measures that directly enlarge entitlements, and intangibly through the behaviour of public officials), and can also enable the scaling-up of micro level social capital by supporting the existing social networks.

The results presented here concentrate on micro-level social capital, and particularly on trust dynamics among members of two savings and credit schemes aimed at combating financial exclusion in two rural areas located in the Oaxaca and Puebla states of Mexico. Information was collected about some features of members' trust of other members, groups' representatives and the wider community. These are believed to constitute an essential determinant of the success of group-based microfinance institutions. The aim of the present paper is to throw some light onto the complexity of such dynamics, by identifying commonalities and differences in 'trusting attitudes' among members of the two schemes.

Information was also collected regarding the group-level characteristics connected to the group's functioning. Such characteristics include both group-level design features (group's duration, membership stability, meeting's frequency, representatives' and members' attendance and participation, presence of joint liability), and group members' characteristics (homogeneity across members of income, gender, religion, ethnicity, type of production). Together with trust indicators, these served to address issues such as the relationship between in-group bonding versus bridging with outsiders, and homogeneity versus heterogeneity as factors of group's success (Portes and Landoldt, 1996; Grootaert, 1998; World Bank, 2000).

The paper includes a brief review of trust definitions and related issues. This is done in a step-wise progression from instrumental and simple concepts of trust towards more holistic approaches, in order to set the stage for the empirical study that follows. The data from the latter is then briefly described, followed by the actual analysis of the trust variables, in the form of a factor analysis. The final section summarises the results obtained, and draws implications.

Concepts of Trust

A brief survey of recent literature shows that a number of definitions and ways of fostering trust are put forward in connections with particular issues, varying from the conditions for creating cohesive communities to issues arising in the context of economic transactions.

Putnam does not actually provide a consistent definition of trust. For Putnam social capital is trust, norms and networks. Trust is however produced by norms and networks; only certain norms are conducive to trust, and only certain networks are promoting good norms. In particular he believes that horizontal networks are good for building social capital (his 'networks of civic engagement'), whereas vertical networks are not suitable for building it. Horizontal networks are based on equal-to-equal relationships, their crucial feature being, borrowing from game theory language, that of increasing the interconnectedness of encounters (games), and through this of fostering robust norms of reciprocity. In such networks communication and information about trustworthiness of individuals is transmitted by means of horizontal interactions that in this way become carriers of experience of past success at collaboration; in Putnam's words they provide a 'culturally-defined template' which serves to support future collaboration (reducing uncertainty and incentives to defect).

This circularity of Putnam's argument – trust generates norms that generate trust – is present also in Fukuyama (1995), who maintains that trust is based on commonly shared norms, but also defined as the expectation that arises within a community of 'regular, honest, and co-operative behaviour' by its members. The scope of investing in social capital is that of creating a 'moral community', but such investment cannot be the result of individuals' rational investment decision. It consists instead of habituation to the moral norms of a community that makes possible the existence of generalised trust. Fukuyama further complicates his argument about trust by advocating the necessity of hierarchies (due to the fact that 'people cannot be trusted at all times to live by internalised ethical rules and do their fair share', p. 25, 1995).

More precise, and consequently conflicting views on trust are provided within economic approaches to trust. Neoclassical theory sees trust as 'a particular level of subjective probability with which an agent assesses that another agent or group of agents will perform a particular action, both before he can monitor such action (or independently of his capacity ever to be able to monitor it) and in a context in which it affects his own action' (Gambetta, 1988, p. 217). The crucial conditions here are connected to the impossibility of monitoring other agents' behaviour, which is affected not just by non-trustworthiness, but also by the existence of a non-congruence between individual and moral values (otherwise declarations of intent would automatically translate into the corresponding actions, eliminating the problem). The nature and role of trust are therefore of an instrumental non-material resource in which people explicitly invest with the purpose of building a reputation for honesty. The latter in turn makes possible co-operative behaviour, and with it the emergence of stable structures for transacting.

Transaction costs analysis almost does away with trust altogether. The accent is rather on investigating the costs of planning, adapting and monitoring under alternative governance structures providing the structure in which transactions can occur. Trust itself gets defined by default by the type of relationship exogenously existing among trading parties, and although the existence and importance of personal trust between individuals (based on absence of monitoring, and a favourable and forgiving attitude) is acknowledged, the attitude which is believed to be associated with the majority of transactions (involving individuals and institutions) is in essence pure calculativeness. This attitude means that individuals involved in the relationship are aware of the set of possible outcomes and the corresponding probabilities, and therefore take cost-effective actions to try to avoid hazards and enhance benefits (Williamson, 1996).

In an attempt to reduce the level of abstraction that allows such rigid separation between attitudes and exchange environments, Ben-Porath (1980) applies transaction costs theory to the analysis of family businesses and networks. To do so, he explicitly needs to account for the identities of the parties involved and to bonds between them which are not captured in a calculative exercise,[1] other than those of the 'generic' kind.[2] By addressing the interwoven nature of personal and economic transactions which are characteristic of such family contexts, it becomes obvious that the identity of the people engaged in a transaction are a major determinant of the institutional mode of transaction. The family connection possesses various specific characteristics. On the one hand, it extends over a long time of unspecified duration. On the other, it encompasses a wide range of activities, which are contingent, general rules or principles guiding behaviour. The elements of the family 'contract' are highly interdependent, no balancing of the exchange is foreseen, and enforcement is mostly internal. Basically, the family contract, which is embedded in the identity of the partners, has the effect of creating a collective identity that affects the transactions of each member with people and institutions outside the family. His approach shows how the characteristics of personal trust-based transactions impinge upon the manifestations of the identity of individuals in the economic activities they engage in.

Neo-institutional theory provides a yet more articulate vision of trust. The latter is indeed seen as the solution to the problem of transacting which is basically about processes of trust building and networks of co-operating agents (be they individuals or institutions). Smith-Ring (1997), for example, suggests that networks are actually a product of the presence of resilient trust and the processes that lead to its formation. Fragile trust exists *a priori* and people tend to rely on it for occasional contacts, whereas resilient trust emerges in groups of people involved in both formal and informal processes of transacting, if people employ connected ways of learning in the common processes of sense making, understanding, and commitment (for a similar distinction between minimal and extended trust in the context of development, see Humphrey and Schmitz, 1998). The essence of his approach is that where trust does not already exist, it may emerge from formal and informal processes of transacting. Where trust does exist, those same processes provide opportunities for economic actors to deepen the levels of trust that exist between them, or to destroy it. Another step forward into more explicit treatment of trust building is provided by Casson (1991 and 1995), who assumes trust as assumed as the fundamental basis of co-operation among individuals in social groups. Successful leadership is identified as that which is capable of engineering trust among the group members Leaders can, by performing certain actions, increase their value in the group members' eyes and increase the probability of them spontaneously performing the same action.

Focusing even more explicitly on social behaviour, the embeddedness approach explicitly attributes the production of trust to 'concrete personal relations' and structures of them, which are defined as networks (Granovetter, 1985). The typical economic reason for building a reputation analysed in the game theoretic approach, by which incentives to avoid malfeasance in exchange relationships are well represented by the costs of losing future exchanges, is regarded in this approach as an 'under-socialised conception of reputation', and one that does not capture the true value of it (which, as shown in what follows, is also not so easily determined). Treatment of reputation as a generalised commodity defined as a ratio of cheating to opportunities of cheating does not capture one important determinant of the value of continuing relations (or repeated games). These provide important sources of information (which is still the determinant of a need for trust if transactions are to take place at all) because of a list of motives that are both economic and non-economic. Firstly, information derived from past personal dealings with somebody is cheap to gain, compared with information from other sources. Secondly, the reliability of such information is higher. Thirdly, the incentives not to discourage future transactions are higher where there already is a continuing relationship in place. These are the pure economic motives with which game theory deals as well, but to them must be added another non-economic motive and it is that 'continuing economic relations become overlaid with social content that carries strong expectations of trust and abstention from opportunism' (Granovetter, 1985, p. 490).

A critical approach to Granovetter's account of embeddedness is provided by Platteau (1994) who observes that the contention that in modern market economies trust is essentially produced by dense interpersonal networks supported by effective codes of 'limited group morality' is not able to provide a complete answer to the problem of market order. Self-established spontaneous rules for the co-ordination of the market mechanism are not sufficient to handle the complex informational problems of large societies. Conscious co-ordination efforts and external sanction systems (which he classifies as institutions) are also needed to establish an appropriate social structure, capable of developing self-enforcing mechanisms in which the market mechanism can display beneficial effects. Generalised morality in this framework is needed in order to reduce enforcement costs deriving from external sanctioning, and reduce the necessity of external sanctioning altogether. Referring to Mauss (1950), Platteau describes the exchanges of gifts in traditional societies as a means for creating personal relationships and manufacturing trust beyond the community space. As in Hirschman (1958), he defines as traditional those societies in which individuals occupy definite positions in the social matrix, and in which the discharge of their functions serves to confirm or manifest their socially differentiated existence rather than generate it. In the capitalist market-based society described in Marx's work, by contrast, people can exist socially only after having objectified themselves in money values, so that individuals are abstract actors (in the sense that they are not socially differentiated before entering into the exchange process). Platteau distinguishes between limited-group morality, restricted to people with whom one has close identification, and generalised morality, which is applicable in an abstract manner to people in general. A generalised morality becomes social capital, and is capable of sustaining order in the marketplace, if the concern for others is based on identity or loyalty feelings towards a large reference group actually encompassing all the relevant market transactions. In his comment on Platteau's survey, Moore (1994) points out how reputation mechanisms at the institutional and inter-business level must also be an essential feature in the explanation of the social content of market relations. In a more recent contribution, Moore synthesises his view on the role of trust in market creation as follows: '(increases in) trust and market order may not be very dependent on (increases in) generalised morality, but may be developed on the basis of personal relationships within narrow and specific social and economic networks; and therefore the prospect for creating market order might be relatively bright even in societies apparently characterised by low levels of trust and generalised morality' (Moore, 1999, p. 74). A crucial point in his contribution is the distinction provided between the different fundamental natures of trust and of sanctions, since the former refers to mental states, whereas the latter are more akin to institutions (arrangements to enforce contracts). Furthermore, he points the attention to the need of differentiating concepts of trust according to the different domains of social relations one is referring to (within firms and other organisations, or in inter-firm relations etc.). For these reasons, it can be assumed that very often variations in measured levels of trust reflect primarily differences in institutional effectiveness.

This brief list of approaches illustrates how trust is conceived of in different ways according to the specific issues of interest (from social cohesiveness, to economic transactions, to leadership). The social scientific literature at large does indeed recognise trust is a multidimensional phenomenon, connecting individuals in various ways according to the contexts in which their interactions occur (see for example Seligman, 1997).

Accordingly, trust is seen here as highly context specific (to individuals, situations and places) and it is believed that a more relevant question than 'how much' a person trust, it is 'who' they trust and 'how' and 'when' that we should be asking. This would in turn mean that a number of dimension should be assessed, and at the individual level.

In the study, a selection of indicators believed to be specific to the issue of trust among members in a group participating in a savings and credit scheme have been selected. To then operate a meaningful reduction to few significant variables, factor analysis is employed, precisely to identify some common dimensions among respondents of each scheme. Place specificity is also taken into account by analysing separately the two regions were the communities are located, and making then comparisons across the resulting factors.

The Field Study

The field study has then been carried out based on interviews with two MFIs and with members of their borrowers' groups, in the Puebla and Oaxaca states of Mexico. Information was collected on the design of the institutions and the groups' repayment rates, and, from the households, on household livelihoods, access to credit, perceived impact on income, consumption and production, households characteristics, and group's characteristics. The core questions aimed at measuring household' trust in group's representatives, in other group members, and in the wider community.

The research was carried out in co-operation with AMUCSS (Asociatión Mexicana Uniones de Crédito Sector Social), a Mexico City-based NGO with much experience in rural credit, currently offering services (help with accessing funds from supporting programmes, managerial and accounting services, training of credit promoters) and co-ordination activities to MFIs predominantly operating in rural areas, with the aim of ensuring the viability of such schemes (introduction of accounts-keeping criteria with an eye to the future conversion to formal providers for the better established schemes) and actively engaging in the establishment of links with formal financial institutions (such as development banks).

The information collected within this study was of interest to AMUCSS, as it is currently piloting a project for the creation of Bancos Campesinos (Rural Banks) in poor indigenous regions based on aforementioned existing schemes, and trying to diffuse among them the principles of open credit (oriented to the borrowers and not to a specific activity, and available all year long), graduation of users to larger credits, gradual expansion with savings and capitalisation (aiming to reach users-ownership of the schemes, see also Johnson, 1998), use of a vast array of material and social collateral mechanisms (group responsibility for default always present in all schemes), active participation of scheme users, geographical proximity of the services offered and information dissemination, aim of financial viability (to be achieved in approximately five years, even if they observe that most schemes actually require seven-eight years), and gender orientation for access equity (Bancos Campesinos, AMUCSS Project).

Two existing savings and credit schemes, one in the Oaxaca region (six year old scheme conducted within the federation of social solidarity 'Zapata Vive' in San José Tenango, a 10 year old farmers organisation) and one in the Puebla region (two year old scheme conducted within the co-operative SCARTT of Cuetzalan, a 20 year old farmers co-operative). These two schemes were chosen because Oaxaca scheme did not have a very good repayment performance whereas the Puebla scheme was considered rather successful, so that they offered the possibility of performing an investigation across different scenarios. In both cases, 50 questionnaire-based interviews with members of the scheme were carried out.

Data Overview

The following table presents a summary of the collected information divided in four main categories: income-related variables, household characteristics, group's characteristics, and trust variables. The first column presents the name of the variable, the second column contains variable description, the third indicates the unit of measurement and the final two columns report the number of observations available for each of the two sub-samples.

Most variables have a dichotomous nature, since respondents were asked to agree or disagree with statements (credit access and design variables, credit impact, some household characteristics and the group characteristics), other variables are instead continuous (most income-related variables, head of family age). The five trust variables are taking the form of Likert scales, a widely used method for measuring psychological phenomena in attitudinal surveys (see Hofstede, 1980).

Table 5.1 List of variables

Variables	Description	Dominion	Oaxaca N.	Puebla N.
Income-related				
LANDQ	Hectares of cultivated land (hectares)	0.25-5	49	36
LANDP	Property of land (0 = communal, 1 = private)	0,1	45	31
YRATIO	N. of months of high income in n. of months of low income	0.125-2	49	37
EXPPFM	Monthly household expenditure (pesos/n. of family members)	50-600	35	32
Household characteristics				
HFAGE	Age of Head of Family	18-80	44	34
HFSEX	Gender (0 = man, 1 = woman)	0,1	45	36
HFPRIM	Primary education (0 = no, 1 = yes)	0,1	44	33
HFSEC	Secondary education (0 = no, 1 = yes)	0,1	44	33
Group characteristics				
MSTAB	Stability of membership	0,1	49	36
HY	Income homogeneity of group members (yes = 0, no = 1)	0,1	49	37
HG	Gender homogeneity of group members (yes = 0, no = 1)	0,1	49	37
HR	Religion homogeneity of group members (yes = 0, no = 1)	0,1	49	37
HP	Production homogeneity of group members (yes = 0, no = 1)	0,1	49	37
HE	Ethnicity homogeneity of group members (yes = 0, no = 1)	0,1	49	27
FREQ	Meetings frequency (times per annum)	0-1	24	37
ATT	Respondent's attendance at meetings (no = 0, yes = 1)	0,1	49	35
RS	Representatives' participation in meetings (no = 0, yes = 1)	0,1	49	36
MS	Other members' participation in meetings (no = 0, yes = 1)	0,1	49	36
JLIAB	Respondent's awareness of joint liability in the group (no = 0, yes = 1)	0,1	49	34
MHELP	Belief that group members help each other (no = 0; yes = 1)	0,1	49	36
PARTORG	Participation in other organisation in the community (number)	0-3	50	37

Variables	Description	Dominion	Oaxaca N.	Puebla N.
Trust variables				
ADJTR	Trust in Representatives (0 = not at all, 1 = not much, 2 = partially, 3 = yes)	0,1,2,3	49	37
ADJTM1	Trust in other members (0 = not at all, 1 = not much, 2 = partially, 3 = yes)	0,1,2,3	49	37
ADJMT	Belief that members trust respondent (0 = not at all, 1 = not much, 2 = partially, 3 = yes)	0,1,2,3	49	37
ADJTM2	Belief that other members are honest with respondent (0 = not at all, 1 = not much, 2 = partially, 3 =yes)	0,1,2,3	49	37
ADJTN	Trust in non-members (0 = not at all, 1 = not much, 2 = partially, 3 = yes)	0,1,2,3	49	37
DEFAULT	Has there been default in your group? (no = 0, yes = 1)	0,1	0	37

* All adjusted-trust measures have been corrected with individually specific propensity to trust, i.e. the average respondent's score across trust questions.

The preliminary data analysis (simple association patterns between variables) indicated that in Oaxaca stability of group membership is low and it relates negatively with attendance at meetings, awareness of rules and perception of solidarity. It also relates negatively with representatives' and members' activity. This is problematic, since the scheme stresses the importance of groups' stability, and suggest that there are problems of institutional design, in that this feature might be ill suited to the local conditions. In Puebla, conversely, stability is high and positively associated with awareness of rules and member's activity, whereas it relates negatively with representative's activity. This suggests further that representatives are perceived differently in the two localities, and in particular the more stable groups in Puebla seem to prefer less leadership and more members' direct control.

The association patterns between trust variables suggest that in both subsamples in-group 'bonding' takes place at least partly at the expense of 'bridging' with outsiders. This suggests the existence of a trade-off between bonding and bridging that needs to be further assessed.

Analysing Trust Dynamics: Factor Analysis

As suggested in section 2, the trust variables collected are all capturing different dimensions of a general psychological phenomenon, which might be defined 'trusting attitude'. This section reports results from the analysis carried out in order to isolate significant trust dimensions which might help clarify both the nature of trust in each of the sub-samples considered, and the differences between them.

Factor analysis is a method that, given the presence of more variables measuring the same phenomenon, allows reducing them in just a few underlying explanatory new variables. The technique aims at explaining the covariance structure of the variables, assuming the existence of a statistical model that explicitly takes errors into account. The statistical model assumes that, given n variables, there are m underlying factors and each observed variable is a linear function of these common factors, each weighted with a factor loading (the loading of the variable on the factor), and a residual. Factors are extracted in decreasing order of importance, which is by decreasing proportion of common variability in the original variables accounted for. In the present case, it is hoped to identify the main factors characterising 'trusting attitude' in the two sub-samples, and to be able to find a meaningful interpretation of their composition, as reflected by the factor loadings' sign and magnitude.

In order to achieve more easily interpretable loadings, rotations of the plane defined by the main factors can be performed, with the aim of spreading the loadings' magnitudes for each factor, so that the most relevant ones can be clearly recognised. The goal of all of these strategies is to obtain a clear pattern of loadings, that is, factors that are somehow clearly marked by high loadings for some variables and low loadings for others.

In what follows, results of factor analysis on the data for the trust variables are presented for each of the two sub-samples (Oaxaca and Puebla). In each case, two factors are extracted, and factor loadings from each variables are presented, with significant ones highlighted. Alongside the factor loadings from the unrotated factors extraction, loadings from the most helpful rotation (varimax in Oaxaca and biquartimax in Puebla) are also presented, and comments on the factors' extraction order and on their compositions are then made on their basis. A study of the differences in trusting attitude among the two sub-samples is then carried out by means of multivariate regressions performed with the identified factors as dependent variables.

Factors Extraction: Oaxaca

	Factor Loadings (Unrotated) (data_oax.sta) Extraction: Principal components (Marked loadings are > .700000)			Factor Loadings (Varimax normalized) (data_oax.sta) Extraction: Principal components (Marked loadings are > .700000)		
Variables	Factor 1	Factor 2	Variables	Factor 1	Factor 2
MHELP	0,33	0,57	MHELP	0,11	0,65
ADJTR	**0,97**	-0,04	ADJTR	**0,93**	0,30
ADJTM1	**0,97**	-0,04	ADJTM1	**0,93**	0,30
ADJMT	-0,63	0,62	ADJMT	**-0,80**	0,37
ADJTM2	-0,18	**0,82**	ADJTM2	-0,45	**0,71**
ADJTN	-0,62	-0,70	ADJTN	-0,34	**-0,87**
Expl.Var	2,81	1,88	Expl.Var	2,70	1,99
Prp.Totl	0,47	0,31	Prp.Totl	0,45	0,33

The first trust factor extracted in Oaxaca appears to capture a person's general trusting attitude towards the group, its principal components being trust in representatives and trust in other members. The connection between trust in representatives and in other members supports the hypothesis that leadership and bonding are connected. Distrust by other members is also a component in this factor, which can then be defined as 'trust without mutuality'.

The second factor extracted seems to be referred more to the group level, and is composed of belief in other members' honesty and distrust of non members. This factor confirms the existence of a bonding versus bridging issue, and in particular that in group-bonding is in part based on not bridging with outsiders. To reflect this, the factor is named 'exclusive cohesion'.

In summary, trusting in Oaxaca appears to be a combination of two factors, 'trust without mutuality' and 'exclusive cohesion', the first of which dominates in the explanation of the observed trusting patterns in this sub-samples. The composition of the first factor confirms the hypothesis of a direct relationship between leadership and bonding in this sub-sample, whereas the existence and composition of the second confirms the hypothesis on a trade-off between bonding and bridging. To further confirm these findings, and their comparative relevance, they will also have to be cross-checked with results from the other sub-sample.

Factors Extraction: Puebla

Further to the factor loadings from the unrotated extraction, a different factor rotation (Biquartimax normalised instead of Varimax) was chosen here because it helped to isolate the factors' components.

The first factor extracted in this case is composed of trust in other members and distrust of non members. This helps to identify it as the 'exclusive cohesion' factor identified also in Oaxaca, even though with less importance (see different extraction order there). This confirms the hypothesis of the existence of a trade-off between bonding and bridging, and also that this is more the case in Puebla than in Oaxaca. Moreover, note that in the present case a further 'exclusion' dimension to this factor emerges, and namely distrust of representatives. This confirms the hypothesis that representatives are considered as outsiders in Puebla, and that there exists a direct relationship between leadership and bonding in Oaxaca which takes the opposite sign in Puebla.

Factor Loadings (Unrotated) (data_pue.sta) Extraction: Principal components (Marked loadings are > .700000)			Factor Loadings (Biquartimax normalized) (data_pue.sta) Extraction: Principal components (Marked loadings are > .700000)		
Variables	Factor 1	Factor 2	Variables	Factor 1	Factor 2
MHELP	-0,47	-0,57	MHELP	-0,24	-0,69
ADJTR	**-0,70**	0,28	ADJTR	**-0,76**	0,02
ADJTM1	**0,84**	0,23	ADJTM1	**0,71**	0,51
ADJMT	-0,09	**-0,83**	ADJMT	0,20	**-0,81**
ADJTM2	0,65	-0,21	ADJTM2	0,68	0,02
ADJTN	-0,69	0,29	ADJTN	**-0,75**	0,04
Expl.Var	2,32	1,27	Expl.Var	2,19	1,39
Prp.Totl	0,39	0,21	Prp.Totl	0,37	0,23

The second trust factor in Puebla consists only of a perception of distrust by other members, and is therefore named 'Perceived distrust'. This factor appears to differ substantially from the first factor identified in Oaxaca, so that no comparison will be attempted here.

Regression Analysis of Trust Factors

Once individuated some significant factors describing trust patterns in the two places, a further step in the analysis is required, in order to look at the factors more closely and in particular at their relation with other variables of interest. In particular, it is necessary to address the existence and sign of the relationships between trust factors and those variables that are believed to relate to them. The latter includes both individual and group characteristics, the first since they describe the background of the respondent, and the second because they describe the functioning of the particular group the respondent belongs to. Whilst carrying out such an investigation, particular attention should be devoted also to assessing differences between similar factors across places.

Regression analysis of 'trust without mutuality': Oaxaca To analyse the impact of various potentially related variables on the first trust factor, a multivariate linear regression has been performed, with 'trust without mutuality' as the dependent variable. Case-wise selection of missing data takes place in the original specification, under the assumption that the questionnaires which are more completed have been done more scrupulously and therefore the data excluded is the less reliable. This implies that the specification includes only observations that are available for all the included variables.

To analyse 'trust without mutuality', explanatory variables connected to income, head of family characteristics and participation in other social organisations are included. Alternative specifications with such variables (from each group) have been attempted, and the most significant results are reported here. The results include number of observations, list of variables, variables' estimated coefficients with their significance, overall significance, and the result of normality tests. The alternative specifications tested included the following variables among the regressors (right-hand-side, or independent variables):

- income-related variables: LANDQ, LANDP, YRATIO, EXPPFM
- head of family characteristics: HFAGE, HFSEX, HFPRIM, HFSEC
- others: PARTORG.

The most significant specification:

N = 44	Regression Summary for Dependent Variable: 'trust without mutuality' FACTOR Oaxaca			
	Estimated Coefficient B	Standard Error of B	t(37)	p-level
Intercept	0.73	0.70	1.04	0.31
LANDQ	-0.26	0.11	-2.23	0.03
YRATIO	-0.65	0.41	-1.57	0.13
HFAGE	0.03	0.01	3.45	0.00
HFSEX	-0.47	0.26	-1.81	0.08
HFPRIM	-3.18	0.80	-4.00	0.00
PARTORG	0.36	0.14	2.54	0.02
Goodness of fit	$AdjR^2 = 0.35$ $F(6,37) = 4.86$ $p < .00095$			
Normality	Kolmogorov-Sminorv test: OK			

The 'trust without mutuality' factor is negatively related to the income-related variables (LANDQ, YRATIO), and to primary education so that, in general, the better-off the respondent, the less trusting. Secondly, it is positively related to head of family age, whereas the presence of a female head of family relates negatively to this factor. Finally, the 'trust without mutuality factor' relates positively to participation in other organisations: the more involved in other social groups the respondent, the more trusting of others and persuaded that others do not trust her.

Regression analysis of 'exclusive cohesion': Oaxaca To account for this factor, which is believed to represent a dimension associated with the group's characteristics, some of the variables representing the latter are also included.

Alternative specifications were tested including the following variables among the regressors (right-hand-side, or independent variables):

- income-related variables: LANDQ, LANDP, YRATIO, EXPPFM
- head of family characteristics HFAGE, HFSEX, HFPRIM, HFSEC
- group characteristics: MSTAB, HY, HG, HR, HE, RS, MS, PARTORG.

The most significant specification:

N = 45	Regression Summary for Dependent Variable: 'exclusive cohesion' FACTOR Oaxaca			
	Estimated Coefficient B	Standard Error of B	t(40)	p-level
Intercept	0.48	0.30	1.63	0.11
LANDQ	-0.42	0.10	-4.39	0.00
HFSEX	0.70	0.23	3.09	0.00
MSTAB	-0.59	0.27	-2.16	0.04
RS	0.31	0.22	1.45	0.15
Goodness of fit	**AdjR^2 = 0.5** F(4,40) = 11.958 p < .000			
Normality	Kolmogorov-Sminorv test: OK			

The 'exclusive cohesion' factor relates negatively with quantity of land cultivated (the only significant income-related variable). It relates positively with the presence of a female head of family. As for the effect of group's characteristics, membership stability (which is low in this sub-sample) is negatively related to exclusive cohesion, whereas representative's activity relates positively.

Regression analysis of 'exclusive cohesion': Puebla To account for this factor, which is believed to represent a dimension associated with the group's characteristics, some of the variables representing the latter are also included.

Alternative specifications were attempted with the following variables among the regressors (right-hand-side, or independent variables):

- income-related variables: LANDQ, LANDP, YRATIO, EXPPFM
- head of family characteristics HFAGE, HFSEX, HFPRIM, HFSEC
- group characteristics: MSTAB, HY, HG, HR, HP, HE, RS, MS, PARTORG.

The most significant specification:

N = 34	Regression Summary for Dependent Variable: 'exclusive cohesion' FACTOR Puebla			
	Estimated Coefficient B	Standard Error of B	t(28)	p-level
Intercept	1.16	0.29	3.99	0.00
LANDQ	-0.38	0.21	-1.80	0.08
MSTAB	0.89	0.41	2.17	0.04
HY	-0.64	0.45	-1.42	0.17
HR	-1.02	0.36	-2.86	0.01
PARTORG	-0.29	0.18	-1.66	0.11
Goodness of fit	**AdjR^2 = 0.46** F(5,28) = 6.6104 p < .00035			
Normality	Kolmogorov-Sminorv test: OK			

The 'exclusive cohesion' factor relates negatively to LANDQ, the larger the area of cultivated land, the more 'exclusive cohesion' prone the respondent. It relates positively with stability of membership in groups and negatively with members' homogeneity with respect to income and religion. Finally, exclusive cohesion relates negatively with participation in other organisations.

Regression analysis of 'perceived distrust': Puebla The original specification included the following variables among the regressors (right-hand-side, or independent variables):

- income-related variables: LANDQ, LANDP, YRATIO, EXPPFM
- head of family characteristics: HFAGE, HFSEX, HFPRIM, HFSEC
- group: MSTAB, HY, HG, HR, HP, HE, RS, MS, PARTORG.

The 'perceived distrust' factor relates positively with income stability, the better off the respondent, the higher perceived distrust. As for groups' characteristics, it relates negatively with membership stability, and income homogeneity, whereas it relates positively with religious homogeneity and participation in other social organisations.

Regression Summary for Dependent Variable:
'perceived distrust' FACTOR Puebla

N = 35	Estimated Coefficient B	Standard Error of B	t(29)	p-level
Intercept	-0.01	0.37	-0.01	0.99
YRATIO	0.46	0.32	1.45	0.16
MSTAB	-0.90	0.42	-2.14	0.04
HY	-1.36	0.46	-2.92	0.01
HR	0.56	0.30	1.85	0.08
PARTORG	0.43	0.16	2.71	0.01
Goodness of fit	\multicolumn{4}{c}{$AdjR^2 = 0.45$ F(5,29) = 6.5221 p < .00035}
Normality	\multicolumn{4}{c}{Kolmogorov-Sminorv test: OK}

Summary of Factor Analysis Findings

The following table provides a summary of the study of trust patterns:

Table 5.2 Summary of trust patterns

Factors		OAXACA	PUEBLA
Exclusive cohesion factor	Order	Second: 'exclusive cohesion'	First: 'exclusive cohesion'
	Differences	- better-off respondents are less exclusive cohesion prone - the presence of a female head of family enhances exclusive cohesion - exclusive cohesion decreases with membership stability - the more active the representatives, the higher exclusive cohesion	- better-off respondents are more exclusive cohesion prone - exclusive cohesion increases with membership stability - exclusive cohesion decreases with higher income and religious homogeneity of group members - exclusive cohesion decreases with taking part in other organisations
Distrust factor	Order	First: 'trust without mutuality'	Second: 'perceived distrust'
	Similarities	\multicolumn{2}{l}{The better off the respondent, the more he/she perceives distrust}
	Differences	- the presence of a female head of family reduces trust without mutuality - the older the respondent's head of family, the more trusting the respondent - the more involved in other social organisations the respondent, the more trusting	- perceived distrust decreases with membership stability - perceived distrust decreases with income homogeneity and increases with religious homogeneity - perceived distrust increases with participation in other social organisations

The existence and composition of the 'exclusive cohesion' factor in both subsamples confirms the hypothesis of a trade-off between bonding and bridging; moreover, from the factors order emerges that this trade-off is a more relevant component of trust in Puebla than in Oaxaca.

In Puebla distrust of representatives emerges as a further 'exclusion' dimension to this factor, which confirms the hypothesis that representatives are considered as outsiders in this sub-sample. Together with the composition of the 'trust without mutuality' factor in Oaxaca (based instead on trust of representatives), this confirms the hypothesis of a direct relationship between leadership and bonding in Oaxaca, and an inverse one in Puebla.

Better-off respondents appear to score lower on both trusting factors in both Oaxaca and Puebla. Regarding the exclusive cohesion factor, in both Oaxaca and Puebla membership stability appears to play a role, although with opposite effects: this confirms the idea that stability should probably not be considered as a univocally positive feature. Similarly, members' homogeneity appears to matter for this factor in Puebla, whereas in Oaxaca matters representatives' activity (indicator of leadership), re-enforcing the above observations regarding factors' composition.

The other two factors extracted do not coincide, and therefore no meaningful comparison can be attempted. However, note the effect from membership stability and participation in other social organisations in enhancing perceived distrust in Puebla, confirming the relative closure of members of this scheme. Conversely, taking part in other organisations enhances trust without mutuality (more specific investigation is required to establish which component of the factor it affects).

Conclusions

The chapter addressed the issue of analysing trust dimensions in the context of group-based microfinance. Having acknowledged the multidimensional nature of trust, and particularly its context specificity, the study assessed the common patterns emerging from measuring several dimensions of trust among members of groups participating in two savings and credit schemes. Factor analysis was deployed to identify some common dimensions among respondents of each scheme.

The presence in both sub-samples of an 'exclusive cohesion' factor, based on trust in group members and distrust of outsiders, was interpreted as a symptom of the existence of a trade-off between in-group bonding and bridging with outsiders. The fact that such a factor was preponderant (as reflected in the extraction order) in Puebla, and less important in Oaxaca, was then taken as evidence that the aforementioned trade-off was a more fundamental component of trust dynamics in Puebla. In the latter sub-samples, moreover, representatives were also considered as outsiders, whereas in Oaxaca trust of representatives was the basis of the trust factor 'trust without mutuality'. Such evidence was taken to confirm the hypothesis of a direct relationship between leadership and bonding in Oaxaca, and an inverse one in Puebla. The role of membership stability was found to differ dramatically across the two sub-samples (a result that holds across the whole data analysis), and it was therefore suggested that institutional design should take this feature into account, remembering that in the study areas in Oaxaca live many resettled people, who may naturally find it difficult to form stable groups and might for this reason prefer to 'try out' belonging to different ones (see Barr, 1999).

Perhaps the most important implication deriving from these results concerns the need to approach generalised trust measurements (of the kind used to make statements about the existence of social capital in communities) with a certain degree of scepticism. The present analysis supports the assumption that context (in terms of specific domains in which individuals interact) matters and shapes the nature and extent of trust among the individuals involved (and their trust of others in general), producing quite different pictures even within a 'high' or 'low' trust environment.

A more general implication of this study is that it lends support to the view that successful (in terms of developmental impact and viability) microfinance schemes tend to be integrated in wider development programmes, and to be, at least to some extent, 'users-owned'. This calls into question not just views on the role of financial intermediaries in fostering access to financial markets, but more fundamentally ideas about what the conditions for success of developmental projects are. In particular, this study contributed to the literature arguing that success is influenced by participants' trusting attitudes towards both the local community and the institutions addressing financial exclusion, and suggested the need for more careful examinations of such attitudes.

Appendix – Associations Between Variables

Credit access and design variables – Oaxaca

Variables	Yates-corrected χ^2	φ^2	Outcome
DELAYS & FINPUN	36.07 (.000)	0.49	Strong negative correlation
DELAYS & REPLOSS	1.46 (0.226)		No association
DELAYS & REFLOAN	6.89 (0.0087)		No association
FINPUN & REPLOSS	64.23 (.000)	0.674	Strong negative correlation
REPLOSS & REFLOAN	21.14 (.000)	0.263	Strong negative correlation

Credit access and design variables – Puebla

Variables	Yates-corrected χ^2	φ^2	Outcome
FINPUN & REPLOSS	27.45 (.000)	0.405	Strong negative correlation
REPLOSS & REFLOAN	1.89 (0.1697)		No association

Group's characteristics – Oaxaca

Variables	Yates-corrected χ^2	φ^2	Outcome
MSTAB & ATT	44.62 (.000)	0.483	Strong negative association
MSTAB & RS	11.38 (0.007)	0.131	Weak negative association
MSTAB & MS	11.38 (0.007)	0.131	Weak negative association
MSTAB & JLIAB	41.87 (.000)	0.454	Strong negative association
MSATB & MHELP	25.78 (.000)	0.284	Strong negative association

Group's characteristics – Puebla

Variables	Yates-corrected χ^2	φ^2	Outcome
MSTAB & ATT	6.22(0.0126)		No association
MSTAB & RS	14.06(000)	0.222	Strong negative association
MSTAB & MS	8.38(0.0038)	0.1384	Weak positive association
MSTAB & JLIAB	9.49(0.0021)	0.1602	Weak positive association

Trust variables – Oaxaca

Oaxaca					
Spearman Rank Order Correlations					
	ADJTR	ADJTM1	ADJMT	ADJTM2	ADJTN
ADJTR	1.00	1.00	0.53	0.40	-0.75
ADJTM1	1.00	1.00	0.53	0.40	-0.75
ADJMT	0.53	0.53	1.00	0.55	-0.70
ADJTM2	0.40	0.40	0.55	1.00	-0.80
ADJTN	-0.75	-0.75	-0.70	-0.80	1.00

Trust variables – Puebla

Puebla					
Spearman Rank Order Correlations					
	ADJTR	ADJTM1	ADJMT	ADJTM2	ADJTN
ADJTR	1.00	-0.13	0.01	-0.28	-0.16
ADJTM1	-0.13	1.00	0.35	0.37	-0.77
ADJMT	0.01	0.35	1.00	0.18	-0.50
ADJTM2	-0.28	0.37	0.18	1.00	-0.52
ADJTN	-0.16	-0.77	-0.50	-0.52	1.00

Notes

1. Due to their intrinsic nature, and not to bounded rationality on the part of who performs the calculation.
2. Typical in this approach of the culture that does not refrain opportunism.

References

Bancos Campesinos, *Una alternativa financiera para los pobres rurales*, AMUCSS Report.
Barr, A. (1999), 'Familiarity and Trust: an experimental investigation', Working Paper CSAE, Oxford.
Ben-Porath, Y. (1980), 'The F-Connection: Families, Friends, and Firms and the Organisation of Exchange', *Population and Development Review*, 6, pp. 1-29.
Casson, M. (1991), *The Economics of Business Culture*, Clarendon Press, Oxford.

Casson, M. (1995), *Entrepreneurship and Business Culture*, Edward Elgar, Aldershot.
Cruz Hernandez, I. (1994), *Las Uniones de Credito en Mexico*, Cuaderno AMUCSS.
Cruz Hernandez, I., Ramon Braujos, G. and Martin Zuvire, L. (1996), *Las Uniones de Credito Campesinas y el Neoliberalismo Mexicano*, Cuaderno AMUCSS.
Della Giusta, M. (1999), 'A Model of Social Capital and Access to Productive Resources', *Journal of International Development*, 11, pp. 921-934.
Fukuyama, F. (1995), *Trust*, Free Press, New York.
Gambetta, D. (1988), *Trust: Making and Breaking Cooperative Relations*, Cambridge University Press, Cambridge.
Geertz, C. (1962), 'The Rotating Credit Association: a "Middle Rung" in Development', *Economic Development and Cultural Change*, 10, pp. 241-263.
Gore, C. (1997), 'Irreducibly Social Goods and the Informational Basis of Amartya Sen's Capability Approach', *Journal of International Development*. 9, 2, pp. 235-250.
Granovetter, M. (1985), 'Economic Action and Social Structure: the Problem of Embeddedness', *American Journal of Sociology*, 91, 3 (Nov), pp. 481-510.
Grootaert, C. (1998) 'Social Capital the Missing Link', Working Paper No. 1, Social Capital Initiative, World Bank.
Hirschman, A.O. (1958), *The Strategy of Economic Development*, Yale University Press, New Haven.
Hofstede, G. (1980), *Culture's Consequences: International differences in work-related values*, Sage, Beverly Hills CA.
Hulme, D. and Mosley P. (1996), *Finance against Poverty*, 2 Vols, Routledge, London.
Johnson, S. (1999), 'Evaluation of Microfinance Projects', *Development in Practice*, 9, 4, pp. 488-490.
Johnson, S. and Rogaly, B. (1997), *Microfinance and Poverty Reduction*, Oxfam, UK and Ireland.
Matin, I., Hulme, D. and Rutherford, S. (1999), 'Financial Services for the Poor and the Poorest: Deepening Understanding to Improve Provision', Working Paper No. 9 Finance and Development Research Programme, Institute for Development Policy and Management, University of Manchester.
Mauss, M., *Essai sur le Don*, Presses Universitaires de France.
Moore, M. (1994), 'How Difficult is it to Construct Market Relations? A Commentary on Platteau', *Journal of Development Studies*, 30, 3, pp. 818-830.
Moore, M. (1999), 'Truth, Trust and Market Transactions: What Do We Know?', *Journal of Development Studies*, 36, 1, pp. 74-88.
Platteau, J.-P. (1994), 'Behind the Market Stage Where Real Societies Exist', *Journal of Development Studies*, 30, 3, pp. 533-577 and pp. 753-817.
Portes, A. and Landolt P. (1996), 'The Downside of Social Capital', *The American Prospect*, 26 (May-June).
Putnam, R. (1993), *Making Democracy Work: Civic Traditions in Modern Italy*, Princeton University Press, Princeton NJ.
Seligman, A.B. (1997), *The Problem of Trust*, Princeton University Press, Princeton NJ.
Smith Ring, P. (1997), 'Processes Facilitating Reliance on Trust in Inter-Organisational Networks', in M. Ebers (ed.), *The Formation of Inter-Organisational Networks*, Oxford University Press, New York.
Stiglitz, J. (1990), 'Peer Monitoring and Credit Markets', *World Bank Economic Review*, 4, 3, pp. 351-366.
Van Bastelaer, T. (1997), 'Does social capital facilitate the poor's access to credit?', Working Paper No. 8, *Social Capital Initiative*, World Bank.

Williamson, O.E. (1996), *The Mechanisms of Governance*, Oxford University Press, New York.
World Bank (2000), *World Development Report 2000/2001*, The World Bank, Washington, D.C.

Chapter 6

Constructing Alternative Circuits of Value – The Case of Local Currency Systems (LCSs)

Roger Lee, Andrew Leyshon, Theresa Aldridge, Nigel Thrift, Jane Tooke and Colin Williams

Introduction

The widespread emergence of localised circuits of exchange in the form of Local Currency Systems (LCSs)[1] in many countries of the developed world over the past 20 years or so, raises a range of questions concerning the nature of social responses to processes of uneven development, social and economic marginalisation and the ever-more intense disciplining of economic behaviour by processes of neo-liberal capitalist globalisation. But, considered as more or less spontaneous and positive responses to these circumstances, the emergence of LCSs also points to a set of wider and more fundamental range of questions concerning cultural constructions of 'the economic', the potential, even within a highly-regulated and deeply embedded capitalist system, for people to make their own histories and geographies, and the place of economic activity in the various forms of sociability which give shape and meaning to social relations. Not surprisingly, then, the potential of LCSs for local regenerative development has been recognised by policy makers – both national and local – although, at present, this potential remains largely latent rather than realised.

This chapter, which draws on research conducted in the UK during the period 1997-2000 intended primarily to consider Local Exchange and Trading Systems (LETS) as possible vehicles for tackling social exclusion (see, for example, Williams 1996), argues that the potential of LCSs for local development cannot be separated from the significance attached to them and interpretation of them by their participants and potential participants. In other words, their potential is closely connected to the wider questions outlined above. Such questions are, of course, posed by all forms of economic activity. But the spontaneity, autonomy, scale and, for the most part, embryonic nature of most LCSs exposes these questions rather more clearly than is the case in more highly institutionalised, regulated and ritualised formal circuits of economic activity. An exploration of these questions also begins to reveal the kinds of institutional support which the making of, and engagement in, economic activity implies.

The remainder of the chapter is in three parts. Part 2 outlines the nature of LCSs, and seeks to identify their distinctive features by considering them as monetary networks. Part 3 analyses three variants of LCSs in the form of LETSystems, LETS schemes and Time Dollars. LCSs are revealed as socially constructed economic geographies which seek to foster and encourage processes of consumption, exchange and production that conform to norms that are morally acceptable to their administrators and participants, and which at the same time bring about 'progressive' social and economic change. This part of the chapter also considers (some of) the various and contested interpretations of 'appropriate' economic behaviour which practitioners, involved in these processes of construction, place upon them. Part 4 concludes the chapter by raising questions about the barriers which limit the potential of LCSs to act as effective economic geographies operating in parallel with but separate from the mainstream, given that their current contribution to the material reproduction of social life is, even in the most effective systems, marginal.

Local Currency Systems

In this chapter, we use the term local currency system (LCS) generically to refer to a set of local circuits of production, consumption and multilateral exchange. For many of their advocates, LCSs are intended to work *in conjunction* with the formal economy and to be connected to it in various ways in order to facilitate their extension and credibility. However, LCSs are also intended to operate *in parallel* to the formal economy through the use of alternative means of exchange, or currency. The local or community currency created in this way is not formally exchangeable with a national currency, but in many cases may be closely related to national currencies in terms of nominal value. Most LCSs use a locally identified form of currency for exchange, which may circulate physically, in the form of cheques registered centrally, or in virtual form, as debits and credits within electronic accounting programmes. These accounts are made public to members of LCSs and the possibilities for exchange, along with the information transfers necessary to enable it, are also registered centrally in a directory or through a registry. The intention is that processes of production, consumption and exchange that would not be possible or that would be unacceptably transformed by the social and financial relations of reproduction within the formal economy may be facilitated within LCSs by the provision and use of an independent currency which comes into existence only as a result of the agreement of participants to engage in exchange with each other.[2] Thus, access to formal money need no longer be a necessary prerequisite for participation in economic activity.

Local currencies facilitate the production, exchange and consumption of services and self-produced or self-earned goods (such as second-hand goods, for example) across the network of members within the LCS. Thus, although they may currently be restricted in geographical scale, exchange within LCSs is, in theory at least, not constrained by the spatial limitations inherent within barter exchange (that is, the bilateral exchange of one good for another) (See, for example, Leyshon, 1995). Rather, insofar as information about the LCS network, which is comprised of its members and the commodities and services that they wish to trade, is kept up-to-date and accurate by the registry or published in a directory of offers and wants provided to all members, the local currency acts as a localised form of *monetary network*. This network offers information not just about the possibility of individual transactions (sale and purchase) but also about the extent (diversity, size, geographical range) of those possibilities and so offers some of the pre-requisites for the functioning of independent economic geographies. This idea is developed in more length in the next section of the paper, which examines LCSs as monetary networks according to the categorisation developed by Nigel Dodd (1994).

LCSs as Monetary Networks

Dodd's notion of a monetary network is particularly valuable in attempting to understand the dynamics of LCSs. Dodd's purpose in developing the concept of the monetary network is to attempt to provide a flexible but robust theory of money that is 'sufficiently abstract to enable ... cases to be compared without generalizing to such an extent that important variations cannot in fact be accounted for or explained' (Dodd, 1994, p. xxvii). He argues that all monetary systems contain five essential abstract qualities: (i) a system of *accountancy*, which enables 'money' in the network to function as a medium of exchange, a store of value, and measure of account, the three concrete requirements of all money forms; (ii) a system of *regulation*, to protect and defend these functions of money; (iii) *reflexivity*, by which past experience of the network enables participants to develop expectations of the future which, in combination with a system of regulation, enables the network to develop as a means of deferred payments and thus to project forward in time; (iv) the existence of *sociality*, so that it is possible for information about exchange and value to circulate between actors within the network, and; (v) *spatiality*, which means that monetary networks will have specific types of territoriality. According to Dodd, these abstract properties are required for a monetary system to be brought into being and, in combination, enable money to work in a wide range of forms, in different places and at different times. The concept is of considerable utility for the analysis being pursued here because variations in the relative strength of the abstract qualities of monetary networks can be advanced to explain why some monetary forms are more extensive and more durable than others, while it is also suggestive of a proliferative and multiple understanding of monetary systems. The theory of monetary networks admits that there may be many competing monetary networks in existence at any one time, each with distinctive systems of accountancy, regulation, reflexivity, sociability and spatiality.

As monetary networks, LCSs are distinctive from the formal, state-regulated mainstream monetary system along all five of the abstract properties identified by Dodd (Table 6.1):

Table 6.1 Monetary networks and Local Currency Systems (LCSs)

Dimension	LETSystems	LETS schemes	Time Dollars	National currency
Accountancy	Measure of exchange; measure of value; ~~Store of value~~, (Social capital?)	Measure of exchange; measure of value; ~~Store of value~~, (Social capital?)	Measure of exchange; measure of value; ~~Store of value~~, (Social capital?)	Measure of exchange; measure of value; Store of value, ~~(Social capital?)~~
Regulation	Low	Low	Moderate	High
Reflexivity	Low/moderate	Low	Moderate	High
Sociality	Low	Low	Moderate	High
Spatiality (length of network)	Moderate-long	Short	Moderate	Very long
Theories	Self-organization, systems theory and cybernetics, evolutionary, community development	Community, Social capital, Ecological and green, anti-market, Third Way	Social capital, community	Neo-liberal
Morality	Libertarian	Mutuality	Mutuality	Market
Links to social policy communities and agendas	Weak	Strong	Strong	Moderate
Emotional investment	Low	High	Moderate	Low

- The system of *accountancy* revolves around a special, local credit money operating quite independently of the 'legal tender' of the mainstream economy.[3] Such local money serves as a measure of value and a medium of exchange, but it does not function very well as a store of value. No interest can be earned on credit accumulated, and the system is an accumulation of credits with no external value other than when they are activated through expenditure; that is, money in LCSs has to be in action to be worth anything.

- LCSs have a fairly informal system of *regulation*. They rely primarily upon good will and the collective moral suasion of the LCS as a whole. The central regulatory problems facing LCSs is the problem of the 'free rider'; that is, an individual who accumulates large debts through purchasing goods and services through the system but who makes little or no attempt to reduce their debt through undertaking work for other members of the system, and/or who leaves the system or the area before doing so.

- The issue of *reflexivity* relates here to the problems of creating trust and of generating expectations of the long-term survival of LCSs into the future. From an economically rational perspective, without sound expectations that credits accumulated within LCS will retain their value or be expended in the future it will be difficult for actors to engage with the network or justify spending much of their time earning local currency.

- The *sociality* of such systems is partly institutionalised, especially at the local level. Many LCSs are linked to larger, national organisations but these organisations have only very limited scope to engage in the promotion or regulation of transactions. In some LCSs, a local office may help to encourage contact between members by advertising the goods and services offered and sought by LCSs members and by organising trading meetings which act like a kind of trade fair for members. Such activities help to disseminate information about exchange through the network, but active trading itself is intended to drive the circulation of information through the network.

- LCSs tend to have quite constrained *spatial* boundaries. Although LCSs exist world-wide, and so in that respect are part of long networks, each operates as an inherently local institution, signified by the way LCSs often draw upon specific local features or sayings to name the unit of currency used. Therefore, while LCSs are able to create a financial space that is in many ways alternative to monetary mainstream, the majority of these networks simply do not extend very far. Their limited spatial reach acts as a constraint upon their effectiveness, for they are limited to utilising the resources that exist within their area and are in danger of being hostages to the places in which they are formed.[4]

Whilst this is an adequate description of LCSs as a generic group, there are important differences between the LCSs that have important implications not only for their strength and durability, but also for their ability to carve out separate spaces of economic and social action. The next part of the chapter draws attention to these differences by focusing in turn upon three particularly important forms of LCS: LETSystems, LETS schemes, and Time Dollars (Table 6.1).

Contested Economic Geographies of Social Reproduction: LETSystems, LETS Schemes, and Time Dollars

In as much as they are geographical circuits of consumption, production and exchange, LCSs constitute *economic geographies*, and to better understand their dynamics necessitates moving beyond the theory of monetary networks and its tendency towards abstraction (for a discussion, see Leyshon, 1997). LCSs represent attempts to *construct* circuits of social reproduction operating across space and time which, in turn, requires a mode of understanding which moves beyond an attempt to develop essential, abstract representations of money, value and information, and to deal instead with the embodied and performative processes of monetarisation, value construction and calculation as they are practised within LCSs (Thrift, 1996; Power, 1997). This is not to say that the theory of monetary networks is not of use in analysing LCSs. But while such abstract properties may exist in ideal cases and, indeed, even within the minds of the designers and architects of LCSs, the practices of participants within LCSs reveals messier and often contradictory uses and understandings of money and value.

There is an inherent materiality and practicality about such circuits of social reproduction (Figure 6.1). They are constituted in and by the continuous flow of value through consumption, the exchange of labour power for production and the exchange of value embodied in commodities so facilitating further consumption. In order to enable social and material survival, circuits of social reproduction have to sustain the delivery of this flow of value, in appropriate quantities and distributions.

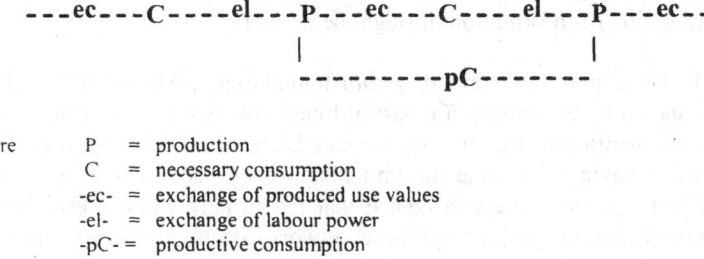

where   P   = production
        C   = necessary consumption
        -ec- = exchange of produced use values
        -el- = exchange of labour power
        -pC- = productive consumption

Figure 6.1 A circuit of social reproduction

Value may be thought of as relations and things which, through the material and social practices of consumption, exchange and production, come to be regarded as useful, helpful, uplifting or, more narrowly but more generally, as functional.[5] Thus as circuits of social reproduction, LCSs – like all economic geographies – necessarily involve complex and influential intersections of material *and* social relations and practices in the formation and definition of value. Material relations involve the practice and co-ordination of circuits of consumption, exchange and production. Social relations are the circuits of authority and direction through which some social sense is made of, or imposed upon, these material practices. They are, in effect, social relations of reproduction which involve the power to control and direct the forces of production (people and the material objects used in consumption, exchange and production) engaged in the circuits of material practice. The contemporary world is dominated by capitalist relations of social reproduction based on the separation of labour and capital. These social relations are extended and imposed upon social reproduction – although not without resistance – by financial and commercial institutions operating over multiple scales from the individual to the global. Such institutions define highly focused notions of value directed at profitability and accumulation and use them to constrain and direct capitalist circuits of social reproduction.[6] In this way, the social and material dimensions of social reproduction are mutually formative and inseparable.

Nevertheless, there is a limit to the promulgation of alternative values which is set by the inputs necessary to sustain social reproduction. Bowring (1998), for example, suggests that:

> although the self-limitation of needs is a vital cultural and political project, [it] is unlikely to succeed if people are not rewarded for their self-restraint with an expansion in disposable time. Given the meagre capital resources – and relatively low productivity levels – of the local economy, it is unlikely that ... small-scale, self-sufficient communities ... would have much spare time to devote to labour-intensive, non-essential cultural pursuits or to pioneering entrepreneurial projects. Maintaining the tension between the micro-social activities of local trading systems and the more efficient and productive functioning of the macro-economic system is thus crucial to the protection of individual liberties and of the space for innovation, imagination, and experimental change.

Thus, although LCSs offer great scope for the practice of alternative values and so open up a range of political possibilities (North, 1999), there is an uneasy and hotly contested fault line between LCSs and formal circuits of social reproduction.

This contested relationship is linked, in turn, to the distinction between LETSystems, LETS schemes and Time Dollars and, more broadly, to the distinction between LCSs as economic geographies and as social geographies.[7] It also raises the question of the distinction between financial capital and social capital in LCSs. Although LCSs crave business involvement, they have no mechanism for conventional accumulation. For those active in LETS schemes and Time Dollars this is largely irrelevant because the establishment of community relations and the possibilities of reaching out to others are seen to be more important goals and objectives. It is the production and accumulation of forms of social capital[8] which provides the major criterion of evaluation for such circuits of social reproduction.

In order to illustrate some of the tensions and contradictions within and between LCSs, we now turn our attention to three distinctive forms of LCSs: LETSystems, LETS schemes and Time Dollars.

LETSystems and Amoral, Libertarian Geographies

Its designers define a LETSystem[9] in the following way:

> A LETSystem, Local Exchange Trading System is a self-regulating network which allows its users to issue and manage their own money supply within the boundaries of the network.

The LETSystem accounting service maintains a system of accounts for its users. A LETSystem has the following essential characteristics:

1. A service in the community

Administrative costs are recovered, in the internal currency, from each account according to the cost of service. The service operates on a not-for-profit basis.

2. Consent is required at all times

There is never any obligation to trade.

It is the account holders who have control over the movement of money into and out of their accounts. The administration can only act (sic) on the instructions of the account-holder who is making a payment.

All accounts start at zero, no money is deposited or issued.

3. Key information is available to all account holders

Any account-holder may know the balance (the degree of commitment) and trading volume (the level of participation) of any other account on the system.

4. A convenient measure

The unit of account is a measure equivalent to pound sterling.[10]

5. Your money belongs to you

Your money is personal, in every way your own money. No interest is charged or paid on balances.

A personal money network that adopts all of the above criteria and agreements is a LETSystem (see http://www.gmlets.u-net.com/design).

Thus, LETSystems are accurately named: they represent an attempt to develop an efficient and effective means to transmit information about exchange in a community currency across a network. It is, in effect, very similar to the monetary transmission services provided by the formal financial system, and within LETSystems these services are provided at cost, and do not rely on the goodwill of volunteers. LETSystems set out to form trading links and developmental resources with local business and the voluntary sector, and their quest for efficiency has led to the promotion, as local money, of electronic technologies such as smart cards, examples of which are already in use for many forms of local interaction within certain communities. Such developments have the potential of enabling money within the LETSystem monetary network to interact relatively freely with other monetary networks and, insofar as LETSystems moneys generate benefits for locally-controlled processes of economic development, they are capable of challenging the hegemony of (national) money within other (non-local) monetary networks.

The emergence of LCSs (and the various forms of currency that pre-dated them) were a direct result of a failure of engagement in circuits of social reproduction. As

Michael Linton, who invented LETS in British Columbia and has since promoted them world-wide, succinctly argues about the origins and benefits of the first LETSystem with which he is most directly involved:

> First there was some money, then there was no money, then there was.[11]

In the early 1980s the Comox Valley region was severely economically depressed and the response was the Comox Valley LETSystem, which was 'designed and implemented' by just a dozen or so people, including Linton.[12] This response demonstrates the possibility for local pro-activity presented by LCSs but, at the same time, it also points to the need for the design and implementation of an institutional and transactional infrastructure which is largely self-sustaining:

> ... what we're doing has got to be practical and viable.[13]

For the designers of this system, the overriding objective was to:

> Do it well, do it so that it pays for itself.

The performance of the system is probably less than one per cent of capacity – BUT it still pays its way.
A money system that needs grants of volunteers to operate is a boat that don't float (sic).[14]

This emphasis upon practicality and viability raises an important distinction within the world of LCSs. It is the difference, as a leading UK proponent of LETSystems put it,[15] between planning and design:

> ... with planning you're trying to influence everything that goes on all the time, but with design, you're trying to set something up that is inherently self-manageable.

This encapsulates one dimension at least of the distinction between LETSystems and LETS schemes. The former are concerned with design; the latter tend towards 'planning' or at least intervention. But this raises a deeper issue because the construction of monetary networks which work – in terms of sustaining a monetary system and in which confidence[16] is largely unquestioned – is no easy task. The infrastructural fabric of conventional money networks extends from central banks and their international co-operation down to the probity and effectiveness of financial and retail institutions. It enables money to circulate in unproblematic ways which appear almost invisible to its users. Such an infrastructure is difficult to replicate outside the framework of state regulation and all the resources devoted to it, and without the complex and extensive network of financial institutions which, for self-interested reasons, maintain (but also often undermine) the effectiveness of the mainstream monetary system.[17]

Thus a major pre-occupation of those involved in LETSystems remains the provision of appropriate infrastructure (see, for example, http://www.driveout.

demon.co.uk/mrs2.html). The primary purpose of this infrastructure is to facilitate the emergence and practice of multiple currencies so as to break the power relations associated with dominant currencies. The infrastructure of LETSystems is designed to transmit information between participants and to facilitate trading. It is intended to be almost entirely (but not quite) neutral with respect to the social objectives of involvement in LETSystems. The point of this infrastructure (e-mail and other forms of electronic communication, smart cards etc.) is to facilitate multiple networks of interactions within multiple currencies. This is what Michael Linton calls 'a means to pure exchange':[18]

> LETSystems should be considered as essentially value free mechanisms that enable the community to realise their own directions.[19]

For a UK-based advocate of LETSystems,

> [It is] the philosophical thing that attracts me ... [it] is still the idea of Adam Smith's invisible hand, so that you don't get things like the state trying to interfere too much in people's daily lives ... one of the reasons I get attracted to things like LETS [is] because ... it's more a tool box approach for me.[20]

And the notion of community here is neither pre-determined, for 'a community is what its elements do'[21] nor is it necessarily defined only in terms of its place boundedness. In short, the objective of LETSystems is monetary diversity for use in ways that people who wish to see fit. There is, therefore a powerful political message here, concerned with issues of personal autonomy, responsibility and community:

> ... and there's the thing about individuality as well as the State. There's the thing about personal freedom as well as the advantages for people acting collectively and in terms of community ... nobody in LETS should be coerced into doing anything and so it's about freedom of choice, freedom of association, but it's also about the benefits of collective activity.[22]

Thus, the highly political objective of multiple community currencies is to overcome the power relations and constraints inherent in the scarce medium of mainstream money. By this means the objective is to unlock the development potential of local economic geographies.

> The potential for the full space of exchange to be filled/fulfillable is only consistent (sic) with multiple currency options. Anyone can then do what they want, unrestricted by any lack of a suitable medium.[23]
>
> We are so accustomed to a singular money that we tend to bundle conventional monetary values into exchange as a whole without seeing what relates to the means and what to the matter of exchange. My view of community money systems – IN PLURAL – is that they reduce the politics to close to nothing. This is, I agree, very political (original emphasis).[24]

... exchange is (possibly) never value free, but the mechanism is. This is because it isn't singular and constrained, as with conventional money. Conventional money, as a commodity in itself, introduces power relations. Community money IF PLURAL – does not ... the consequences of the scarce medium are power relations (original emphasis).[25]

It is important to stress here that this project is indeed 'very political' not merely because of the power relations inherent in the scarcity and singularity of official currencies. Rather, it derives from the significance of money as a means of carrying and imposing capitalist relations of social reproduction and from associated practices of regulation – including monetary regulation – in the capitalist state. The provision of multiple currencies serves to contest the dominance of the (capitalist) social relations sustained and extended across exchanges in mainstream money. This is not a simplistic attempt to challenge capitalist relations of production and the imperatives of accumulation by means of regulating exchange relations. It is, rather and much more ambitiously to try to demonstrate that, given the convincing availability of a multiplicity of currency systems from which can choose with confidence, it is possible to practise different forms of social relations in production and consumption. The objective here is not 'pure exchange' – an impossibility – but a challenge to the singular constraint of, and Foucauldian disciplining carried out by, conventional money and the power relations that are reproduced through it. However, the provision of multiple currencies creates, in effect, a market in currencies that may lead in the short or medium term to diversity but which, in the long term, is likely to lead to a uniformity induced by inter-currency competition.

Indeed, there are strong echoes here of the arguments made by monetary libertarians such as Hayek and White. Both have advocated that the control of currencies be located in the hands of non-state institutions, although in each case the justification has been in the interest of controlling inflation and monetary stability, rather than local economic self-determination (Dodd, 1994, pp. 36-40). Their arguments for making non-state institutions responsible for the issue of currency is to place the process in the hands of economic actors that are less powerful than states and who, therefore, are more easily disciplined by the 'market' to ensure that the management of currencies is not subverted for 'non-economic', 'political' purposes. The parallels with the arguments advanced by advocates of LETSystems are striking in this regard.

As well as pointing to the potential for the creative use of productive energy and the satisfaction of otherwise unrequited wants and needs embodied in LCS, this central concern for multiple currencies underlies the amorality of the philosophy of LETSystems. The general ethos of LETSystems is libertarian, no matter what the views and objectives of particular systems may be, and which produces a set of potentially unsustainable contradiction within. One geographical consequence of this is that trading between systems is inappropriate, not least because of the potential leakage of money out of local systems[26] and the associated patterns of uneven development to which such leakage may give rise. Individuals can, however, belong to as many systems as they wish and the effectiveness of LCSs is dependent in part on their ability to engage in the production, consumption and trading of a wide range of values. This, in turn, implies the desirability of non-local exchanges. One way around this problem is the establishment of further infrastructure in the form of multi-registry procedures that operate independently of local systems.[27]

A further point to note about the amorality inherent in the construction and objectives of LETSystems is the failure/reluctance to get LETSystems easily onto the policy agenda and the hostility which attempts to proselytise the LETSystem model have generated. For example, consider this exchange with a leading UK proponent of LETSystems:[28]

> A: It's a subversion. It's not good enough. For some people in this country, it's not good enough to have something innovative that attempts to re-engineer what's basically a social construct, this thing 'money'. It's not good enough to do that, to improve the financial relationship between individuals, to give individuals and organisations a chance to increase their business and liquidity and their personal well being. That's not good enough.
>
> Q: Why?
>
> A: It's not moral enough. We're adopting a systems approach. We're a bunch of engineers, right? We've got no morality. I've talked to people in the City of London ... [who say] 'I really like this work you are doing. It's such a change to help you out doing this'. It's not good enough that I'm adopting the systems approaches, because I'm still working within a market framework. I'm still advocating enterprise. I'm advocating freedom of association ... but the other big thing is 'not invented here' ... You've got to be very careful about it. 'Not invented here.' You put those two things together – and the third thing is, because LETS has got into this awful voluntary sector positioning, we're seeing the systemic problems of a sector in there.

This exchange reveals a double process of resistance to the incorporation of LETSystems within the wider economy and polity. On the one hand it reveals within LETSystems the tendency to reject formalised state involvement in community development for the libertarian reasons outlined above and, on the other, a resistance to the incorporation of spontaneous institutions like LCSs into state policy:

> ... in a LETSystem, it's not my job to carry out the government's social exclusion agenda. It's the same with the credit unions. Why is it the job of these people who are volunteers ... why is it all of a sudden our job to deal with social exclusion?[29]

LETS Schemes and Moral Geographies[30]

Against the more formalised model of LETSystems, those who advocate LETS *schemes* as autonomous social alternatives, argue that monetary integration with the formal financial system, and the concern for the provision of a pure means of exchange at cost, would destroy the very basis of the attraction of LETS *as* alternatives. Indeed, it is the notion of *alternative* rather than *parallel* currencies which motivates many LETS schemes. They operate with local currencies which may be related to pounds sterling but they are, in any case, run in a much more dirigiste fashion by volunteers who may form a core group to direct and facilitate the LETS. Compared to LETSystems, LETS schemes are, therefore, in certain ways more coercive. 'Socials' and 'trading days' are held, for example, to facilitate trade and certain kinds social objectives – such as facilitating the social inclusion of various marginal groups. Social agendas of this sort may compete with trade as the driving force within the scheme.[31] LETS schemes have, therefore, a far more pronounced moral agenda than do LETSystems. They reflect a response not merely to the lack of money, scarcity and the power relations inherent in a singular, highly regulated monetary system but also to the perceived social inadequacies of the prevailing monetary and market system. Thus, whereas LETSystems are underpinned by notions of libertarianism and self-organisation, LETS schemes are animated more by sentiments of mutuality, self-help and communitarianism.[32]

Thus, the ways in which economic activity carried out in LETS schemes are justified can reflect ecologically-sustainable values, a desire to foster social capital within local communities, or the foregoing of efficiency and choice in favour of a lower material standard of living in order to free up time to engage in alternative activities. By contrast, within LETSystems, the question of the social objectives of engaging in a LETS is hardly relevant. The point is to provide multiple currencies and an efficient and effective means of exchange as an alternative to formal money. The implication here, of course, is a rejection of certain formal state structures and centralised policy prescriptions and administration.

The desire within LETSystems to create an unincorporated infrastructure for exchange draws attention once again to the difference of approach not only to the practices of LCSs but to their objectives. This difference revolves around the extent to which economic geographies are socially constructed, and the degree to which such geographies *should* be consciously and purposively constructed to achieve particular pre-given goals. For LETSystems, there are, as we have seen, no or minimal moral obligations; for LETS schemes, the alternative moralities of exchange are paramount.

In what follows, therefore, we examine various aspects of LCSs to draw attention to four ways in which economic life in LETS is performed and constrained through social action.

First, as a social process, economic activity depends upon the development of confidence, co-operation, trust, understanding and social divisions of labour. Thus, whereas the architects of LETSystems are concerned with the efficiency of their systems and the development of confidence in the multiple currencies made available through them at a systemic level, for those involved in LETS schemes it is the cultivation of personal trust and finding an alternative to the impersonal nature of the formal economy that offers an important motive for participation:

... when you phone someone in the Yellow Pages [you] are purely communicating on an economic level. I might want something that you've got ... [but] we don't have to get

> involved with each other personally ... With LETS you join a community, where trading, by its very nature, takes place and involves society. You 'phone somebody up, invariably on Friday. You may speak to the wife or the husband ... you may get their children. They may only be able to do the things that you want them to do, or you for them, in private ... so what's happening is [that] trading activity is taking place in another time and space than it normally takes place.[33]

> Well, we don't agree with the kind of society we've got now, the economic or the social ideas that are about. We feel that there should be as much equality as possible in society, and the idea of LETS as an alternative trading system or a kind of barter was very appealing [as was] community. I like that aspect of meeting people and helping each other and the informality, in a way, that [we are] trading through.[34]

The development of LCSs beyond a desire for greater social contact within a community has been in response not only to the failures of circuits of social reproduction but, as many interviewees have indicated, to the possibilities generated by their construction to conduct economic activity in ways more acceptable to their participants.

> ... I suppose that I've always been involved in radical politics since, I guess, the early 1960s in many ways, and this, to my mind, the whole market global economy, seemed something that wasn't doing local economies very [much] good, and [there was a] need to look for other ways of ... how to relate to one another but to keep the economy within the local community ... [35]

> ... people are able to share things within the LETS community that they wouldn't otherwise contribute or share. I mean sharing ... in a sharing environment. Even [obtaining] services that sterling buyers would be looking for.[36]

And LETS schemes enable their participants to act in ways which offer some resistance and develop alternatives to global market capitalism in the face of its perceived fragility, albeit in a mundane and 'slow-burn' kind of way:

> I think the main thing that grabbed me about it was in the beginning, was just that feeling of somehow taking control ... I had a feeling that eventually, at some point, [formal] currencies would get into a mess ... I had a feeling there'd be crashes and ups and downs and inflation and all that sort of thing, and I just thought that with LETS you can be separate from that really. So, you're taking some responsibility, because you feel so helpless don't you? And I suppose, in everything that I'm doing, I like to feel I'm kind of ... I'm doing it, I'm not having it done to me. I suppose that's what I felt about LETS really, and I thought, well, if you get a scheme going now when things are reasonably okay ... and then if things do suddenly get bad you've got it there ready blossom and expand, whereas if you suddenly got it going in a kind of crisis, I thought it would be a lot more difficult.[37]

Observations such as this underline the point that participation in circuits of social reproduction involves a simultaneous engagement in both social and material relations.

However – and this is the second way in which social actions shape LCSs – as repositories of diverse social relations and objectives which contest, in a variety of ways, mainstream economic geographies, certain forms of LCS suffer from an institutional thinness bordering on the non-existent. This is a lack that generates a number of contradictions.[38] LCSs are intended to be spontaneous in the sense that their existence is very largely a function of the activity of exchange. The economic practice of LCSs is based not on slotting into a pre-existing set of economic and social relations but upon the active practice of matching wants and needs with the skills and time to satisfy them. As and when trading takes place, LCS exist; outside this practice they do not. This was remarked upon directly by one of our informants, a leading figure in the organisation of Stroud LETS, who observed that, unlike formal money, LCSs are, in effect, zero-sum games, that are not generative of money in themselves:

> If everybody sits around waiting until they're in credit nothing would ever happen at all because the two things have to be in balance. One lot have to be in the minus situation and the other have to be in the plus situation, and they have to be – I mean, I hope, presumably they are – I haven't looked through the whole account, but one would imagine that the two numbers are exactly a balanced at all times. They have to be and it is certainly a mistake to think that being in a minus situation is a bad thing. It's not a bad thing ... [39]

> ... the other big thing is money creation ... how money is actually created which is something that nobody, as far as I can make out, hardly ever thinks about (sic). When you ask them they haven't the faintest idea, and that's very interesting. Whereas LETS is created at the point of use, as far as I understand [mainstream] money, it's created when you borrow it. Which is why it's highly inflationary ... [40]

Furthermore, for many LETS schemes in particular, the thing that binds them together is a concern for alternative forms of economic, social and ecological relations and the ability to practice such alternatives through personal, or close to personal, trade. There is relatively little institutional infrastructure. In the case of LETS schemes, the infrastructure involves a centrally issued directory and a computer based accounting system normally maintained by volunteers. The institutional thinness of such arrangements is revealed over and over again by LCS participants not knowing, for example, how to record transactions, or of being unaware of an central administration, and by frequent complaints amongst those who are aware of the inadequacies of the central processes of administration, and of the people that staff the office.

Nevertheless, the spontaneity of exchange depends in part on the extent to which trading is possible and this, in turn, is a function of the size of the group and, more particularly, its diversity (range of goods and services traded) and the intensity of involvement (regularity and amount of trading) by its participants. The personalised nature of economic transactions in LETS schemes increase the need for central co-ordination and initiative. There is constantly a need to try to stimulate and extend trading in order to more effectively achieve the objectives of the group involved. As indicated above, such pressures frequently elicit a response from a 'core group' which then is subjected to pressures of time, since they work on a largely voluntary basis, and so produce and reveal the institutional thinness characteristic of LCSs. Furthermore, the emergence and activities of the group produce a vertical element of power relations which sits uneasily alongside the intended horizontal and mutually negotiated relations of exchange generated amongst its participants.[41]

A third aspect of the social construction of economic geographies is that the effective performance of economic activity depends upon a widely-based understanding and acceptance – even if that acceptance is imposed by some kind of force – of what economic activity is, what its objectives are and how its achievements or lack of them will be assessed. Within LETS schemes, for example, there is a great deal of debate about the value of time; whether more highly-'skilled' should be paid more per unit of time than less 'skilled'; what the significance of qualifications may be in terms of pricing; how the quality and efficient organisation of economic activity may be real drawbacks to the extension of LETS schemes. It is clear from the comments of practitioners that conflict over pricing policy (that is, whether skill should be recognised as a major factor in pricing) is a real disincentive to trading and hence to the extension and intensification of activity in LETS schemes:

Q: Do you think that there ought to be a standard rate introduced in the LETS?

A: I am in two minds about that. I can see that in an ideal world, yes, there would certainly be a standard rate. Or you may find that if you did that then the more professional people, who have had to lay out considerable sums and time to acquire certain skills, would find it not worth their while, but I can perfectly see that in a socialist world there should be an equal rate for everything. But that's not the way ... People are conditioned by the present capitalist system and [one cannot] assume that you can just switch on and off. I don't think that's possible.[42]

Q: Do you think that there are some groups of people, for example, someone who hasn't been employed for a while, who'd have problems actually pricing their skills, and maybe undervaluing their skills?

A: No, because, I mean, everyone knows what shop workers get paid, or unskilled workers get paid.

Q: Do you think that LETS should challenge those values at all?

A: No, it's like a market-place isn't it? So, you know, you've got to say. 'I'll work for this much', and if no-one will employ you, you've got to drop your price haven't you? So, LETS is still working in the real world.[43]

I know [that] in Mendip LETS the view there was ... [that] an hour of one person's time is worth an hour of another person's time, it doesn't matter what you are doing. And I was doing acupuncture then, and I had a babysitter, and in some way it didn't feel quite balanced for me, because somebody could come and do four hours of babysitting – and that's quite nice – two hours you're sitting reading a book, and I mean, that's fine, but for me to do four acupuncture treatments – four people – you can't [do it]. You know, it's not quite the same. So to me that's one of the difficulties which is just the nature of life. You have to address these issues.[44]

Clearly, although many of those involved in co-ordinating LETS schemes envisage the creation of an economic system with different values to the mainstream economy, our research suggests that trading within them is drenched in the conventions of the mainstream market economy. This tension produces conflict within those individuals who wish to further the aims and objectives of the LCS, but who wish to avoid selling themselves short:

> I just pitch [my rate] roughly at what everybody else is doing on the grounds that you don't want to be undercutting people, because that's an un-neighbourly thing to do, but on the other hand you don't want to price yourself out of the market. So I see that as straight economics really, that you price yourself roughly in the middle of the range. I tend to be down the lower end of the range, and I must admit that I don't update it often enough, so I think that I'm still charging about 10 or 12 LETS an hour, which is probably far below the professional rate by now. I expect [that] in the big outside world people are charging at least £15, if not £20 an hour for professional services of all kinds ... [45]

There is also evidence that the insertion of bureaucratic understandings and attitudes influence the way in which apparently spontaneous trading takes place. In Stroud, for example, administration is carried out by an office with a distinct location, staffing and institutional set up. A number of interviews revealed that 'the office' practised a view of LCS that was far more like that found within the formal economy, especially in relation to attitudes to debt:

> People always say to me, 'What do you do when somebody goes off and leaves the scheme owing loads of LETS?' It has happened that people have gone off, [with] small amounts [of debt] actually. I don't think it's a big problems really. I really don't. It could be just as much of a problem, in a sense, if they went off with a big credit actually ... but I think what they say in theory, the practicalities of it are, that you distribute that minus or plus throughout the group just to make the numbers balance up. Whether they are actually doing that ... ? I don't think they are in the office ... you do have to change your whole way of looking at money, I think. It is very easy to get stuck in old patterns of thinking ... you really need that same feeling to permeate throughout because, if it doesn't, the wrong messages get put out really, and I think that's happened in Stroud LETS actually. And I don't want to actually get to the office folk too much, because I think it's a bit sad really, their attitudes. But equally I don't want them to walk out, because I don't want to go and do what they do all the time – I haven't got time! (laughs).[46]

This draws attention to a fourth point relating to the social construction of the economic. What is thought of as 'value' is very much a social construct. Material things are endowed with social value as a result of prevailing social norms. Thus, within contemporary capitalist society, the primary determinant of whether something is valuable or not is measured in terms of its contribution to profitability. Trying, for example, to gain employment without possession of currently valued (i.e. potentially value-producing) skills – no matter how the skills that you do have may have been valued in other spaces and times – is extremely difficult. Not surprisingly, the lack of such skills is a cause of much unemployment – especially long-term unemployment. What is happening here is that the criteria of value operated within the labour markets in which unskilled people seek work simply negates the skills that they do possess. As a result, it also negates the productive work, consumption and exchange that could otherwise take place.[47]

Within LETS schemes, there is the possibility of establishing relations of exchange which deliberately and consciously set out to pursue alternative values. Thus individuals who would otherwise have difficulties gaining access to the formal labour market may be accommodated easily within the informal atmosphere of work within a LETS scheme. This seems especially true of work carried out for the LCS itself and, indeed, the personal challenge of selling goods and services across the LCS may act as a further disincentive to engagement. It is for reasons such as these that certain LCS practitioners actively reject the notion of currencies as mediating relations, preferring to see LCS as a relatively (but only relatively) formalised means of favours.

Similarly, single-purpose LCSs or schemes with a single, clearly identified focus within a more general scheme may reflect the deliberate attempt to side-step the evaluations inherent in the mainstream economy and use a local currency to enable those other wise marginalised to engage in informal activity.[48] We now move on to the third and final variant of LCSs considered in this chapter: Time Dollars.

Time Dollar Schemes and the Regulation of Social Capital

The first Time Dollar scheme was developed in the late 1980s by US academic, Edgar Cahn, in Washington DC. Within this type of LCS the unit of exchange is an hour of time expended in working for someone else. Therefore, to this extent at least, Time Dollars are potentially the most economically radical and socially progressive of all LSCs, for they equalise skills and pay rates through the measure of time. These schemes are explicitly designed to encourage the growth of social capital within often deprived and marginal communities:

> People earn Time Dollars by helping others. They can then either spend the Time Dollars to get help for themselves or their families, or they can donate their Time Dollars to individuals or groups in need of help. Computerized Time Dollar accounting systems help mobilize human resources to provide direct service. Programs operating in 38 states and three countries are generating hundreds of thousands of hours, reinforcing a norm of reciprocity, rewarding altruism, and building trust among strangers. Time Dollars are more than simply an inexpensive way to expand specialized social service programs with volunteers. They do something else. The Time Dollar currency enables human beings to redefine themselves as assets, each and every one with something

special to contribute – regardless of what the market economy says. When all hours are valued equally, when the tasks are essentially those which families and neighbors have always done for each other, when the obligation to repay is backed by a moral norm of reciprocity rather than a legal norm of coercion, one is outside the realm of the Internal Revenue Service, outside the market economy, and outside the constraints of feasibility imposed by market wages and the availability of tax dollars on building social capital (Cahn, 1999).

Thus Time Dollars are similar to LETS schemes in as much as they share goals of fostering social inclusion, mutuality and self-help within local communities. Moreover, at least to gauge from Cahn's pronouncements about Time Dollars existing outside the market economy and their distance from the surveillance and influence of the Inland Revenue System, they would seem to share with LETS schemes a rejection of the values and morality not only of the market, but also of the panoptic tendencies of the welfare state.[49] However, in practice, Time Dollar schemes represent a more directed and centralised monetary network than do LETS schemes because of two distinctive features of their organisation. First, each Time Dollar scheme has a central office that acts as a clearing house for the scheme as a whole. When people want jobs done, they phone into the office, which then attempt to put wants and offers together, usually through a series of telephone calls. This differs from the reliance upon a registry or printed directory as is the case with both LETSystems and LETS schemes respectively, or the need to negotiate directly with counterparties. This enables the administrators of the scheme to exert a strong influence over the scheme, including direct attempts to accelerate turnover by putting members in contact with one another, a task which is made easier by the use of a bespoke software programme – timekeeper – which contains information on all the members of the scheme, their wants and offers, and their current balance of Time Dollars. Secondly, and relatedly, the high level of central control over the system makes possible and is reinforced by the regulation of members, all of whom are subject to a police check before joining, while those who offer childcare are subject to further checks and scrutiny. In undertaking these regulatory tasks, the administrators of Time Dollar schemes argue that participants are more likely to engage in trading with counterparties that have effectively 'pre-approved'.

In the case of the Time Dollar scheme that we investigated in the UK – Fairshares – this centralised and paternalistic approach to trading activity was underscored by it being underwritten by a Local Authority for a three year trial period, and by the fact that focus groups with participants revealed that a major role of the scheme was as an unofficial adjunct to the welfare state, as participant assisted sick or elderly members in meeting appointments with various branches of the National Health Service, or to circumvent the isolation and loneliness that disablement and age can bring:

> I've been in Fairshares for about two months ... I basically moved into the area after becoming disabled and didn't want to be stuck in the house, and also recognising the needs that I had and finding ways of meeting those needs. It was the Health Resource Centre that got me involved with Fairshares.[50]

I have needed help because I've needed to get about. I've needed to go to the hospital – Frenchay and Gloucester – and I've needed transport because both my daughter and her husband work and so I can't call them. I've got a little battery runabout which I can run round and do my own shopping and that kind of thing, but I wouldn't like to go to Gloucester in it because I don't know whether I'll get back![51]

The system was seen to be adequate as a framework through which people felt able to ask for (paid) favours to be done for them, and to create the possibility to reciprocate such favours across the schemes as a whole. However, the imposition of a standard hour rate for all work was seen to be limiting, in that it prevented the membership of participants who would provided valued and much needed skills. As was witnessed in the case of LETS schemes, the conventions of the market were taken for granted by many of the participants in Time Dollar schemes too:

Q: What about ... the shortages of people like the electricians and plumbers and carpenters. How would you get those sorts of people into Fairshares? Why aren't those people joining Fairshares?

A: Well, partly I should think, to be honest, it it's your trade you're not going to do it for free (sic) are you? I mean, quite honestly, you might go and put an old lady's electric light bulb in or mend a fuse for somebody, but you're not going to do anything really serious in the way of electrical work. It wouldn't be fair on the trades people.[52]

... if we had a solicitor, we could get him (sic) to give some advice of what procedure we could take on a certain case ... he could tell us what to do and where to go and his service may be valued at £25 an hour or £30 an hour, but he would give you a few minutes telling you what you could do. That's if we had a solicitor ...

But of course they did not, nor were they likely, if the following example is any guide. In some cases, people within the scheme clearly had valuable skills which were in demand, but they were not prepared to trade them in the fear that to do so would mean foregoing 'real' income:

I'm a translator and I was asked, 'Could I translate [for someone]?' And I said that for teaching I would come and give a hand happily, but I certainly wouldn't do it on a professional basis ... [53]

Thus, for some participants, the striking of a standard rate for work at one hour per unit effectively devalued the currency that made it not worth expending effort for. This problem was exacerbated by the fact that participants who worked full-time had much less free time, and while might have welcomed the use of other people's time to undertake certain tasks and services on their behalf, they discovered that they did not have the time to fully participate, to reciprocate and to earn Time Dollars, particularly when, as above, they were unable to make their professional skills available for purchase within the scheme.

Conclusions

All economic geographies are social constructs and LCSs are no exception. Indeed, precisely because of their small scale and the prior thought (whether in the form of design or planning) that informs their practice, LCSs open a window onto the nature of this process of social construction and the contested diversity of practice to which they give rise. One of the more intriguing aspects of trying to understand the nature of LCSs – especially to their participants – is the assessment of the significance of their 'economic' or reproductive characteristics.

As argued above, LCSs are economic geographies and yet, although they may have enormous potential to act as parallel currency systems and have demonstrable capacity to incorporate those people otherwise excluded from formal economic engagement, their material contribution in these regards is, as yet, highly limited. Only a tiny proportion of the UK population belong to a LCS, and an even smaller proportion are active participants, for whom LCS transactions make up only a small part of their material requirements. For example, a national survey of LETS scheme co-ordinators within the UK revealed that, on average, members made between one and five trades per annum, and that a third of members were not actively trading (Tooke, 1999). Meanwhile, LETSystems are, even according to their advocates, currently located at the foot of the 'S'-shaped curve of innovation.

Under these circumstances, questions about barriers to LCS development and about limits to their developmental potential arise. Internal barriers are associated with the institutional structure and practice of LCSs whilst external barriers are associated with the economic, political and institutional environment in which LCSs are located and unfold. A number of such barriers have been discussed in the paper. However, a narrow focus on barriers implies a relatively unproblematic acceptance of the economic nature and existence of LCS and does not necessarily address the nature of LCS as social organisations. It may well be that the major barrier to LCSs as developmental alternatives lies less in their institutional and economic shortcomings as in their identity as institutions of membership and social solidarity rather than as circuits of social reproduction. This raises wider questions of the nature and direction of the causal relations between culture and economy (see, for example Ray and Sayer, 1999) which lie beyond the scope of this chapter but it also broaches the issue of the possibility of economic geographies of this kind and hence of their potential for alternative forms of development. This is a big issue. It helps to explain the antagonism that exists between the proponents of various forms of LCSs as well as and it represents a challenge to the mainstream acceptance of the social economy as realistic strategy for poverty alleviation and social exclusion.

Notes

1. The term Local Currency System is coined in this chapter to refer to a range of different local or community currency schemes, including LETSystems, LETS schemes and Time Dollars. For an introduction to LCSs, see Douthwaite (1996), Boyle (1999) and Croall (1997).
2. However, for some LCS practitioners, the notion of currencies regulating exchange between participants is abhorrent. They would interpret LCSs more as a weakly-institutionalised system of favours.
3. For example, Pounds sterling, US dollars, French Francs, Italian Lira etc.
4. However, for many participants, it is precisely the shortness of the network that is the primary purpose and advantage of LCSs. This may be for explicitly communitarian reasons, or for reasons connected with a desire to keep money circulating locally so preventing or limiting uneven development associated with the emergence of geographies of comparative or absolute advantage or financial and corporate geographies of profitability.
5. In capitalism, for example, value is defined in terms of profitability although the precise measurement of profitability is contested and debated by financial consultancies. See, for example, T. Lester, 'Value ratios need a rationale', *Financial Times*, 13 October 2000, p. 18.
6. But, more generally, the social relations of reproduction both shape and are shaped by contested understandings and practices of relations of gender, ethnicity and religion as well as by contested moral and political relations such as nationalism, socialism and liberalism. Thus the notion of value – so central to materiality – is itself constituted in and through the social relations which define the social objectives of social reproduction and guide the trajectory of its circuits.
7. This is an important issue not taken up in this chapter. It is addressed by R. Lee, A. Leyshon and N. Thrift, 'Non-economic economies: culture and economy in local currency systems', forthcoming.
8. But see the critique of social capital in a developmental context by Fine (1999).
9. LETSystems are associated especially with Michael Linton, who founded the first LETS on Vancouver Island, off British Columbia in 1983.
10. Within the UK.
11. Michael Linton e-mail interview 21 August 2000.
12. Ibid.
13. Interview 20/22 May 2000.
14. Michael Linton e-mail interview 21 August 2000.
15. Interview 20/22 May 2000.
16. Confidence rather than, for example, trust is seen by LETSystems designers as a crucial ingredient of their success.
17. Some measure of what is involved here may be gained from an appeal to banks and building societies launched in September 2000 by the Association of British Credit Unions for 'about £15 million to establish a national organisation ... providing computer systems, treasury management, payment services and marketing support' (J. Wilman, 'Financial exclusion targeted by credit unions', *Financial Times*, 11 September 2000, p. 3).
18. Michael Linton e-mail conversation 29 August 2000.
19. Michael Linton e-mail interview 21 August 2000.
20. Interview 20/22 May 2000.
21. Michael Linton e-mail conversation 29 August 2000.

22 Angus Soutar interview 20/22 May 2000.
23 Angus Soutar interview 20/22 May 2000.
24 Michael Linton e-mail conversation 6 September 2000.
25 Michael Linton e-mail conversation 29 August 2000.
26 However, there is a potential contradiction here. Local circuits of social reproduction may, in fact, be highly regressive and environmentally harmful. The geography of production based upon the principles of comparative or of absolute advantage may be more desirable in social and environmental terms than geographies of local autarky. Consider the social and ecological disasters of the Maoist 'cellular economy' which was similarly motivated by a disavowal of comparative advantage over space (see, for example, Cannon and Jenkins, 1990). Such social and environmental objectives would not, however, be imposed by LETSystems.
27 Thus, multi-registry trading may come to exceed local trading if participants perceive an advantage to such non-local practice and which would, in effect, encourage the movement of money between local economies, thereby raising the spectre, for some advocates of LCSs at least, of the reintroduction of comparative advantage.
28 Interview 20/22 May 2000.
29 Ibid.
30 In addition, see, for example, Lee (1996).
31 An example of a social agenda is the singular adoption of time as the basis for pricing exchange, thereby equalizing skills and compensating for pay rate differentials within the mainstream economy. (However, a standard hourly rate was used in only one LETS in our nationwide survey and, as we indicate below, was resisted by those that saw LETS schemes as parallel rather than alternative economic entities: see below.)
32 The desire for the creation of a more humane and supportive community expressed by many of the respondents in LETS schemes within our research are strongly reminiscent of arguments for greater levels of communitarianism made by the likes of Amitai Etzioni (see, for example, Etzioni, 1995).
33 Stroud case study, transcript 6.
34 Stroud case study, transcript 12.
35 Stroud case study, transcript 5.
36 Stroud case study, transcript 6.
37 Stroud case study, transcript 21.
38 The avoidance of contradictions like this is imperative for the designers of LETSystems.
39 Stroud case study, transcript 21.
40 Ibid.
41 However, these power relations may be resisted even by major participants in LETS schemes.
42 Stroud case study, transcript 7.
43 Stroud case study, transcript 16.
44 Stroud case study, transcript 19.
45 Stroud case study, transcript 13.
46 Stroud case study, transcript 21.
47 This is an example in practice of the social assessment of what is valuable. It is in other words an example of evaluation based on criteria that are socially established.
48 For example, since the mid-1990s Stirling and Alloa LETS has run an internal project, LETS Make it Better, dedicated to developing ways in which individuals with mental health problems can participate within LETS (C. Manley and T. Aldridge, 'Can LETS Make it Better? A Stirling Example', forthcoming).

49 This implicit critique of the role of the state in local development and its surveillance tendencies are particularly interesting in light of Roy Boyne's wider argument that state surveillance, welfarism and social democracy run-hand-in-hand (Boyne, 2000). According to Boyne, 'it may follow that the ethical and philosophical underpinning for a substantial critique of surveillance may not exist in a welfare-type society, that we can see surveillance as an ineluctable facet of social democracies, which are therefore bound to be surveillance societies' (p. 292).
50 Fairshares focus group 1, 23 February 2000.
51 Fairshares focus group 3, 25 February 2000.
52 Ibid.
53 Ibid.

References

Bowring, F. (1998), 'LETS: an eco-socialist initiative?', *New Left Review*, 232, 91-111.
Boyle, D. (1999), *Funny Money: In Search of Alternative Cash*, Harper Collins, London.
Boyne, R. (2000), 'Post-panopticism', *Economy and Society*, 29, pp. 285-307.
Cahn, E. (1999), 'Time dollars, work and community: from "why?" to "why not?"', *Futures*, 31, 5, pp. 499-509.
Cannon, T. and Jenkins, A. (eds) (1990), *The Geography of Contemporary China*, Routledge, London.
Croall, J. (1997), *LETS Act Locally: The Growth of Local Exchange Trading Systems*, Calouste Gulbenkian Foundation, London.
Dodd, N. (1994), *The Sociology of Money Economics, Reason and Contemporary Society*, Cambridge Polity Press, Cambridge.
Douthwaite, R. (1996), *Short Circuit: Strengthening Local Economies for Security in an Unstable World*, Liliput, Dublin.
Etzioni, A. (1995), *The Spirit of Community: Rights, Responsibilities and the Communitarian Agenda*, Fontana, London.
Fine, B. (1999), 'The developmental state is dead – long live social capital', *Development and Change*, 30, pp. 1-19.
Lee, R. (1996), 'Moral money? LETS and the social construction of local economic geographies in southeast England', *Environment and Planning A*, 28, pp. 1377-1394.
Leyshon, A. (1995), 'Annihilating space? The speed-up of communications', in J. Allen and C. Hamnett (eds), *A Shrinking World?*, Oxford University Press, Oxford, pp. 11-54.
Leyshon, A. (1997), 'Geographies of money and finance II', *Progress in Human Geography*, 21, pp. 278-289.
North, P. (1999), 'Explorations in heterotopia: Local exchange trading schemes (LETS) and the micro-politics of money and livelihood', *Environment and Planning D - Society and Space*, 17, pp. 69-86.
Power, M. (1997), *The Audit Society: Rituals of Verification*, Oxford University Press, Oxford.
Ray, L. and Sayer, A. (1999), *Culture and economy after the cultural turn*, Sage, London.
Thrift, N. (1996), *Spatial Formations*, Sage, London.
Tooke, J. (1999), Evaluating LETS as a means of tackling social exclusion and cohesion: co-ordinators survey, Internal Project Report.
Williams, C. (1996), 'Local exchange and trading systems (LETS): A new form of work and credit for the poor and unemployed', *Environment and Planning A*, 28, 8, pp. 1395-1415.

PART III

SOCIAL CAPITAL IN THE PATHWAYS OF LOCAL DEVELOPMENT

Chapter 7

Social Capital in the Development of the Agro Nocerino-Sarnese

Anna Bull and Matteo Frate

Introduction

On the basis of both theoretical and empirical works it is possible to argue that development depends upon a multiplicity of factors. Until recently great importance was attributed to specifically economic and technological factors, totally neglecting the social and institutional context within which the dynamics of development unfolded. Today numerous scholars and politicians acknowledge the crucial role played by synergic relations between all factors and actors directly and indirectly involved in a process of sustainable development (in an economic, social and environmental sense).

Thanks to many scholars, among whom Amartya Sen stands out, today we no longer refer to development as economic growth but – and this is how we use the term in this chapter – as the process through which more and more people gain access to a whole range of capabilities and opportunities. The concept adopted is very wide and contains within itself the idea of development as improvement in the quality of life. It takes into account factors beyond an increase in income levels, including health conditions, education, security, the environment, individual freedom, institutional efficiency etc. This new concept of development implies changes in the unit of analysis and the sphere of intervention of economic policies, focusing attention upon the socio-economic context. The context in turn changes from area to area, nevertheless it can be described and analysed on the basis of two macro variables, the institutional set up and social capital, that is to say, the interrelations that exist between the various actors.

The importance of the context is increasingly being recognised by Italian policy makers, too. In the last few years many public policies in support of development in the South aimed explicitly at influencing the context. The old generalised or sectoral, top-down interventions were replaced by a new type of policy-making which encourages a bottom-up participation of as many actors as possible both in the decision-making process and in the monitoring of the degree of efficiency and efficacy of the policies themselves. These changes had the obvious aim of transforming state aid from pure welfare measures to factors capable of generating new businesses and employment, but also civic, social and environmental betterments. A clear effort was made to intervene upon the deepest distortions of Southern Italian society, promoting a better performance of public institutions and encouraging civic society and the citizens to regain confidence in themselves and to participate actively in determining and implementing a new process of development. In particular, institutions were goaded into giving up clientelist, bureaucratic and corporative criteria, replacing them with new criteria of efficiency and efficacy in the provision of services. In other words, the new type of intervention is not directed at distributing funds, but at producing positive externalities capable of convincing economic and social operators that it would be in their interest to invest in a particular area (Ministero del Tesoro, 1999).

This chapter is divided into two parts. In the first part, based critically on Putnam's work on civic traditions in Italy (Putnam, 1993), we attempt to construct a theory of social capital capable of exploiting to the full the holistic features of this concept. We are particularly concerned with identifying in which conditions social capital can have a positive effect on local development or, on the contrary, negative effects such as clientelism, corruption and criminality. In developing the concept, the influence of social capital on developmental paths is linked to the institutional context which characterises a certain area.

Governance is determined by a mix of shared and acknowledged, formal and informal, rules and behaviour, which constitute the framework, or the *rules of the game* within which the socio-economic dynamics unfolds. Out of the combination of the type of governance and social capital, different contexts emerge which can promote development or, on the contrary, can lead to situations of conflict or exclusion. Alternatively, and this is the case in many areas of the South of Italy, a context may emerge which promotes coping strategies on the part of social actors.

In the second part, the theoretical approach is applied to the analysis of a specific area in the South: the Agro Nocerino-Sarnese (ANS). On the basis of official documentation and statistics, as well as a series of interviews with local actors, we analyse the changes undergone by the local context during the last few decades. In this area apparently conflicting phenomenons developed such as: a decisive rise in the level of consumer goods accompanied by an equally substantial rise in the level of unemployment; the consolidation of a proto-district in the agroindustrial sector able to compete in all foreign markets despite the massive presence of organised crime. These and other contradictions can only be understood if we bear in mind that social capital and the type of governance characterising a given area can simultaneously produce both positive and negative effects.

Thus, during the 1980s a tight network of contacts and relations was utilised to the exlusive benefit of a small part of the local community, giving rise to a perverse interrelationship between the political, administrative, entrepreneurial and working classes and causing a profound distortion in the process of development. However, since 1993 various exogenous and endogenous factors have produced a slow process of change, such as: a turnover in the local political class; the imprisonment and confessions of many local bosses of the *Camorra*; the end of the policy of extraordinary state intervention in the South. In other words, the *rules of the game* have changed making it more difficult to utilise public resources (economic, social and environmental) for particularistic ends. There has also been a change in the type of social capital present in the area, with an increase, albeit slight, in transversal, cross-cutting relations. In this way the local context has started to produce some positive effects upon the developmental path.

The process of change has only just started and can lead to two contrasting scenarios: a new type of development accompanied by diffused wellbeing; or increased recourse to coping strategies. We conclude by stressing the fragile nature and uncertain outcome of the new processes of change. In particular, preliminary results of our research lead us to believe that the perverse networking which had developed during the 1980s has not been completely dissolved and that therefore the political-economic-criminal bloc may yet take advantage of the loss of moral tension in the institutions and in civic society registered in the last two or three years.

Social Capital

Putnam's Theory

An interesting starting point for an exploration of the literature concerning social capital (SC) is Putnam's work (1993a, 1993b, 1995a, 1995b and 1996) from which the so-called 'neo-Tocquevillean' school has developed.

When talking about SC, Putnam refers to trust, social rules, civic networks, factors which improve the efficiency of social organisation by stimulating agreed decision-making processes (1993a). Moreover, such processes facilitate social cooperation and coordination providing widespread benefits (1993a and 1993b). One of Putnam's theory's basic assumptions is that SC can solve dilemmas inherent to collective action. Besides, SC embedded in norms and civic networks seems to work as a precondition for economic development and for effective institutional performance (1993b).

Trust According to Putnam, one basic component of SC is trust (1993a). Trust facilitates social cooperation by making formal control over accepted deals unnecessary. Putnam does not refer to blind trust, but to the possibility of foreseeing the behaviour of independent actors. This means that you trust someone because you expect that he will honour his promises. These expectations are based either on personal knowledge or on the sense of reliability generated by norms of reciprocity and civic networks, in other words associational membership. Norms of reciprocity and civic engagement are needed to shift from bounded trust to generalized trust.

Putnam's conclusions are that when the number of associations is higher people are more used to trusting reciprocally and this leads to a situation of generalised trust (1993a). In short horizontal networks are developed, which can be helpful to solve local problems, increase resources and knowledge so as to favour good governance and economic performance.

Criticism to neo-Tocquevillean arguments Putnam's intuition that civic engagement is a key factor in the developmental process is still valid. But some points remain unclear: are all associations equal? Are vertical associations not capable of civic engagement? How is it possible to shift from reciprocal trust to generalised trust?

Membership in the Klu Klux Klan (KKK) would certainly create trust among clan's members but not between them and the outside. Moreover affiliation to the KKK will not have positive effects on the community: KKK's goals are antithetical to social welfare. The same might be said of the Mafia: an association which surely owes its strength to internal loyalty ties. But is this a generalised trust? Certainly not. Empirical researches and judicial inquiries have shown clearly that *mafiosi* only trust their closest collaborators. This means that not every kind of association generates trust, and seldom they lead to generalised trust;[1] as a matter of fact, many of them produce mistrust and disadvantages for the community, rather than benefits.

The neo-Tocquevillean civic voluntarism model is based on the assumption that motivation and capacity to take part in politics have their roots in the fundamental non-political institutions with which individuals are associated during the course of their life. This model has several limits, the most evident one being that it does not consider any kind of social organisations different from the American ones (Edwards and Foley, 1998, p. 134).

An analysis based on Putnam's scheme would inevitably lead us to underestimate the level of civicness of many communities. For instance, many of Southern Italy's bars might be assimilated to Putnam's trust-building associations. In bars people meet, exchange favours, make deals, interact and build durable relationships on the basis of generalised trust. Similarly, Putnam neglects the important role, in terms of promoting generalised trust and civicness, played by public squares and buildings' courtyards in most Southern communities. People living in Neapolitans courts or alleys have been helping each other for ages, and establishing a dense net of trust-based relations, while never affiliating to formal associations.

The thesis that vertical associations are not capable of generating generalized trust is also not convincing. The formal vertically-structured organisation of many Catholic associations leads Putnam to think that they are not capable of generating civicness. Indeed, he assumes that vertical relations between Church hierarchies and believers are stronger than horizontal links of brotherhood between the believers themselves. This way of reading Catholic associations' role leads to a misinterpretation of the Roman Catholic Church's role in Southern Italian society, which is not simply a spiritual one.

One final ambiguity in Putnam's work relates to the way trust is built and preserved within the community: focusing on civic engagement as the basis itself of generalized trust, Putnam is led to the blind alley of historical heritage. In his analysis SC derives from trust, and the latter is the outcome of complex, long-aged processes shaping different civic traditions and moral systems.

Putnam's recourse to historical heritage is of little help in justifying differences in civic engagement between regions, especially between Southern regions sharing the same historical background. When taking present structures as irrelevant, Putnam runs into a logical circularity: SC is simultaneously cause and effect of heritage (Portes, 1998, pp. 19-20).

A Dynamic and Contextualized Theory of Social Capital

Putnam's research, and the ensuing debate, have had the undeniable merit of drawing attention to the importance of collective action and social actors for properly working economic, political and social processes – thus for development itself. But Putnam's theory also draws a line between communities that have inherited SC and others that, not sharing the same luck, have remained underdeveloped (Edward and Foley, 1998, p. 128). Within each community, it also assumes that only horizontal organisations create SC, while vertical and informal ones are excluded – thus more limits are added to the theory's own heuristic significance.

The civic engagement that Putnam identifies is only one tile in the mosaic of developmental processes, as it is a small part within the whole social sphere. The social sphere is in constant interaction with the economic and political ones. Interactions, as well as motivations for social actions, are part of a dynamic process, that is, they change with time and according to variations in the socio-economic ad political context (Edwards and Foley, 1998, p. 128). Therefore if SC is meant as the set of interrelations occurring between these three spheres, the quantity of SC existing in each community is not a fixed amount, and it varies in a continuous process that social actors contribute to shape – while being themselves influenced by it (Granovetter, 1972, p. 345).

Holding steadily to the importance of context and the dynamism of social relations, and trying to overcome the main weaknesses in Putnam's theory, we come here to the definition that follows:

> SC is the set of formal and informal relations existing at a given time between the members of a community. These relations allow the coordination of collective actions and the achievement of shared goals. SC, like any other kind of assets, is not distributed uniformly among all members of a community and it is not even used univocally for the well being of the whole community. The features of existing relations and their distribution influence individual behaviour and determines the quantity and quality of a community's economic, institutional and social activity, that is of its development. Moreover these relations, though built in one specific sphere, produce their effects also in the other spheres.

In a definition of SC as inherent to relations between factors (individuals, organisations, institutions) we want to highlight that SC depends strongly on the context in which it works. The context here is not considered uniquely as heritage from the past, but as 'conditions of possibility' for collective action (Pantoja, 1999, p. 18).

As a matter of fact, one of the most interesting contributions that the theory of SC can give is its explanatory capacity with respect to a local system's adaptability to changing external and/or internal conditions. In order to achieve hoped-for social, civic and economic results, the existence and availability of needed social, civic and economic (pre)conditions is helpful, but it is not sufficient. Human behaviour should also be considered, and the way in which it determines, through social interaction, a learning and changing process that leads to actual outcomes (Falk and Kilpatrick, 2000, p. 89).

In order to analyse the dynamic processes through which SC is constituted and transformed we have to refer to multi-dimensional and multi-level analysis schemes. These analyses can be helpful in understanding the structure of incentives/disincentives that actually regulate access to resources (assets) and control over them. The identification of depth, width and patterns of distribution of SC is important because SC is not homogeneously distributed within the community: the question is then *who* has access to it and *what* they use it for (Edwards and Foley, 1998, p. 130). A dynamic analysis of SC leads us to understand how it is created, destroyed and re-created again while the community undergoes developmental processes. The dynamic process is characterized by conflict cycles and co-operational ones. 'Rules of the game' and generalized trust are continuously changing, advancing or regressing according to variations in their social background (Pantoja, 1999, p. 5).

Dangers SC, like any other kind of asset, might be used to benefit the whole community or to satisfy particularistic interests. A dense SC can produce innovation, political and economic development, but it can also determine conformism, conservatism or even corruption and/or illegality. Therefore, SC does not necessarily lead to economic growth and widespread improvements in quality of life; it is frequently a source of trouble (Portes and Landolt, 1997). Authors like Coleman (1988, p. 105) have been aware since the first formulation of the concept that SC might also have a 'dark side'. In Coleman's view SC is an ethically and morally neutral resource. Putnam, on the contrary, assumes that the concept must necessarily have a positive ethical and moral connotation, thus reducing its heuristic value (Edwards and Foley, 1998, p. 131).

Diversion: Many societies are characterized by two kinds of SC, one of which is productive while the other is perverse. In such cases two scenarios are possible: in the first scenario, with positive SC, a virtuous circle is established: the institutional background, cultural patterns and 'rules of the game' stimulate economic development. Those organisations that are positively involved in this process favour institutional changes that in turn strengthen the developmental process. But a different scenario might also be figured out, with negative SC: networks, vertical relations, informal norm, political activity, the legal system, and, more generally, the whole social system favour rent seeking and/or opportunistic or criminal behaviour that constitute a constraint to production and innovations. As organisations growing successfully in this environment get stronger, and even more unprincipled, they reinforce those social norms that lead to the diversion of formally accepted rules of the game. Thus productive activities are hindered and opportunities of development become restricted (Rubio, 1997, p. 815).

In this case benefits deriving from SC are usurped by individuals and/or organisations that use it cynically to increase their power. Macroscopic examples of this situation are all the world's *mafias*, internally close-knitted and well organised, and ferociously fighting anyone who interferes in their business. More simply, social networks can be used to establish relations based on patronage, corruption, favouritism and so on. In virtually all regions of the world, regardless of their level of wealth, SC is frequently diverted from the path that leads to widespread welfare.

Exclusion: Exclusion is complementary to diversion. Contrary to Putnam's view, SC can be an exclusive good rather than a public one, meaning that it can be the prerogative of bounded groups whose members share the same norms, or benefit from a special mutual trust, or are integrated in the same social nets (De Renzio, 1998). In some cases, someone's SC means social exclusion for others (Portes and Landolt, 1997). So we should consider this asset not as a *public good*, but as a *club good* owing to which members of the club enjoy a special status that they do not share with strangers (Harriss and De Renzio, 1997).

Closure to the outside: The case is possible that SC grows despite being based on a network of social interactions which is peculiar to a narrow group. If this happens, SC might multiply dangers rather than amplifying developmental opportunities. A wide stock of SC operating in enclosed environments can powerfully restrict individual freedom, both actually limiting free action and hindering the reception of hints and information from the outside. This happens also in the economic sphere. Many entrepreneurs are subject to absurd or inefficient rules imposed by the group they belong to.

Another negative aspect in 'enclosed' SC is that a group can put direct or indirect pressure on individuals so as to discourage them from trying to improve their social status. This is a typical situation for those groups whose strongest internal ties is the disadvantaged position of its members within the community. Here the group fears that its internal solidarity might be affected by socio-economic improvements in the lives of some members: once the basic link disappears, solidarity within the group might fade. Normally self-defensive responses to this danger are based on programmatic discouragement to socio-economic mobility (Portes and Sensenbrenner, 1993, pp. 1342-1345; Portes, 1998, p. 17). This leads to a 'lie-back' (non-reactive) attitude: politicians, entrepreneurs, workers, citizens settle for their present condition, fearing the damage they might suffer from someone else's betterment. This negative feature of SC is the main support to workers and entrepreneurs' corporative attitudes. Perverse norms established within a group can hinder rises in productivity of even willing workers; ostracism is the price paid by those who break the rules and commit themselves to work.

In summary we can say that social capital is a resource that facilitates or hinders individual access to other social, economic and political resources. Through specific actions, people can achieve certain goals, which may make SC productive or at times destructive (Pantoja, 1999, p. 20).

Interrelations Although trust is a key component of SC, in a dynamic and contextual analysis of SC we should rather focus on the role of social networks.

In his well-known article on embeddedness, Granovetter (1985, p. 348) argued that trust is the result mainly of social relations within the community; as a matter of fact, most types of behaviour are deeply rooted in interpersonal networks. Similarly both Coleman (1988) and Portes (1998) maintain that SC resides in the structure of relations between individuals. To have access to SC, people have to interact; from interaction, that is from relations with other people, they derive the greatest advantage.

As shown above, SC depends on the complex and dynamic process of social interrelations developing through a given period of time, and it is essential to the quality of developmental processes investing the whole community. We can identity four kinds of interrelations: face-to-face (bonding), horizontal (bridging), vertical (linking) and cross-cutting.

Face-to-face interrelations: The simplest way of interacting is through face-to-face relations, that is relations based on physical proximity lasting through time. Usually these relations, of kinship, neighbourhood, fellowship etc., are characterised by very intense interaction, which makes them the basis of social, economic and political life. Their major limit is that they rely heavily on contiguity; therefore these relations are likely to create closure towards the outside.

Horizontal interrelations: These interrelations develop between equals: people belonging to the same class, sharing the same status etc. Both individuals and groups are concerned. Typically, these interrelations are established between members of non-governmental associations or organisations; but they don't necessarily need formalised structures to develop. Horizontal relations may be considered weak ties, as opposed to face-to-face relations that are typically strong ties. Their major limit is that they only occur within or between groups of peers.

Vertical interrelations: These interrelations develop between individuals and groups in asymmetric, hierarchical mutual position; indeed they are typical of formalised associations and organisations. Like horizontal relations, they may develop directly or by means of one or more intermediaries. Their major limit is that they often stick to formal rules that hinder any fruitful exchange of information, knowledge or resources; in case of conflict between two different levels in the hierarchy, the subordinate cannot do anything but execute orders. One typical example of situations of this kind is represented by laws that are passed without being supported by an adequate popular consensus: people take them as an imposition, and try by all means to elude them.

Transversal interrelations: According to Narayan (1999, p. 7), cross-cutting ties refer to 'social relations in informal or formal voluntary groups and networks characterised by heterogeneity of membership, that is to say, ties that cut across ethnic, gender, caste, class, wealth, religion, location or any other characteristics which distinguish social groups'. Cross-cutting relations link people belonging to very different groups and social classes, thus they allow the exchange of information and knowledge and favour processes of social redistribution. Thanks to cross-cutting relations politicians, entrepreneurs, citizens, associations etc., come in touch with each other so that the principle of accountability becomes really operative.

These cross-cutting interrelations facilitate co-operative agreements that enhance each actor's abilities and specificities, regardless to the sector the actors themselves belong to. Cross-cutting ties have helped the growth of new supranational and interclass associations that play a crucial role in the new global politics.

In brief, face-to-face interrelations relate to interpersonal relations (micro level); horizontal ones pertain to groups (meso level); vertical ones operate between the various social strata and between these and the institutions (macro level). Transversal relations operate at all three levels linking the various foci of the existent social network. All types of interrelations are extremely important for the development of a community, but transversal relations are the most difficult to create: these are relations capable of transforming trust, reciprocal collaboration, solidarity etc. from being circumscribed to being generalised. Thanks to cross-cutting interrelations social networks become thicker, filling the gaps within face-to-face, horizontal and transversal relations.

The role of institutions Social interrelations are the main source of SC but state institutions[2] can also play a crucial role in laying out the basis of generalised trust, especially when social structure is weak.

Levi (1996, p. 50), as opposed to Putnam, maintains that effective political performances may be the source of trust and not only the result of the community's level of civicness. Under certain circumstances, state institutions can constitute the required complementary basis for the emergence of generalised trust. On the contrary, the neo-Tocquevillean model assumes that both motivation and capacity to take part in politics have their roots in the fundamental non-political institutions with which individuals are associated during the course of their lives. The opponents of the 'civic voluntarism model' try to understand the ways in which the political system might be made more responsive to organised societal demands, more accountable to societal scrutiny, more open to profound differences within society (Edwards and Foley, 1998, p. 134).

Since historic inheritance was considered as the main source of SC, the role of political factors in explaining development processes has been severely undervalued. As Trigilia (1999, p. 11) correctly suggests, owing to underestimation of politics we fail to determine under what conditions SC has a positive effect on local development and when, on the contrary, it produces negative effects such as patronage, corruption or criminal economy. Therefore we have to focus on the ways in which constitutional and political structures design state-society relations, that is, we should consider the political context in which SC operates, so as to determine how SC can lead to different paths of development.

Depending on the prevailing combinations of a state's organisational capacity, its engagement with and responsiveness to civil society and economic actors we may have a range of different roles of state-society relations in development. Starting from the most desirable situation, institutions may be: developmental, weak, predatory or collapsed (Woolcock, 1998).

Developmental Institutions: Institutions are development-oriented when they have dense interrelations with all associations and groups within the community, and they use institutionalised channels for the continual negotiation and re-negotiation of goals and policies. In other words, when all stakeholders are involved in the decision-making process. In such institutional framework the exercise of individual and collective freedom is not only permitted, but strongly encouraged.

These institutions are part of a well-organised and efficient bureaucratic structure able to ban corruption and patronage. In addition, institutions provide a positive environment for economic activities through encouraging co-operative behaviour, minimising the potential for corruption and malfeasance and ensuring flexibility in objectives and actors.

Weak Institutions: A weak institutional structure is able to pass good laws but not to ensure their observation. It is characterised by bureaucratic administration where too much depends on the voluntary action of civil servants rather than on the effectiveness of the system. The result is a state that responds slowly if at all to citizens' demands, is largely indifferent to the plights of vulnerable groups and is inept in supporting businesses seeking to be competitive in world markets.

Above all, weak institutions are unable to provide their citizens with the needed sense of security, so that Mafia and militia groups emerge to provide private protection in place of designated public institutions.

Predatory Institutions: A state can be absolutely distant from society's needs: a government bureaucracy ineffective and corrupt operates freely without being held accountable to citizens. In such a situation civil servants seek to use their connections with the economic sector and civic society to maintain their personal power. Predatory institutions have a hostile attitude towards any activities of voluntary associations since these constitute a threat to their power. Consequently they do not accept any control from associations or individuals. These institutions can function quite well, but they only serve the powerful and not all citizens; indeed they often make deals with organised crime. Needless to say, this combination is hardly conducive to developmental outcomes.

Collapsed Institutions: In this case, state institutions fail completely to guarantee public order and the enforcement of even basic laws. Institutions delegate their functions to a violent and powerful elite. Moreover, this is a situation in which criminal organisations operate freely and without fear of punishment, and sometimes they even obtain sufficient power to impose their own law and order.

Four different situations As seen above, SC can sustain and amplify either developmental processes or underdevelopment and distorted growth. SC's effects vary according to quantity and quality of economic, political and social interactions, as well as to the latter's institutional background.

Different combinations of these two elements give origins to a number of situations that communities or geographical areas may experience. In Figure 7.1, following Narayan (1999) and Woolcook (1998), we draw a Cartesian system showing graphically these different situations. Horizontal axis measure qualitative and quantitative variations in interactions. For the sake of simplicity, only cross-cutting interactions are shown, as they are the most complex and significant in terms of development. As Narayan puts it, 'cross cutting ties between groups open up economic opportunities to those belonging to less powerful or excluded groups. They also build social cohesion, a critical element in social stability and economic welfare over any extended period. Social cohesion requires not just high social capital within groups. It also requires dense though not necessarily strong cross-cutting ties among groups' (Narayan, 1999, p. 2).

Vertical axis register qualitative/quantitative performance of institutions. Four typical situations emerge: widespread social and economic welfare, exclusion, conflict and coping strategy.

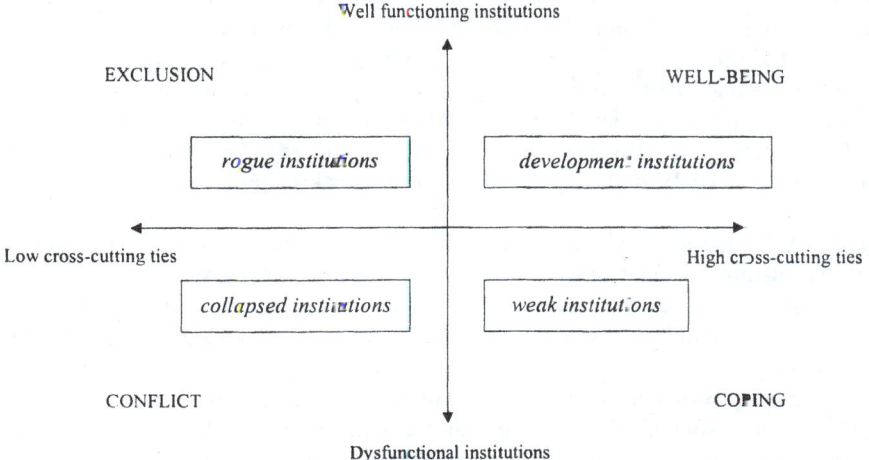

Figure 7.1 Relationship between cross-cutting ties and governance

Source: Adapted from Narayan (1999) and Woolcock (1998).

Widespread welfare: A situation of widespread social and economic welfare is the outcome of an institutional apparatus acting within an environment characterized by a wide stock of interrelations, especially of the cross-cutting kind. In this situation there is synergy among the economic, political and social spheres, a sort of cross-sectional cooperation exploiting and enhancing individual actors' specificities. All the actors are involved and participate in decision-making, and they also have real control of the apparatus that is held accountable for its performance. The result is a *milieu* that encourages greatly sustainable economic development. Specifically, three environmental features are developed, that Brusco (1999) recognises as basic to this kind of development: (1) a blend of strong competition and great deal of cooperation, that generates trust through decreasing transaction monitoring costs; (2) a balance between conflict and participation that prevents paternalism on the part of the entrepreneurs, and guarantees a full involvement of the employees in the enterprise's choices, especially related to innovation; (3) strong connections between the local sources of expertise and the system of codified knowledge that is science and technology. In this scenario we have a virtuous circle where welfare becomes more and more widespread and social, political and economic institutions progress daily thanks to synergies created between them.

Conflict: Opposite to the situation depicted above is a scenario in which conflict prevails. This situation occurs when the institutional apparatus is close to collapsing, while social networks are marked by very scarce interrelations, especially of the cross-cutting kind. The result is a diffused political, economic and social instability, that leads to amoral individualism. In this scenario the leading (ruling) groups are completely separated from ordinary people, while they join forces with criminal organisations. Criminal groups grow stronger because they are the only ones that can guarantee order and security, high levels of earnings for their affiliates and subsistence level for their hodmen, often made up of teenagers.

This vicious scenario can be modified only by reducing the power of the criminal group and promoting participatory peace-making policies.

Exclusion: Scenarios in which latent conflict and exclusion prevail are the result of working institutions that favour only a few, within a context marked by little interaction. This is a situation of great instability because a few powerful and wealthy groups stand against a mass excluded from decision-making processes and fighting for survival.

Exclusion grows also because disadvantaged groups have no contacts with one another. Being isolated, these groups can't obtain the information and knowledge they need to develop. As coded knowledge is not integrated into local knowledge, economic and social conditions remain stagnating.

This scenario can be modified by creating mechanisms of inclusion and connection between groups. It is also necessary that generalised economic opportunities are created, so as to really guarantee diffused access to political, educational, financial and other institutions.

Coping strategies: In this scenario formal interrelations are almost non-existent because of the poverty of institutional apparatuses. Prevailing informal interrelations guarantee survival for the unsupported mass of the population. The society takes the shape of an hour-glass: within the ruling (dominant) group there are intense interactions and the same is for the mass, but the two groups are linked by the thinnest tie (Rose, 1995). Established relations are typically based on patronage; in this situation Banfield's *amoral familism* flourishes.[3] People lacking even the basic familial safety net are left completely abandoned and wanting in resources. Institutional weaknesses allow the diffusion of illegal micro or macro-activities. Smuggling, tax evasion, illegal work expand. Criminal organisations enjoying complete freedom of movement extend their control to legal or semi-legal activities. The resulting economic effect is stagnation. Industrial workers adopt corporative attitudes, entrepreneurs show a low propensity to risk; thus investment is weak and productivity very low.

This scenario can be modified by exploiting civil society's potential and supporting the few working institutions. The interrelations between institutions and civil society must be specifically addressed: vertical and cross-cutting interactions must be strengthened to become resources for change.

Social Capital in the Agro Nocerino-Sarnese

Methodology

In this section we will apply the theoretical structure worked out so far to verify the role played by SC in the development of a particular area in Southern Italy: the Agro Nocerino-Sarnese (ANS). Using the case-study methodology we explore what kind of SC exists in this area, what is the institutional context in which it operates and what results, if any, it has produced. We will also assess the extent to which changes in the SC and in the institutional structure have affected the development path during the last few years.

The empirical evidence used in this chapter derives from different sources: semi-structured interviews, direct observation, analysis of official data and documents. We also make use of the already existing literature that explore problems similar to those troubling ANS.

We planned to interview 30 local actors. When we wrote this chapter we had already interviewed 20 local actors: 4 entrepreneurs; 3 politicians; 5 members of local civil society; 2 trade unionists; 3 representative of R&D centres; 2 managers of the Territorial Employment Pact; 1 journalist.

Interviews have been conducted using a framework composed by three sets of questions. The first one aimed at investigating how people perceive the actual situation in the Agro. We tried to understand strengths and weaknesses of the area as they are perceived by local inhabitants. The second set of questions has been used to single out what strategy social actors adopt in the particular context in which they operate. Specifically, if and why they assume a position of *conflict*, *exclusion, coping* or *well being*. The object of the third set of questions was to analyse the kind of interrelations actors operating in a specific sphere (economic, political or social) have with members of the other spheres and what results are pursued thanks to these interrelations. In particular, our aim was to find out whether and when relations were face-to-face, horizontal, vertical, or cross-cutting.

A warning is necessary: the actual social situation is extremely complex. Here we present an interpretation that is the starting point of a wider research aimed at analysing the typology of SC that exist in this area and the rules it plays so as to find out if it works towards development or against it or if SC simply does not play according to any rule.

Background Analysis

The ANS area extends over roughly 161 sq. km, covering the territory of nine municipalities in Salerno's Province: Nocera Inferiore, Nocera Superiore, Pagani, Angri, Scafati, S. Egidio del Monte Albino, S. Marzano sul Sarno, S. Valentino Torio, Sarno. This area lies within the wide River Sarno's plain, between the two urban poles of Napoli and Salerno.

The resident population amounts to 232,435 people (ISTAT, 1991), which makes up about 24 per cent of the whole Province's population; the annual increase rate is nine per cent, much above the national average.

The high fertility of the Agro plain allows intensive farming: vegetables, tomatoes, tobacco and fibres for textile production. Indeed, the availability of raw materials attracted, in the mid-19th century, some Swiss entrepreneurs who established an important textile and hemp industry. At the beginning of the 20th century a new sector, canned vegetables production, began to flourish. This sector has been growing in importance throughout the century, and it has favoured the development of engineering and packaging industries, as well as haulage companies and service providers.

At present there are 11,936 enterprises in the area, employing 49,800 workers. Most enterprises are small-sized, employing three workers on average. The textile and hemp industry has become marginal, while the canned vegetables production has developed into an agroindustrial district which has been recently recognised as one of the few industrial districts in the South of Italy.[4] About 80 per cent of the canning industry in the Salerno area concentrates in ANS. The main output is a range of tomato sauces and, in a lesser quantity, peas, beans, purees and fruit juices. The area's total sales amount to 1,000 million Lira per year, one third of the province's total turnover, more than 60 per cent of which is composed of export sales. Most of the district's production is seasonal, concentrated between June and September; during this period, the total work-force rises from 3,000 to more than 10,000 people. The leading company in the district is 'La Doria', with a sales volume of 5,000 million Lira, employing 250 regular and 750 seasonal workers.

Although nearly one third of the whole Italian canned vegetables production comes from the ANS area, this sector is undergoing a severe crisis due mainly to the wide predominance of mono-product enterprises, to entrepreneurs' low propensity to innovation and to the products' low added value. Further weaknesses are the sector's atomisation and the absence of economies of scale the endemic shortage of business services providers and the lack of adequate infrastructures, that hinder the reduction of management costs and the exploitation of new markets. The whole set of infrastructures falls far below national average standards.

Table 7.1 Population and education, 1991

Municipalities	Population	Density of population	Graduate	Diploma holders	Illiterate
Angri	29,753	2,178	784	4,276	1,003
Nocera Inferiore	49,053	2,331	1,826	8,348	2,621
Nocera Superiore	22,325	1,594	434	3,156	1,005
Pagani	33,138	2,906	821	4,313	1,887
S. Egidio	8,188	1,305			
S. Marzano	9,556	1,862	119	738	736
S. Valentino	8,203	944	92	642	568
Sarno	31,509	788	536	3,199	2,641
Scafati	40,710	2,253	952	6,342	871

Source: ISTAT (1991a).

The weaknesses of the canning industry in the ANS area become particularly evident when analysing the dynamics of commercialisation. The producers depend on large distributors or commercialisation businesses, not located within the area, for both domestic sales and export; this determines a subordination of the producers to the distributors. Furthermore, the maturity of most products and some non-cooperative attitudes prevailing among ANS enterprises lead to high competition on prices; this competition is even more intense because of foreign low-price producers (Spanish, Portuguese, Greek, Israeli) that have entered the market. This mix of factors renders the main economic sector in the ANS area quite weak.

As canned vegetables production is seasonal, the labour market is strongly distorted: work is temporary and uncertain. Only in the summer, during the so-called *tomato season*, the unskilled work-force nearly reaches full-employment, while the abundant educated and/or trained work-force have difficulty in finding even temporary jobs. When the food-processing period is over, unemployment goes back to its striking average standards: the unemployment rate is around 40 per cent, but rises to 47.6 per cent among women, and exceeds 64 per cent among young people (ISTAT, 1991).

It should be noted that these figures do not consider the diffusion of irregular jobs, which is actually quite difficult to quantify. Recently it has been estimated that irregular workers amount to 50 per cent of the total unemployed work-force.

Table 7.2 Population and labour market, 1991

Municipalities	Population	Employed	Unemployed (%)				Enterprises		Institutions	
			Total	Female	Male	Juvenile	Number	Employed	Number	Employed
Angri	29,753	7,113	39.3	47.8	34.1	68.2	1,557	4,344	26	814
Nocera Inferiore	49,053	12,238	36.3	45.4	31.6	66.1	2,541	6,415	45	2,297
Nocera Superiore	22,325	5,584	34.9	48.0	29.0	62.4	984	3,967	12	195
Pagani	33,138	7,135	46.1	55.7	41.2	74.2	2,397	5,349	26	350
S. Egidio	8,188	1,699	46.7	53.1	44.0	70.6	500	1,619	3	68
S. Marzano	9,556	2,641	42.2	43.3	41.3	69.3	513	1,096	14	53
S. Valentino	8,203	1,862	46.7	53.3	42.6	71.1	445	983	7	80
Sarno	31,509	6,859	45.3	49.4	43.0	72.4	1,554	3,397	9	892
Scafati	40,710	10,077	38.6	46.7	34.3	68.2	1,445	4,590	30	510
ANS	232,435	55,208	41.3	47.6	36.0	64.5	11,936	31,760	172	5,259

Source: ISTAT (1991a and 1991b).

The diffusion of illegal work is amplified by: the atomisation of business units, mentioned above; the weakness of trade unions, at the local level; the new standards of flexibility imposed by the enterprises, that need to cover their costs and to bridge the efficiency gap; the importance that agriculture and constructions – sectors in which illegal work is massively present – still have as main sources of employment; the presence of criminal organisations that control the labour market as one of their basic and more profitable businesses; the specific features of some re-distributive policies targeted to industrial workers, and the distortions in their management (Ministero del Tesoro, 1999, p. 7). The situation of irregularity is worsened by the presence of immigrants who are employed for exhausting, scarcely remunerated and frequently illegal jobs.

A few statistics highlight a situation of diffused juvenile discomfort: 2,271 cases of children having problems with the educational system, 185 minors denounced to Judicial Authorities in 1995, 445 minors left in charge of Social Assistance, 81 children who have been institutionalised. Drug abuse is also very common; drug addicts registered at the SERT service number 1,096 (Ministero del Tesoro, 1999). Environmental conditions are close to collapse: the area is well-known for its beautiful landscape, fertile soils, important archaeological sites, but these beauties are threatened by wild urbanisation processes and unmonitored pollution. The river Sarno, which flows across the plain, is one of the most severely polluted rivers in Europe. Moreover, owing to an unplanned urban development, some of the most polluting plants have been incorporated within or lie very close to residential areas.

In the area, criminal organisations – and especially the *Camorra*[5] – still represent one of the main constraints to territorial development and to the diffusion of a consolidated condition of security and law enforcement. The *Camorra*, unlike the *Mafia*, is strongly locally-rooted. At the same time, its control over the territory is fragmented, because of the separation and bloody conflicts between the *Cosche* (criminal clans): we should thus follow Isaia Sales (1992), and talk of a plurality of Camorre. This criminal business-like organisation controls public aid to development as its main activity, in a pervasive but not showy way that makes it difficult to identify its presence. It fascinates mainly the young, because of the easy and fast money that it guarantees in a context where it is very difficult, if not impossible, to find a legal job.

Social Capital During the 1980s

During the 1980s and early 1990s, in the ANS area a dominant bloc emerged, whose exclusive purpose was to enrich and to increase its own members' power. Most of the local political elite belonged to this bloc, together with some entrepreneurs and members of criminal organisations. The group aimed at diverting the consistent flow of money directed to the development of the South to their own exclusive advantage.

The bloc leaders were the politicians, who were ready to take any risk just to obtain greater political and economic influence. They were able to attract large amounts of public money to their constituencies – and their voters. The money was then utilised to finance public infrastructures that, quite often, did not meet any real developmental need; in many cases, these public works were left unfinished. By this, the politicians ensured great earnings to themselves, obtained rich orders for their fellow entrepreneurs, gained bids for the benefit of the *Camorra* and provided jobs to their clients – all in return for votes.

Indeed, these years were characterised by what we can label as a 'perverse networking' between dominant politicians, big entrepreneurs and *Camorra* affiliates, all aiming at exploiting public funds and at enforcing their power.

Politicians and *Camorristi* were linked by a relation similar to that occurring between business partners; sometimes this relation was even closer, and quite similar to symbiosis (Figure 7.2).

The relation did not involve single parties or groups of them, but party members or party leaders taken as individuals, without any reference to their ideological affiliation. The sound political-camorristic bloc that had developed relied on a dense net of face-to-face interrelationships. Politicians of any level were involved: from local groups to national élites. Not only were vertical relations very tight, but *camorristi* and the local political class showed them off as a way to increase their own prestige.

It is clear now that until 1993 *Camorra* affiliates had very good relations with local MPs and Ministers – which in some cases were real *Mafiosi*. *Camorra* organisations also controlled many local Towns Councils and enjoyed high-ranking protection from Rome. In 1993 the Ministry of Internal Affairs dissolved almost all local Towns Councils, denouncing *Camorra* infiltrations.[6]

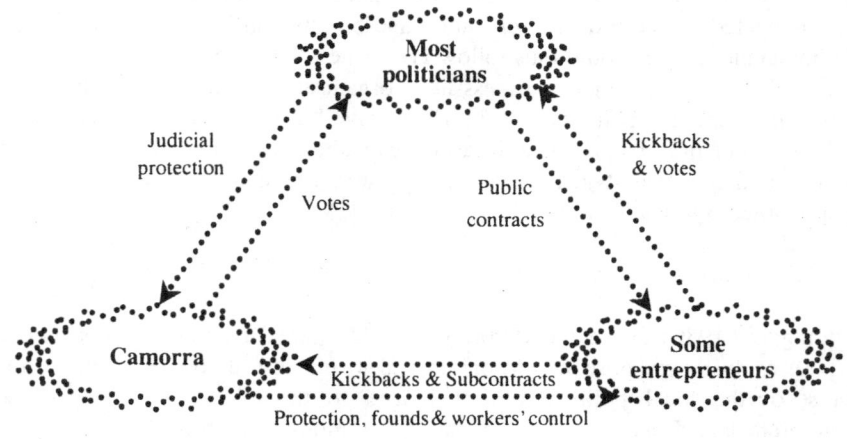

Figure 7.2 ANS during 1980s: perverse networking

Judicial inquiries let us know that administrative acts in Nocera were decided in the private studio of a well-known *Camorra* boss. Mayors and aldermen of Sarno, Pagani, Scafati and Nocera were under the direction of local boss Pasquale Galasso (Commissione Antimafia, 1993, p. 162). Indeed these hierarchical relations worked with profit. All local public bodies were controlled by the political-camorrisite bloc.

A large number of entrepreneurs participated in this bloc and those who were interested in public works were particularly active. Thanks to 'perverse networking', *Camorra* bosses gained total control of public contracts - which meant total control of the local building industry. Wholesale trade, supermarkets and vegetable processing firms were able to ensure to *Camorra* businesses rapid money laundering and easy profits. However, the organisation concentrated particularly on food-processing industries. This sector represented a key to the 'big business' of European Common Agricultural Policy funds. The 'joint-venture' between entrepreneurs and *Camorra* organised a lot of frauds against the European Community (Commissione Antimafia, 1993).

As is well-known, enterprises constantly need licences, permits and other services supplied by the Public Administration. In a context where institutions do not work properly, the enterprises bypass bureaucratic slowness asking favours to corrupt civil servants or to the *camorristic*-bloc's friends, following a tacit agreement on exchange of favours.

Camorra control imposed additional costs to the firms such as '*pizzo*' (monthly 'protection fees'), kickbacks and so on. The result was the introduction of violence and corruption in everyday transactions and through this the distortion of competition. Only few food-processing firms had a legal and transparent ownership and referred to banks or stock exchange to finance their business: most of the others borrowed money from their patrons and 'friends'. The *camorristi* clans, after having financed the entrepreneurs at high interest rates (usury), frequently obtained the ownership of the firms.

The relationship between politicians and entrepreneurs was different for those who were excluded from the 'bloc of power'. Within the bloc typical relations of mutual exchange were characterised by corruption or collusion. Sometimes the politicians were at the same time entrepreneurs and/or *camorristi* and vice versa. Sometimes they tried to keep such double role secret, using a dummy.

The entrepreneurs who did not accept to act in accordance to the rules of the political-camoristic bloc were exposed to hostility, threats or blackmail and, sometimes, violence. In addition, they had to overcome the obstacles originating in a corrupt and inefficient institutional structure.

In the social sphere only few people were members of the perverse networking, the large majority of citizens just endeavouring to maintain their standards of living in such difficult times. In that context the *amoral familism* behaviour became stronger. Families 'withdrew into themselves' and used all available resources to build a safety net. There were no more relations of solicarity, every one trying to find out his/her own coping strategy. Patronage relations with the institutional apparatus became even more frequent.

In addition, relations with the prominent bloc were based on a clear 'exchange of votes': electoral votes in exchange of jobs or access to public resources. Even in the workplace a 'corporative' behaviour was in force, that was characterized by compliance and subjection towards the members of the bloc that guaranteed favours and access to work. Civil servants and legal workers frequently pursued only their own private interests or the interests of their political or *Camorra* referent. Indeed the quality of public services was very low, as it was the productivity of 'corporatist' workers in the firms. Co-operation between the 'corporatist' worker and the entrepreneur did not exist.

The performance of ANS in these years is a clear example of social capital used in a perverse way. The network based on reciprocity and trust between politicians, entrepreneurs and the local population was used for particularistic profits, in opposition to the socio-economic development of the area. The criminal interest of the political-camorristic bloc and the 'withdrawal into themselves' of the population generated a paradox in which public interest seemed in contrast with private interest. The overall result was a period of economic and social stagnation.

We may depict the ANS situation as an hour-glass (Rose, 1995). In the top part of the hour-glass there is a group, the perverse networking, composed of the political camorristic bloc built on a tight net of interrelations. At the base of the hour-glass there is the great majority of the population with no access to public resources or services and without any role in the management of public goods. This second group is composed of entrepreneurs, politicians, associations and citizens that do not belong to the first bloc and who try to defend themselves from its violence and arrogance. The narrow mid-point of the hour-glass represents the few relations and institutions working for the benefit of the whole community.

In conclusion, during the 1980s and early 1990s, the ANS area was characterised by a stock of SC composed prevalently of face-to-face relations. This stock operated within a very weak institutional framework. ANS territory during the 1980s shows a case of SC used by a predominant group against generalised wellbeing and development. Furthermore most of the population used SC to cope with every day problems.

Using the graph presented in the previous section (Figures 7.1, 7.3), we may collocate the ANS case in the bottom left of the fourth quadrant.

Analysis and Empirical Interpretation of the Present Situation[7]

Socio-economic conditions in the ANS area have changed substantially since the late 1990s. This change has been certainly favoured by the new regulatory system that the Italian Parliament recently passed to discipline policies and measures of aid to development. Indiscriminate and massive aid has been substituted by targeted interventions, funded by the EU; the new supportive policy is small-dimensioned, enjoys a more limited financial covering and is submitted to more severe controls (Ministero del Tesoro, 1999).

One further change is due to the fact that some well-known politicians of the area have left the scene after the political and judicial earthquake of *Tangentopoli*.[8]

The political-criminal bloc that operated in the ANS area has been left without its highest-ranking political references: this has led to a turnover in the local political elite, while many *Camorra* bosses have been sentenced to prison. Politicians, entrepreneurs and members of civil society that had suffered the oppression of that perverse networking now enjoy new opportunities and stronger motivation.

In addition to this, the newly adopted incentive policies have created new institutions and diffused new methodologies to support the development process of weak areas: participative and concerted procedures, exploitation and development of local resources have become the leit-motiv of public debates and policies. Local administrations, interest groups, governmental and non-governmental organisations have signed the ANS Territorial Employment Pact which aims at promoting processes of socio-economic sustainable development and at reducing unemployment.

These exogenous and endogenous changes have modified the socio-economic background and the network of interrelations in the ANS area. In brief, the kind of SC which is present in the area has changed.

In the following pages we will try to explain how it has changed what are the new institutional contexts in which it is inscribed and what socio-economic situation has consequently developed.

Interrelation in and between social, economic and political spheres In this section we will investigate the network of interrelations occurring in and between the social, economic and political spheres.

The social sphere is characterised by diffused participation in both formalised and informal associations. Informal associations develop in the shared spaces within residential areas. For a long time people living in ANS have been transforming courts, alleys, balconies and terraces in places where they meet, they interact, they trust and help each other. Frequently children are left in the care of neighbours, whenever their parents are busy or have to be absent for a while. Exchange of information and knowledge, support in economic activities, sustain and help of all kind form the basis of relations between neighbours. Informal groups are also very active in protesting against unpopular measures, in defending public parks and areas, but they are not as effective in elaborating new proposals, or in collaborating with groups that don't belong to the area. They have very limited contact with people and issues that are not the typical ones they are used to. This means that in the ANS area there are intense face-to-face relations, but much weaker horizontal and vertical ones. Cross-cutting relations are even scarcer.

Formalised associations are very different from one another, ranging from social and sporting clubs to cultural and political associations. There are both Catholic and secular organisations, the former being much better organised: groups linked to the Church gather children, young people and adults; they can be spiritually inspired (catechumenal communities), or have educational purposes (Azione Cattolica) or recreational aims. One mentionable Catholic group is the Scout association, which is widespread throughout the area and is linked to similar associations in the whole Western world. When interviewed, the members of this

Association declared their commitment to sustaining and promoting widespread welfare for the whole community. Despite the differences between the groups, they all seem inspired by solidarity values, promoting environmental awareness and encouraging civic engagement. Members are expected by the association to react to difficulties by making the best use of their own resources, without waiting for external help: this enhancement of the self-help principle is proving very important in areas where people are used to being assisted. Indeed, many people interviewed confirmed that they gave their best when their personal commitment was required.

Social inclusion of vulnerable groups is a specific target for most local associations, and especially for their youngest members. Sometimes parents disapprove manifestly of their children dealing with 'risky' mates: as a matter of fact, these associations often fail to bridge the generation gaps through cross-cutting interrelations. Generation gaps, like differences in socio-economic status, are not easy to overcome because the social infrastructures that should help in reaching this goal are missing. Economically and socially disadvantaged households, for instance, are only supported by voluntary associations, with little or no help from social/public assistance. All interventions requiring cooperation between private or public associations and institutions are uneasy: cooperation is sporadic and more formal than substantial. The organisations miss the needed institutional support, and often they fail to involve and mobilize the whole community: therefore, they run the risk of self-closure, or self-exclusion.

Relations within the social sphere, and with the economic and political ones are marked by successive phases of conflict and cooperation. For instance, in a newly urbanized area in the municipality of Angri there has been tension between different social groups, followed by intense collaboration owing to which a yearly *Sagra* is being organised, with full involvement of the whole neighbourhood.

Relations between social and economic actors are very weak. Local groups refer to economic agents only occasionally, in specific circumstances when they need specific help: yearly *Sagra*, events to sponsor, fund-raising for somebody or some purpose etc. Many members of civic organisations think they should deepen their relations with economic agents.

On the contrary, relations with the political sphere and the institutions are kept as formal and detached as possible. Most of civil society fears that politicians might use them. The perverse networking of the recent past is difficult to forget. Still more time and effort are needed before political engagement becomes genuinely committed to territorial development. Many people recognize that they should be more determined in promoting a sense of shared civic awareness. But then they add, partly to justify themselves, that they have to face daily people's attitudes of resignation, due to the malfunctioning of the institutions and the low quality of public services – that people read as the symptom of the 'rottenness' of the political sphere. The most common reaction to this state of things is 'Every man for himself!' In an environment considered as hostile, or at least not favourable, the first thing people think of is creating a safety net for themselves and their family. Therefore relations with the institutions still follow the model of patronage, with people asking for favours and protection for their family.

The ANS's economic sphere is composed of many small micro enterprises, most of which are family businesses. Relations within these units are of the face-to-face kind. This kind of networking allows split-off processes of enterprise creation, in which the steady link between the newly established businesses and their parent firm favours family members or close collaborators. There are several reasons for this organisational choice, and especially the high level of flexibility that it allows. As a result, there is a high enterprise birth-rate, but always in traditional sectors.

Technological innovation is one of the main problems facing ANS enterprises. There are very few private or public R&D centres: only canned-food producers can rely on a public research institute that examines and tests possible product or process innovations. In any case, only a few enterprises refer to the institute, and just for limited services – notably laboratory tests. All the other sectors of production are completely unsupported, and their only way of updating their knowledge and operational organisation is through participation in specialised fairs, which are almost always held in very distant towns and cities. Even for machinery repairing local entrepreneurs resort to specialized workers and spare parts from the North. Some interviewed craftsmen depicted a similar situation for their sector.

All the entrepreneurs complain that the institutions do not cooperate with them to promote R&D. But then they admit that they are unable themselves to collaborate in sharing the unaffordable costs of research and experimentation: indeed, only a few of them let their competitors know what product or process innovations they have introduced in their production. This prevents the diffusion of general knowledge, rather than applying solely to industrial secrets.

On the whole, the ANS economic sphere is characterized by competitive relations that only seldom bring about some kind of cooperation. Cooperative attitudes, that would be very important for balanced economic growth, are not even favoured by the various producers' associations, since these are considered as simple collectors of subscription fees. As a matter of fact, these associations are unable to provide even basic information on laws and regulations, that their members would highly appreciate. Above all, the entrepreneurs need to be informed about sanitary and environmental regulations, because they are subject to periodical controls and they need to meet the required standards; with regard to this, regularized enterprises feel they are disadvantaged in comparison to illegal ones, because they suffer the additional costs of frequently imposed adjustments, and sometimes they are forced to close down their business, temporarily or definitively.

Local economic agents react to public administration's inefficiency with diffused coping strategies: they ask for favours, pay kickbacks, elude norms etc. Unauthorised building, for example, 'copes with' the lack of adequate industrial estates.

Cooperation between entrepreneurs and workers is also difficult to establish. In many workers' views the entrepreneurs only pursue their own private interest. They denounce hardship in working conditions, especially in very small enterprises: long working hours, frenzied work pace, inadequate remuneration. The employers, in turn, claim that the workers do not cooperate and are not committed enough to their job. They add that women workers leave their job once they get married, so that the enterprise loses the money invested on their training. For most entrepreneurs, the high unemployment rates are only apparent: both they and their workers 'benefit' from wide illegal work opportunities, that allow the former to enjoy high flexibility and to evade taxes, the latter to receive the social assistance (unemployment benefits, medical fees exemptions) that they would lose if declared 'employed'.

Relations between workers and entrepreneurs are basically of the face-to-face and vertical kind. There are rare horizontal relations as between equals. Cross-cutting relations, that would link employers, employees, citizens, politicians, are virtually inexistent. The same scheme applies to all other actors in the economic sphere: economic agents do not interact with their peers, especially if not resident in the area and not sharing the same status; while they are to used to vertical relations within the enterprise and the 'filière'.

This kind of network operates in an institutional context that is not able to understand and/or satisfy enterprises' real needs. The coping strategy mentioned above, therefore, responds to the lack of synergy between enterprises, but also to the gaps between these and the institutions. While it appears that some progress has recently been made by both the institutions and the enterprises, in order to improve their mutual relationship, by contrast, improving relations between workers and employers and establishing some contacts with civil society do not seem to be the objects of any special effort.

The institutional sphere is considered the weak point of ANS. Entrepreneurs, civil society members and also some institutions' employees recognise this weakness.

The political class and Public Administration are more frequently criticised. Politicians are considered incapable of doing their job properly, corrupt and not sensitive to local needs. The local people are unable to understand the political decision-making process, in fact they feel excluded by any decision-making process regarding them. To give an example, a local neighbourhood is unable to understand why the local Town Council planned to build a social infrastructure very close to a similar one just completed by the local church. Above all, people considered the slowness of public services as a restraint upon development. An entrepreneur lamented having to wait for two years to have his electrical equipment empowered.

Many people are aware of the great improvement in the institutional and political performance. Recent changes in the local and national political class and the gradual improvement in civic society rules, reduced the power of clientelism. The Territorial Employment Pact of the area is also contributing to introducing concerted and participative procedures in an attempt to build transversal relations between different social actors.

Unfortunately this institution is too young and brittle, sometimes it is unable to promote such complex interrelations and as a result bureaucratic relations are still in force. The banking system can be taken as an example of an actor which is reluctant to change and has preserved its very strong and cumbersome bureaucratic organisation. According to interviewed entrepreneurs, local banks are more similar to branches offering only elementary financial services. None of them invest in

SME start-ups and quite often they create problems for borrowers experiencing a temporary overdrawn account.

Other institutions dealing with research, training and education are seen as quite efficient but not able to answer to local needs. Our on the field research endorse such opinions. While these institutions work efficiently they do not have any relation with the economic sector, civil sector or policy makers and also between themselves. Cross-cutting relations are always missing.

Conclusion

By defining SC as a stock of interrelations which interact in a more or less synergic way, we have been able to analyse the more recent development of ANS. We noted how in this area in the last ten years the institutional context has changed thanks to the weakening of the politico-criminal bloc which had succeeded in capturing many institutions. Despite these changes, many of the actors linked to that speculative bloc, or used to operate according to clientelist and corrupt criteria, are still active in local institutions. This situation constitutes a powerful brake upon the various exogenous and endogenous attempts to make the institutions more efficient, transparent, and responsive to citizens' needs. We are witnessing a tendency towards a substantial improvement of institutional performance. However, there are quite a few risks that the politico-criminal bloc succeeds in re-establishing its position of power thanks to the many people it can rely on who are still active in local institutions. There are still frequent cases of faked public contracts, kickbacks, and similar practices, a clear sign that the old bloc is quite resilient. Nevertheless, improved institutional performance has without doubt been the most significant change of the last few decades.

The stock of interrelations, however, has changed only slightly. Face-to-face and horizontal interrelations have strengthened, while vertical ones have weakened and at the same time modified, especially those between local citizens and political actors as well as local and national institutions. During the 1980s the local people were fully aware of the presence of institutions, parliamentarians and public administrators, even though clientelist relations prevailed. Nowadays, by contrast, there appears to be a diffused feeling of distance, of a deafness of the institutions to the needs of the local community. Transversal interrelations are still scarce goods in ANS. Some associations, politicians, institutions and entrepreneurs understand the importance of being able to establish transversal relations with the other social actors, but they are still in the minority.

From the early 1980s until today the ANS has changed quite dramatically, moving from a phase of deep socio-economic stagnation to one characterised by revival and growth, even though there are still cases of social deprivation, economic and institutional inefficiencies, corrupt and clientelist practices. Many actors continue to adopt a coping strategy with which they try and make use of all available resources to improve their personal situation, as well as that of the family or the group to which they belong. We are still far from a situation of diffused wellbeing deriving from synergic behaviour among all actors.

The progress made by ANS is more in evidence if we look at the graphic (Figure 7.3). Recent improvements in social interrelations and, above all, in the institutional context, allow ANS to move towards a development path leading to diffused wellbeing. Unlike the 1980s, in the last decade SC played a positive role for the development of this area, represented graphically by the shift towards the right.

There is a concrete danger that the current improvement will not last. In this historical phase for ANS, in order to consolidate the tendency towards diffused wellbeing it is crucial to continue to improve the institutional framework. As many interviewees remarked, the redemption of ANS cannot take place without the liberation 'from the slavery of the politico-criminal bloc'.

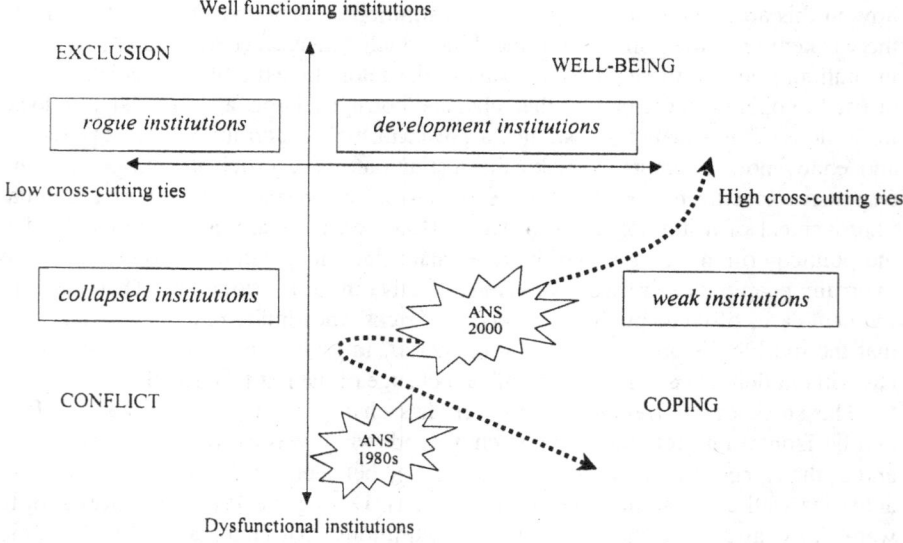

Figure 7.3 ANS's dynamics

Notes

1 It should be noted that generalized trust cannot be considered a must for a well-functioning society. On the contrary, in some cases a lack of trust towards specific institutions or governments is needed to achieve a democratic outcome. In the presence of strong social conflicts political mistrust does not necessarily mean civic weakness or democratic deficit (Edwards and Foley, 1998, p. 133).
2 For institutions we mean all local and national governs, civil services, political parties, banks, stock exchange, employers associations, R&D centres, training and educational centres etc.

3   In Banfield's words (1976), amoral familism aims at maximising the family's own interest taking for granted that others will do the same.
4   See Regione Campania, Delibera Giunta No. 070, 2 June 1997.
5   'The Camorra: it does not have a vertical or hierarchical structure; it has an urban character: therefore geared towards trade and relations with widespread illegality; it is indifferent to political ideologies: its mercenary tradition makes it available to serve whoever can exchange favours with it; even when it has apparently supported political causes it has done so by "tying" itself to individual politicians and not to political parties or lobbies. Its ties to politics are never direct or explicit; it exploits social disorders; it is pervasive: it is cynically and opportunistically present wherever there is something useful to obtain, a service to ensure, a profitable business to do, or a political relation to start; it tries to achieve total control of its territory and it has strong ties with it' (Alfiero, 1995).
6   Scafati and Pagani's Towns Councils were dissolved on 11 March 1993 (Gazzetta Ufficiale, 15 March 1993); Nocera Inferiore's Town Council was dissolved on 14 April 1993 (Gazzetta Ufficiale, 17 April 1993); Sarno's Town Council was dissolved on 23 June 1993 (Gazzetta Ufficiale, 25 June 1993).
7   This section is based principally on interviews made during the second semester of 2000 with local actors. It is also based on the analysis of official documentation and screening of local and national newspapers.
8   The discovery in 1992 of a nation-wide system of corruption and misuse of public funds, that had been linking together politicians and party leaders, public administrators and business people.

References

Alfiero, C. (1995), 'Criminal organisations in Southern Continental Italy: Camorra, N'drangheta, Sacra Corona Unita', in *Atti del 1° Seminario Euriopeo 'Falcon One', sulla Criminalità organizzata*, 26-28 Aprile, Roma.
Allum, P. (1998), 'La DC a Napoli: l'ultima fase - trionfo della macchina politico-criminale', *Nord e Sud*, n.s., XLV, 4-5, pp. 67-87.
Assindustria Salerno (2000), *L'andamento dell'economia in Campania e in provincia di Salerno nel corso del 1999.*
Atkinson, A.B. and Hills, J. (eds) (1998), *Exclusion, Employment and Opportunity*, Working Paper No. 4, Center for Analysis of Social Exclusion, London School of Economics and Political Science, London.
Baculo, L. (1998), 'Patti territoriali, sistemi locali e distretti industriali', *Nord e Sud*, 9, pp. 82-94.
Bagnasco, A. (1977), *La costruzione sociale del mercato*, Il Mulino, Bologna.
Bagnasco, A. (1977), *Tre Italie. La problematica territoriale dello sviluppo italiano*, Il Mulino, Bologna.
Bagnasco, A. (1994), 'Regioni, tradizione civica, modernizzazione italiana: un commento alla ricerca di Putnam', *Stato e Mercato*, 40, pp. 93-103.
Bagnasco, A. (1997), 'Nascita e trasformazione dei distretti industriali', in *Annali della Fondazione Luigi Einaudi*, Olschki Editore.
Banca d'Italia (1998), *Sintesi delle note sull'andamento delle economie delle regioni italiane nel 1997*, Roma.
Banfield, E.C. (1976), *Le basi morali di una società arretrata*, Il Mulino, Bologna.

Barbagallo, F. (1997), *Napoli fine novecento*, Einaudi, Torino.
Barbagallo, F. (1999), *Il potere della camorra (1973-1998)*, Einaudi, Torino.
Barr, A. (1998), *Enterprise Performance and the Functional Diversity of Social Capital*, Working Paper, WPS/98-1, Centre for the Study of African Economies, University of Oxford, Oxford.
Becattini, G. (1987), *Mercato e forze locali: il distretto industriale*, Il Mulino, Bologna.
Besley, T., Coate, S. and Loury, G. (1993), 'The Economics of Rotating Savings and Credit Associations', *American Economic Review*, 83, 4, pp. 792-810.
Booth, J.A. and Bayer, P.R. (1998a), 'Civil Society in Central America: The Dark Side?', *American Journal of Political Science*.
Bourdieu, P. (1985), 'The Forms of Capital', in J. Richardson (ed.), *Handbook of Theory and Research for the Sociology of Education*, Greenwood Press.
Brautigam, D. (1997), 'Substituting for the State: Institutions and Industrial Development in Eastern Nigeria', *World Development*, 25, 7, pp. 1063-1080.
Brown, L.D. and Ashman, D. (1996), 'Participation, Social Capital, and Intersectoral Problem Solving: African and Asian Cases', *World Development*, 24, 9, pp. 1467-1479.
Brusco, S. (1999), 'Trust, Social Capital and Local Development: Some Lessons from the Experience of the Italian Districts', in *Networks of Enterprises and Local Development*, OECD.
Burt, R. (1993), 'The Social Structure of Competition', in R. Swedberg (ed.), *Explorations in Economic Sociology*, Russel Sage Foundations, New York.
Campos, J. and Root, H. (1996), *The Key to the Asian Miracle: Making Shared Growth Credible*, Brookings Institution, Washington, DC.
Cohen, C.J. (1999), *Social capital, intervening institutions and political power*, W.P. Yale University.
Cohen, C.J. and Rogers, J. (1992), 'Secondary Associations in Democratic Governance', *Politics and Society*, 20, pp. 393-472.
Cohn, S.K.Jr. (1994), 'La storia secondo Robert Putnam', *Polis*, VIII, 2, pp. 315-324.
Coleman, J. (1987), 'Norms as Social Capital', in G. Radnitzky and P. Bernholz (eds), *Economic Imperialism: The Economic Method Applied Outside the Field of Economics*, Paragon House Publishers, New York.
Coleman, J. (1988), 'Social Capital in the Creation of Human Capital', *American Journal of Sociology*, 94 (Supplement) S95-S120.
Coleman, J. (1990), *Foundations of Social Theory*, Harvard University Press, Cambridge, Mass.
Collier, P. (1998), *Social Capital and Poverty*, Social Capital Initiative Working Paper No. 4, World Bank, Washington, DC.
Commissione Parlamentare Antimafia (1993), *Camorra e politica - relazione approvata dalla commissione il 21 dicembre 1993*, Laterza, Roma-Bari.
Commissione Parlamentare Antimafia (2000), *Relazione Senatori Lombardi Satriani*, Roma.
Dasgupta, P. (1997), 'Social Capital and Economic Performance', mimeo, Environmentally and Socially Sustainable Development Network, The World Bank, Washington, DC.
de Haan, A. and Maxwell, S. (1998), 'Poverty and Social Exclusion in the North and South', *IDS Bulletin*, 29, 1, pp. 1-9.
De Renzio, P. (1998), 'Capitale sociale e buon governo', *Politica Internazionale*, 5, pp. 97-110.
De Rita, G. e Bonomi, A. (1998), *Manifesto per lo sviluppo locale*, Bollati Boringhieri, Torino.

de Soto, H. (1989), *The Other Path: The Invisible Revolution in the Third World*, Harper and Row, New York.
Del Monte, A. (1996), *Istituzioni, intervento pubblico e sviluppo del Mezzogiorno*, ISPE, Documenti di lavoro, n. 42.
Drèze, J. and Sen, A. (1995), *India, Economic Development and Social Opportunity*, Oxford University Press, Delhi.
Eastis, C. (1998), 'Organizational Diversity and the Production of Social Capital: One of These Groups is Not Like the Other', *American Behavioural Scientist*, 42, 1.
Edwards, B. and Foley, M. (1997), 'Social Capital and the Political Economy of our Discontent', *American Behavioral Scientist*, 40, 5, pp. 669-678.
Edwards, B. and Foley, M.W. (eds) (1997), 'Social Capital, Civil Society, and Contemporary Democracy', *American Behavioural Scientist*, 40, 6, pp. 547-678.
Edwards, B. and Foley, M.W. (1993), 'Civil Society and Social Capital Beyond Putnam', *American Behavioural Scientist*, 42, 1, pp. 124-139.
Elster, J. (1989), 'Social Norms and Economic Theory', *Journal of Economic Perspectives*, 3, 4, pp. 99-117.
Esman, M. and Uphoff, N. (1984), *Local Organizations: Intermediaries in Rural Development*, Cornell University Press, Ithaca NY.
Evans, P. (1989), 'Predatory, Developmental and Other Apparatuses: A Comparative Political Economy Perspective on the Third World State', *Sociological Forum*, 4, 4, pp. 561-587.
Evans, P. (1995), *Embedded Autonomy*, Princeton University Press, Princeton NJ.
Evans, P. (1996), 'Government Action, Social Capital and Development: Reviewing the Evidence on Synergy', *World Development*, 24, 6, pp. 1119-1132.
Falk, I. and Kilpatrick, S. (2000), 'What is Social Capital? A Study of Interaction in a Rural Community', *Sociologia Ruralis*, 40, 1, pp. 38-199.
Feo, F. (1989), *Uomini e affari della Camorra*, Ed. Sintesi, Napoli.
Fernandez-Kelley, M.P. (1995), 'Social and Cultural Capital in the Urban Ghetto: Implications for the Economic Sociology of Immigration', in A. Portes (ed.), *The Economic Sociology of Immigration*, Russell Sage Foundation, New York.
Flora, J.L., Sharp, J. Flora, C. and Newlon, B. (1997), 'Entrepreneurial Social Infrastructure and Locally Initiated Economic Development in the Non-metropolitan United States', *Sociological Quarterly*, 38, 4, pp. 623-645.
Foley, M.W. and Edwards, B. (1996), 'The Paradox of Civil Society', *Journal of Democracy*, 7, 3, pp. 38-52.
Foley, M.W. and Edwards, B. (1997), 'Escape from Politics? Social Theory and the Social Capital Debate', *American Behavioral Scientist*, 40, 6, pp. 550-561.
Franzini, M. (1996), 'Meno trasferimenti più sviluppo? Politici, istituzioni e ritardo del Mezzogiorno', *Meridiana*, 26-27, pp. 75-90.
Franzini, M. (1998), 'Lo sviluppo economico ed il benessere sociale', *Meridiana*, 31, pp. 77-87.
Fukuyama, F. (1995), 'Social Capital and the Global Economy', *Foreign Affairs* September/October, pp. 89-103.
Fukuyama, F. (1995), *Trust: The Social Values and the Creation of Prosperity*, Free Press, New York.
Granovetter, M. (1973), 'The Strength of Weak Ties', *American Journal of Sociology*, 78, pp. 1360-80.
Granovetter, M. (1985), 'Economic Action and Social Structure: The Problem of Embeddedness', *American Journal of Sociology*, 91, pp. 481-510.

Granovetter, M. (1995), 'The Economic Sociology of Firms and Entrepreneurs', in Alejandro Portes (ed.), *The Economic Sociology of Immigration: Essays on Networks, Ethnicity and Entrepreneurship*, Russell Sage Foundation, New York.

Grootaert, C. (1997), 'Social Capital: The Missing Link?' in *Expanding the Measure of Wealth: Indicators of Environmentally Sustainable Development*, Environmentally Sustainable Development Studies and Monographs Series No. 7, The World Bank, Washington, DC.

Harriss, J. and De Renzio, P. (1997), 'Missing link or analytically missing?: the concept of Social Capital', *Journal of International Development*, 9, 7, pp. 919-937.

Hirschman, A. (1984), *Getting Ahead Collectively: Grass-roots Organizations in Latin America*, Pergamon Press, New York.

Hirschman, A.O. (1958), *The strategy of economic development*, Yale University Press.

Hirschman, A.O. (1970), *Exit, Voice, and Loyalty: response Torino decline in firms, organizations, and states*, Harvard University Press.

ISTAT (1991a), *Censimento Generale della Popolazione e delle Abitazioni, 20 Ottobre 1991*, Roma.

ISTAT (1991b), *Censimento Generale dell'Industria e dei Servizi, 21 Ottobre 1991*, Roma.

Jackman, R.W. and Miller, R.A. (1996a), 'A Renaissance of Political Culture?', *American Journal of Political Science*, 40, 3, pp. 632-659.

Jackman, R.W. and Miller, R.A. (1996b), 'The Poverty of Political Culture', *American Journal of Political Science*, 40, 3, pp. 697-716.

Jackman, R.W. and Miller, R.A. (1998), 'Social Capital and Politics', *Annual Review of Political Science*, 1, pp. 47-73.

Kentworthy, L. (1997), 'Civic Engagement, Social Capital, and Economic Cooperation', *American Behavioral Scientist*, 40, 5, pp. 646-657.

Knack, S. and Keefer, P. (1996), 'Does Social Capital have an Economic Payoff? A Cross-Country Investigation', mimeo, Policy Research Department, The World Bank, Washington, DC.

Leonardi, R. (1996), 'Regional development in Italy: social capital and the Mezzogiorno', *Oxford Review of Economic Policy*, 11, 1, pp. 165-179.

Levi, M. (1996), 'Social and Unsocial Capital: A Review Essay of Robert Putnam's Making Democracy Work', *Politics and Society*, 24, 1, pp. 45-55.

Lijphart, A. (1977), *Democracy in Plural Societies: Comparative Exploration*, Yale University Press, New Haven-London.

Loury, G. (1977), 'A Dynamic Theory of Racial Income Differences', in P.A. Wallace and A. LeMund (eds), *Women, Minorities, and Employment Discrimination*, Lexington Books, Lexington MA.

Lupo, S. (1993), 'Usi e abusi del passato. Le radici dell'Italia di Putnam', *Meridiana*, 18, pp. 151-168.

Meldolesi, L. (1998), *Dalla parte del sud*, Laterza, Roma-Bari.

Ministero del Tesoro (1999), *P.O.M.: Sottoprogramma 1, Patto Territoriale per l'Occupazione Agro Nocerino-Sarnese*, Roma.

Mutti, A. (1994), 'I sentieri dello sviluppo' (Recensione a Putnam), *Rassegna Italiana di Sociologia*, 1, pp. 109-119.

Mutti, A. (1995), 'Politiche di sviluppo per le regioni meridionali', *Il Mulino*, XLIV, 1, pp. 83-97.

Mutti, A. (1998), *Capitale sociale e sviluppo. La fiducia come risorsa*, Il Mulino, Bologna.

Narayan, D. (1995), 'Designing Community-Based Development', Environment Department Paper 7, The World Bank, Washington, DC.

Narayan, D. (1997), *Voices of the Poor: Poverty and Social Capital in Tanzania*, Environmentally and Socially Sustainable Development Network, Studies and Monographs Series no. 20, World Bank, Washington, DC.

Narayan, D. (1999), *Bonds and Bridges: Social Capital and Poverty*, World Bank, Washington, DC.

Narayan, D. and Nyamwaya, D. (1996), *Learning from the Poor: A Participatory Poverty Assessment in Kenya*, Environment Department Papers, Paper No. 034, World Bank, Washington, DC.

Narayan, D. and Pritchett, L. (1997), *Cents and Sociability: Household Income and Social Capital in Rural Tanzania*, Social Development and Development Research Group, Policy Research Working Paper No. 1796, World Bank, Washington, DC (also in *Journal of Economic Development and Cultural Change*, July, 1999).

Newton, K. (1998), 'Social and Political Trust', in P. Norris (ed.), *Critical Citizens: Global Support for Democratic Government*, Oxford University Press, Oxford.

Newton, K. (1999), 'Social capital and democracy in modern Europe', in J.W. Van Deth, M. Maraff and Whiteley, P.F. (eds), *Social Capital and European Democracy*, Routledge, London.

North, D. (1990), *Institutions, Institutional Change, and Economic Performance*, Cambridge University Press, New York.

Olson, M. (1965), *The Logic of Collective Action*, Harvard University Press, Cambridge, MA.

Ostrom, E. (1990), *Governing the Commons: The Evolution of Institutions for Collective Action*, Cambridge University Press, New York.

Ostrom, E. (1996), 'Crossing the Great Divide: Coproduction, Synergy and Development', *World Development*, 24, 86, pp. 1073-1087.

Pantoja, E. (1999), 'Exploring the concept of social capital and its relevance for community based development. The case of coal mining areas in Orissa, India', World Bank.

Pasquino, G. (1994), 'La politica eclissata dalla tradizione civica', *Polis*, VIII, 2, pp. 307-313.

PDS Campania (1992), *Rapporto 1990 sulla Camorra*, in I. Sales and F. Barbagallo (eds), L'Unità, Roma.

Piselli, F. (1999), 'Capitale Sociale: un concetto situazionale e dinamico', *Stato e Mercato*, 57, pp. 395-417.

Pizzorno, A. (1999), 'Perché si paga il benzinaio. Nota per una teoria del capitale sociale', *Stato e Mercato*, 57, pp. 373-394.

Portes, A. (1998), 'Social Capital: Its Origins and Applications in Modern Sociology', *Annual Review of Sociology*, 22, pp. 1-24.

Portes, A. and Landolt, P. (1997), 'The Downside of Social Capital', *The American Prospect*, 26, pp. 18-21.

Portes, A., and Sensenbrenner, J. (1993), 'Embeddedness and Immigration: Notes on the Social Determinants of Economic Action', *American Journal of Sociology*, 98, 6, pp. 1320-1350.

Putnam, R. (1993b), 'The Prosperous Community - Social Capital and Public Life', *American Prospect*, 13, pp. 35-42.

Putnam, R. (1995a), 'Bowling Alone: America's Declining Social Capital', *Journal of Democracy*, 6, 1, pp. 65-78.

Putnam, R. (1995b), 'Tuning In, Tuning Out: The Strange Disappearance of Social Capital in America', *Political Science and Politics*, December, pp. 664-683.

Putnam, R. (1996), 'The Strange Disappearance of Civic America', *The American Prospect*, Winter, pp. 34-48.

Putnam, R., with Leonardi, R. and Nanetti R. (1993a), *Making Democracy Work: Civic Traditions in Modern Italy*, Princeton University Press, Princeton.

Ramella, F. (1995), 'Mobilitazione pubblica e società civile meridionale', *Meridiana*, 22-23, pp. 121-164.

Ramella, F. (1997), 'Cittadini e produttori: civicness e sviluppo locale', *Sviluppo locale*, 4, 6, pp. 5-42.

Roberti, F. (1995), 'L'eclissi della legalità. La camorra alle urne', *Nord e Sud*, XLII, 8.

Rose, R. (1995), 'Russia as an Hour Glass Society: A Constitution without Citizens', *East European Constitutional Review*, 4, 3, pp. 34-42.

Rubio, M. (1997), 'Perverse Social Capital - Some Evidence from Colombia', *Journal of Economic Issues*, 31, 3, pp. 805-816.

Sales, I. (1993), *La camorra le camorre*, Editori Riuniti, Roma.

Santacroce, D. (1993), *I miei giorni della Camorra*, Boccia Editore, Napoli.

Sciarrone, R. (1998), 'Il capitale sociale della mafia. Relazioni esterne e controllo del territorio', *Quaderni di sociologia*, XLII, 18, pp. 51-72.

Sen, A. (1997), *Social Exclusion: A Critical Assessment of the Concept and its Relevance*, (mimeo), Asian Development Bank.

Serageldin, I. and Dasgupta, P. (eds) (1997), *Social Capital: Integrating the Economist's and the Sociologist's Perspective*, The World Bank, Washington, DC.

Serageldin, I. and Grootaert V. (1997), 'Defining Social Capital: An Integrating View', paper presented at Operations Evaluation Department Conference on Evaluation and Development: The Institutional Dimension, The World Bank, Washington, DC.

Smith, J. (1998). 'Global Civil Society? Transnational Social Movement Organizations and Social Capital', *American Behavioral Scientist*, 42, 1.

Stiglitz, J. (1996), 'Some Lessons from the East Asian Miracle', *The World Bank Research Observer*, 11, 2, pp. 151-177.

Stiglitz, J. (1998), *Towards a New Paradigm for Development: Strategies, Policies, and Processes*, Given as the 1998 Prebisch Lecture at UNCTAD, Geneva, 19 October.

Stolle, D. and Rochon, T. (1998), 'Are All Associations Alike? Member Diversity, Associational Type and the Creation of Social Capital', *American Behavioural Scientist* 42, 1.

Tarrow, S. (1996), 'Making Social Science Work Across Space and Time: A Critical Reflection on Robert Putnam's Making Democracy Work', *American Political Science Review*, 90, pp. 389-397.

Temple, J. and Johnson, P. (1998), 'Social Capability and Economic Growth', *Quarterly Journal of Economics*, 113, 3, pp. 965-990.

Tendler, J. (1997), *Good Government in the Tropics*, Johns Hopkins University Press, Baltimore.

Trigilia, C. (1992), *Sviluppo senza autonomia*, Il Mulino, Bologna.

Trigilia, C. (1999), 'Capitale sociale e sviluppo locale', *Stato e Mercato*, 57, pp. 419-439.

Uphoff, N. (1993), 'Grassroots Organizations and NGOs in Rural Development: Opportunities with Diminishing States and Expanding Markets, *World Development*, 21, 4, pp. 607-622.

Valenzuela, A. and Dornbush, S. (1994), 'Familism and Social Capital in the Academic Achievement of Mexican Origin and Anglo Adolescents', *Social Science Quarterly*, 75, 1, pp. 18-36.

Waldinger, R. (1995), 'The "Other Side" of Embeddedness: A Case Study of the Interplay of Economy and Ethnicity', *Ethnic and Racial Studies*, 18, 3, pp. 555-580.

Williamson, O. (1985), *The Economic Institutions of Capitalism: Firms, Markets, Relational Contracting*, Free Press, New York.

Woolcock, M. (1998), 'Social Capital and Economic Development: Toward a Theoretical Synthesis and Policy Framework', *Theory and Society*, 27, 2, pp. 151-208.
World Bank (1997), *World Development Report 1997: The State in a Changing World*, Oxford University Press, Oxford.
Zartman, I.W. (1995), *Collapsed States: the Disintegration and Restoration of Legitimate Authority*, L. Rienner Publishers, Boulder.
Zhou, M. and Bankston, C.L. (1996), 'Social Capital and the Adaptation of the Second Generation: The Case of Vietnamese Youth in New Orleans', in A. Portes (ed.), *The New Second Generation*, Russell Sage Foundation, New York, pp. 197-220.

Chapter 8

The Emerging of Different Patterns of Local Development in the Third Italy

Luigi Burroni

Introduction

As is well-known, at the beginning of the 1970s a serious crisis of the fordist model occurred. Several conditions influenced this outcome: the saturation of final markets and their increasing instability and segmentation, together with other conjunctural factors, such as the end of the Bretton Woods system, and the oil crisis of 1973-74. They created strong rigidities, which proved to be an obstacle to competitive strategies based on containment of costs. In addition, the diffusion of flexible, low-cost technology, along with other factors, undermined the foundation of a model characterized by limited flexibility and high volumes of production. Following these changes, intensive restructuring of large-scale enterprises began and new opportunities emerged for the development of competitive models other than fordism, capable of combining considerable flexibility with diversification of products and with a different price-quality relationship.

These changes were so radical that suggested the emergence of a 'second industrial divide'. They brought about new organizational models aimed at combining flexibility and specialization and Italy was a privileged point of view to observe these new trends based on the so-called 'flexible specialization model' (Piore and Sabel, 1984). This form of economic organization had already developed in Italy while fordism was living its golden age, and continued to grow when this model showed the first signs of crisis. This pattern of development was mainly concentrated in the Central and Northeastern regions and it led Italian scholars to design a different map of the Italian economy. There was in fact a progressive shift from a dualistic conception (the developed and industrialized North versus the backward and rural South), to the idea of a 'Third Italy', and the role of the industrial district called attention as its distinct feature.[1]

Many researchers underlined the basic features which characterize the model of the industrial district: a productive structure with a majority of small and medium-size firms mutually interrelated, a limited number of firms which has access to the final market, a wide range of firms specialized in single stages of production etc. Furthermore, some authors stressed that external economies supported this model of productive organization producing collective goods such as training, technological information, export promotion, information on market trends. In a certain sense, it was possible to affirm that external economies represented a competitive advantage that fostered the competitiveness of this kind of local system.

The mechanisms of provision of these local collective goods[2] were of different nature: we can distinguish between communitarian, informal mechanisms and more institutionalized and formalized procedures. In this article, we will focus our attention on the latter, which have been less explored.[3] In particular, we will focus on two main mechanisms. On the one hand, trade unions, employers' associations and local governments favored in fact more formalized co-operation between both workers and small entrepreneurs. A co-operative model of industrial relations strengthened co-operation within firms, which compensated for labour flexibility and redistributed local income through local collective bargaining and social policies. On the other hand, co-operation among trade unions, employers' associations and local governments was important for the production of other kinds of collective goods, through the establishment of specific institutions (*Centri di servizi*) which provided training, export promotion and other services. Thus, this part of the country benefited of the action of local political institution which supported the competitiveness of a model based on networks of small firms strongly rooted in local context.

Nevertheless, since the beginning of the 1990s globalization brought about new challenges for these areas, introducing and intensifying new competitive pressure at international level. This new scenario did not reduce the importance of territorial agglomeration of productive activities (Crouch *et al.*, 2001), but fostered a process of competition among territories (Streeck, 1998). Labour and wage flexibility, high levels of education and training, the necessity of relational formal structures, a high availability of real services, adequate physical infrastructures and other elements became more and more important for the competitiveness of local systems.

The hypothesis developed here assesses that hand in hand with the growth of international pressures there has been a process of reshaping in the models of local governance that characterized the Third Italy. It is possible to identify processes of diversification that fostered the emergence of new 'institutional architectures' that lies behind the provision of local collective competition goods. For this reason, the regions here analyzed do not show the emerging of a process of governance models towards a 'one best way'. On the contrary, homogeneous external pressures create a set of constraints and opportunities, to which regions and local systems react differently according to their institutional assets, to the strategies of their collective actors etc.

Summarizing the results of recent research (Burroni, 2001) which compared Veneto and Tuscany, two regions of the Third Italy often considered as extremely homogeneous, we will try to show the main features of these pathways of diversification, emphasizing how diverse institutional arrangements rule the processes of local governance. As we will see, local governments played a key role in the provision of collective goods in Tuscany, according to a model based on *local concertation* with other collective actors. This model supported the competitiveness of the Marshallian model of industrial districts, here defined as the *localized network of firms* model, based on small firms and on a low level of interfirms hierarchy.[4] On the contrary, *single firms and the associative tissue* play the most important role in Veneto, whilst local governments are definitely non-interventionist. This latter fostered a reorganization of the productive structure leading to the emergence of leader firms, which currently play a relevant role in governance mechanisms, according to a model of productive structure that can be defined as the *localized networked firm*.

In the following paragraph we will analyze the diversity among regional and local political economy, focusing also on the diversification in the industrial relations arena. Then, we will underline the differentiation in the field of productive organization. Finally, we will try to better specify the peculiarities of each model and to emphasize their competitive advantages and shortcomings.

Two Emerging Models of Local Development

Two Paths of Regional and Local Political Economy

The degree of political intervention in the regional economy represents the first important difference between Tuscany and Veneto. Since the beginning of the 1980s, regional government adopted in Tuscany an active role in regional political economy, supporting the provision of *real services*, whilst in Veneto this intervention was delegated to single firms and economic associations. This diversity is well shown by the analysis of investments made by public governments in the two regions (Figure 8.1): in Veneto there was a notable support to the realisation of industrial areas and a notable amount of funds were addressed directly to firms to produce internally the services they need (thanks to credits, direct incentives etc.). On the contrary, in Tuscany a large part of public funds was used directly by local government to set up *Centri di Servizi*, or to produce business services (such as vocational training, information on new markets, technology transfers etc.) in order to support the competitiveness of firms.

This different approach of political economy continues also in the 1990s. As we can see in Figure 8.2, in Tuscany the diffusion of the so-called *Centri di Servizi* (Centres of Business Services) within local manufacturing systems was wider than in Veneto. This is due to the major support that these institutions had in Tuscany: here, conversely to the Veneto case, specific finances were directed to the constitution of these centres *inside* manufacturing areas. Another important cleavage between the two regions is given by the different 'weight' of political intervention in the economy. Adopting the quantity of funds invested by local governments with the aim to support local economy as a proxy of political intervention, it is possible to note the higher degree of intervention of Tuscany political institutions. Conversely, in Veneto regional, provincial and municipal governments address lower funds in supporting local economies (Figure 8.2). These features are tied to the presence of different political subcultures, the socialist and communist (more interventionist) in Tuscany and the catholic in Veneto.

178   *The Institutions of Local Development*

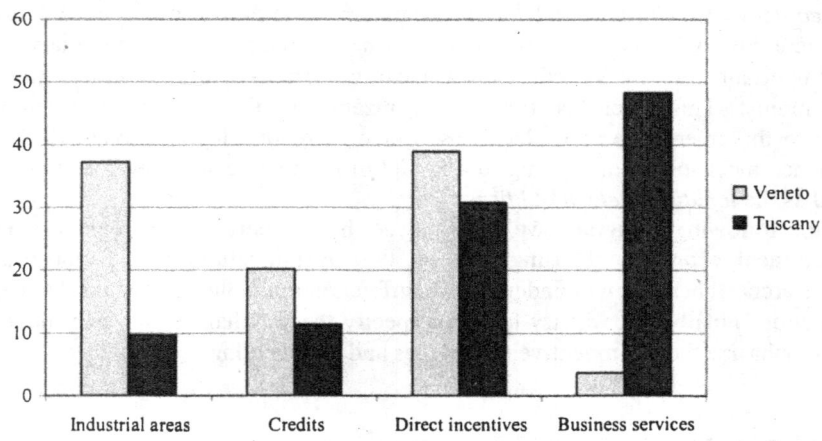

Figure 8.1 Measures of political economy in Veneto and in Tuscany during the 1980s

Source: Freschi (1993).

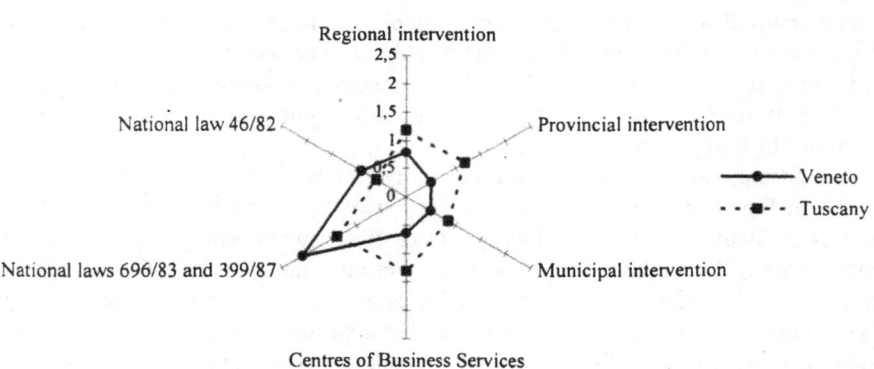

Figure 8.2 Quantitative weight of different intervention of political economy during the 1990s

Source: Burroni (1999b).

It is also worthwhile noting that Veneto benefited from a major amount of public funds connected with national laws (Figure 8.2). Given the fact that often these laws were addressed to finance the mechanical sector, the above-mentioned pattern can be explained with the wide diffusion of mechanical firms in Veneto (higher than in Tuscany). Nevertheless, the diverse weight of mechanical specialization is not sufficient to account for the great difference in the amount of financing.[5] It is possible to find another two additional explanations to this phenomenon. The first is related to the fact that the two regions had two different dominant political parties: Christian Democrats traditionally ruled Veneto, whilst Communist and Socialist Party ruled Tuscany. The major proximity of Veneto local governments to the political party that was dominant at national level (the Christian Democrats) could favor the allocation of resources in this region in exchange for political consensus.[6] A second phenomenon that can help to explain this pattern is the role of business associations. These kind of financial aids are generally obtained directly by firms thanks to the action and co-ordination of local employers' associations. Thus, it seems possible to affirm that the action of employers' associations has been more able to promote and sustain local demand of funds in Veneto rather than in Tuscany. This confirms that employers' associations play a *key role* in Veneto – together with medium and large firms.

Thus, a first cleavage emerges on the models of governance of the two regions: local governments are more active in supporting local economies in Tuscany, aiming at producing and offering real services to firms (directly or through *Centri di Servizi*). On the contrary, regional and local governments adopted a different strategy in Veneto, where the weight of political intervention was lower. In this case, the action of a dense associative network partially balanced the lower intervention of local governments.

The analysis of the local level of governance offers further elements to better specify the relations between institutions and local economic development in the two regions. In Veneto, local governments (at municipal and provincial levels) choose not to support directly local economic actors, according to a 'neo-liberal' outlook: local public administrations 'perceive' economic action as the private domain of entrepreneurs and on the other hand, local entrepreneurs think that politics and bureaucracy are synonyms and that political support to the economic sphere has mainly negative effects. This absence of political support is balanced by the active and strategic role played by economic associations. As it has been shown (Anastasia and Corò, 1996; Diamanti, 1996; Burroni, 2001), a thick associative network provides many local collective goods which are necessary for the competitiveness of small firms. At the same time, leader firms organize the action of a large network of small firms, coordinating the production and the marketing of goods, controlling the quality of production and providing technological innovation through top-down links. In this case, the level of hierarchy is quite high, and the leader firm usually provides competition goods necessary to the competitiveness of the network (information on new technology and markets, financial assistance etc.).

This system is able to produce *club* more than *collective* goods: in fact, the leader firm provides these only to suppliers which are part of its network and not to the entire local community of firms. It is possible to affirm that in Veneto stable and hierarchical networks among firms and a wide group of interests associations 'occupy' the *space* left free by political institutions, according to a model of governance that can be defined as *associative regulation*,[7] where collective actors and 'private governments' play an active role in governing local economies.

Conversely, the most important feature of the model of local governance which prevails in Tuscany is given by the important role played by local governments. Here local institutions directly contribute to the provision of business services, co-ordinate processes of vocational training, favor the establishment of public-private institutions for the provision of real services etc. In this case, the perspective shared by local political administrators is opposite than in Veneto: the economic tissue of small firms is perceived as characterized by a weakness that can be reduced only with direct political support. Also business associations carry out an active role in the governance mechanism, but they are constantly supported – and often coordinated – by local political administrations. Conversely, single firms have in Tuscany a marginal role in the process of local governance, especially for two causes: firstly, as we will see – the average size of firms is smaller than in Veneto and there is a marginal quote of leader firms. These smaller dimensions hinder the economy of scale necessary to produce collective – and also club – goods. Secondly, small-scale firms do not have easy access to the *political space* already occupied by local political institutions and economic associations. Thus, in this case, this resembles a model based on *local concertation*, where the local governments are the most important players in the process of governance.

Summarizing, clear differences characterize the models of both regional and local governance of the two regions; a sort of associative style of governance prevails in the Veneto region, where the lack of intervention of local governments is balanced by the role played by private 'governments' (employers' associations and firms). On the contrary, in Tuscany, public institutions, together with associations, adopt interventionist strategies aiming at supporting local competitiveness.[8]

Two Models of Industrial Relations

The above mentioned differences can be better specified analyzing the industrial relations' arena. There were differences between the models of industrial relations in the two regions even in the previous decades (Trigilia, 1990 and 1992); however, these differences appear to have further increased over time. Currently, two main patterns can be noted. First, in the two regions the decline of membership rates affects trade unions in a different way. Second, trade unions and employers associations of Veneto and Tuscany follow different strategies and logic of action.

As for the first pattern, we can note that membership rate tends to decline both in Veneto and in Tuscany, especially in industrial activities. Nevertheless, trade unions maintain a membership rate higher in Tuscany; moreover, it should be noted that the difference in the industrial membership rate between Tuscany and Veneto arose from 3.2 in 1981 up to six points in 1995. Thus, the decrease in industrial unionization was lower for Tuscany and the relative gap between the two regions in unions' weight increased (Table 8.1).

Table 8.1 Unionization in Veneto and in Tuscany, 1981 and 1995

	1981	1995	Decline of membership (%)
Veneto			
Membership rate in industrial activities	47.5	31.2	-16.3
Total membership rate	43.5	33.3	-10.2
Tuscany			
Membership rate in industrial activities	50.7	37.2	-13.5
Total membership rate	51.0	39.6	-11.4

Source: Argentieri (1997).

Notable differences can be found also in the strategies pursued by trade unions. During the 1990s, in Veneto trade unions sustained an intense development of flexible labour contracts: the growth of part time, apprenticeship and time contracts was here higher, whilst full time contracts were more widespread in Tuscany (Figure 8.3). At the same time, wage levels were lower in Veneto than in Tuscany, both for small and large industrial firms (Figure 8.4).

These data show that the above mentioned process of diversification affects also the industrial relations' arena. In Tuscany there has been a positive association between a lower decrease in unionization, a lower use of flexible labour contracts and higher wage levels, whilst in Veneto a higher decrease in unions' relative weight coexisted with a different attitude towards flexibility's instruments (both of labour and wage regulation).

Changes in Local Organization of Production

Alongside the already shown differences in governance mechanisms, there has been a notable process of diversification in the productive structure of local manufacturing systems in the two regions. At the beginning of the 1990s in Veneto most employees in the manufacturing sector were concentrated in local manufacturing systems with small/medium-sized firms, and local manufacturing systems with small firms in Tuscany.

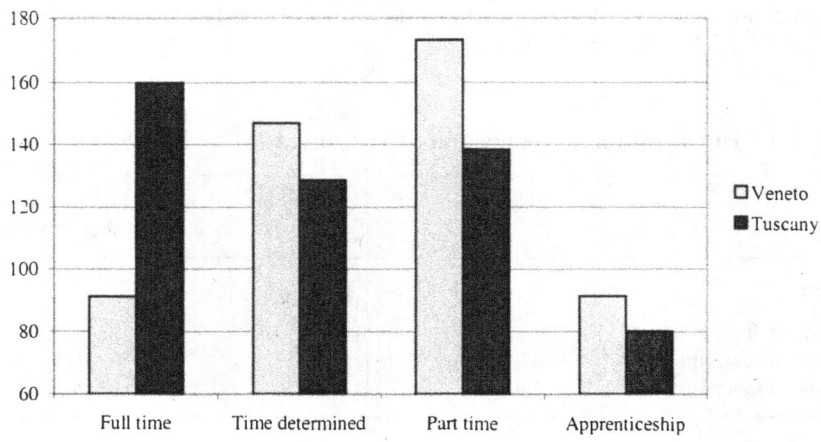

Figure 8.3 Growth of labour contracts for type of contract, 1991-1995

Source: Argentieri (1997).

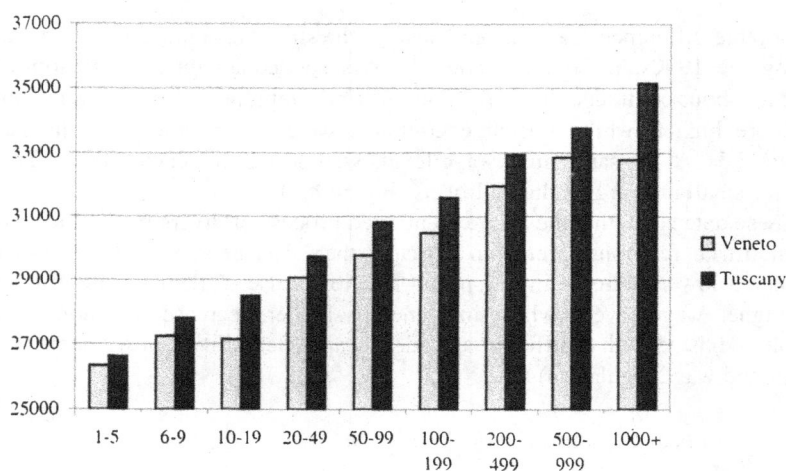

Figure 8.4 Wage levels per dimension of firms, 1995

Source: Istat (1997).

Furthermore, these differences grew in the period 1991-1996: there was in Veneto a large increase in the percentage of employees in systems with small/medium-sized, and also large-scale firms, while in Tuscany there was an increase in the percentage of employees in systems of small firms (Table 8.2). Currently, in Veneto more than 60 per cent of total manufacturing employment is located in local systems characterized by medium firms, and a quite large part of employment is in large firms. On the contrary, in Tuscany a notable part of employment can be found in local systems with small firms (about 75 per cent).

Table 8.2 Number of local manufacturing systems in the two regions and percentage of employees, 1991 and 1996

	Number of local manufacturing systems of small firms (% employees)	Number of local manufacturing systems of small/medium firms (% employees)	Number of local manufacturing systems of large firms (% employees)
Veneto			
1991	35.0 (23.8)	50.0 (57.5)	15.0 (18.7)
1996	25.6 (15.4)	48.8 (64.3)	25.6 (20.3)
Tuscany			
1991	45.5 (63.1)	40.9 (24.3)	13.6 (12.5)
1996	56.5 (75.5)	34.8 (14.9)	8.7 (9.6)

Source: Processed data of ISTAT database.

These features can be observed also looking at the geographical position of local manufacturing systems: in Tuscany there is a higher concentration of manufacturing activities in those systems characterized by small firms, whilst in Veneto manufacturing activities tend to localize in systems of small and large firms. Thus, the two regional economies have two different cores: medium and large-sized firms for Veneto and small firms for Tuscany (Figures 8.5, 8.6).

More qualitative analysis show that these two models are characterized also by a different kind of network between firms (Burroni, 2001). On the one hand, in Veneto there is a more hierarchical model centered on medium or large firms that organize and control a number of subcontracting firms, according to a model that can be defined as *localized networked firm*, which directly play a substantial role in local governance. In this case, notwithstanding the growth of decentralization of production towards low labour costs' countries, the leader firm continue to be *embedded* in the local context, where it maintains ties with strategic subcontractors.

184   *The Institutions of Local Development*

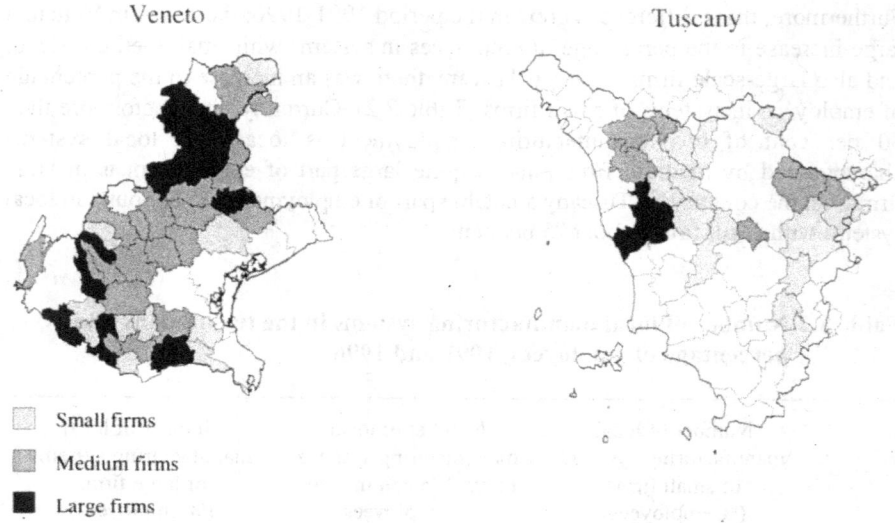

Figure 8.5 Local manufacturing systems per type of firms, 1996

Source: Processed data of ISTAT database.

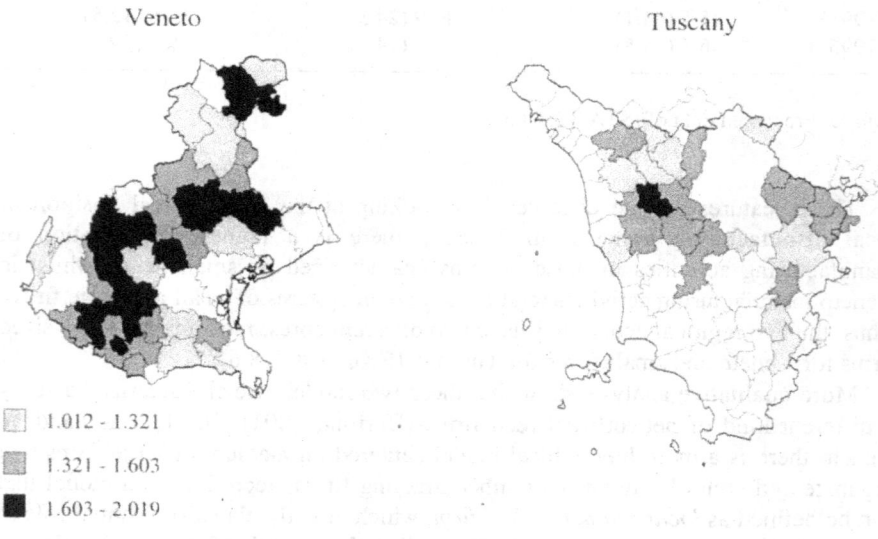

Figure 8.6 Territorial concentration of manufacturing activities (value of the location quotient), 1996

Source: Processed data of ISTAT database.

On the other hand, the Marshallian industrial district – here defined as the *localized network of firms* – prevails in Tuscany, with relation among firms that are characterized by a low level of hierarchy and by horizontal linkages. Finally, it should be noted that manufacturing activities have a different weight in the two regions: in Veneto the majority of local systems have a high quota of manufacture, whilst in Tuscany there are also many local systems specialized in services' activities.[9]

Thus, the organizational model that prevails in the two regions shows relevant differences, confirming that a process of productive and organizational diversification is taking place between the regions of the Third Italy. In Veneto local systems with medium-sized and large firms have become more important, while in Tuscany local systems are mainly composed of small firms, with a productive structure similar to the traditional industrial districts. However, in both cases the relation of firms with the local context and the role played by local external economies continue to be of primary importance.

Conclusion: Different Pathways of Local Development

The main aim of this analysis has been to show the emerging of two diverse models of local governance in two regions that many analysis define as extremely homogeneous (Table 8.3). The persistence of old differences and the growth of new ones support the hypothesis that local economies are reacting differently to the pressures of globalization. Notwithstanding the intensification of international competition, the rise of external decentralization and the growth of mobility for investments and capital, firms continue to be *locally rooted*, even if with diverse model of inter-firms relationship. At the same time, external economies continue to be of primary importance, but in the regions here analyzed they are provided by divergent institutional assets, in which local government, large firms and collective actors play different roles. Here we tried to specify this set of differences focusing the attention on three main spheres.

Firstly, the diverse model of political intervention in the local economy which characterizes most of the local systems of Veneto and Tuscany. We showed that in Veneto, local governments have delegated important aspects of regulation to large firms and to business associations.[10] The delegation of political issues to firms was supported by a widespread presence of locally rooted large and medium-scale enterprises, which directly contributed to the reinforcement of local external economies with the provision of *club goods*. At the same time, business associations played an important role in the provision of collective competition goods such as professional training, information on markets, diffusion of innovation etc. Conversely, in Tuscany, public institutions – in particular local and regional governments – continue to be key actors in the regulation of local economies. In this region, in fact, local administrations have contributed to the creation of collective goods aimed at improving the competitiveness of local systems.

Secondly, as for industrial relations, in Veneto trade unions allowed an intense adoption of flexibility both for labour and wage regulation, which supported the competitiveness of local firms. Since the beginning of the 1990s, there has been a high growth of 'atypical' labour contracts and the wage levels were lower than those of Tuscany, both in small and large industrial firms. In Tuscany, in fact, trade unions adopted more traditional strategies, maintaining also a higher rate of membership rate: higher labour costs and standard labour contracts were here more widespread (Burroni, 2001).

Table 8.3 Model of governance of the two regions

	Importance of local governments in the governance of local economies	Importance of business associations in the governance of local economies	Importance of single firms in the governance of local economies	Models industrial relations at local level	Dominant players of local regulation
Veneto	Low	High	High	Pluralism with strong associations	Business associations and medium-size firms
Tuscany	High	Medium-high	Low	Local concertation	Local governments

Thirdly, as for the productive structure, in Veneto emerged a model that can be defined as *localized networked firms' model*: it is characterized by the presence of a medium or large-size leader firm which organizes and controls the local industrial system. These firms found its main competitive advantages in the specific assets of local context, in which they continue to be embedded, even if practices of decentralisation towards low labour costs countries are emerging. On the contrary, in Tuscany the *localized network of firms* model prevails: it is characterized by the prevalence of small firms tied together by horizontal linkages and where single firms usually do not participate directly to the set up of collective goods.

Naturally, changes in regional models of governance and in productive organization go hand-in-hand. In Veneto the presence of leader firm favored the low degree of intervention of local governments, which in turn reinforce the role of leader firms in governance mechanisms. On the contrary in Tuscany, the prevalence of a small firms' fabric claimed for an active role of political institutions, which through specific policies reproduces this predominance of small firms. Naturally, this does not entail a sort of *iron cage* for institutional change: local actors can play a determinant role in influencing the direction of institutional change.

In conclusion, it seems possible to affirm that the hypothesis presented at the beginning of this chapter is confirmed: global pressures led to a divergence of organizational and local governance models among industrial districts also in the Third Italy, a macro area region usually considered as internally homogeneous. These different institutional architectures seem both able to answer to the new pressures: during the 1990s, in fact, Veneto was one of the most dynamic regions of Italy and performed better than Tuscany. At the same time Tuscany, even if was less dynamic than Veneto, had an increase in GDP per inhabitants and an employment rate higher than the national average (Tables 8.4, 8.5). Thus, even if with different weight, the two regions continue to play a relevant role in the Italian economy.

Table 8.4 GDP per inhabitants, 1995-1999 (Italy = 100)

	1995	1996	1997	1998	1999
Veneto	118.1	118.5	118.7	118.1	117.3
Tuscany	109.1	109.3	109.3	109.6	110.1

Source: Processed data from ISTAT database.

Table 8.5 Extra-agricultural employment rate in 1996

	1996
Veneto	49.7
Tuscany	45.4
Italy	43.1

Source: Processed data from ISTAT database.

However, where there are lights there are also shadows. Both these two models have in fact specific shortcomings related to the long term reproduction of competitiveness. As for Veneto, the prevalent model of governance does not seem particularly able to produce collective competition goods, which are necessary to the long-term reproduction of this type of organization. The model of the *localized networked firm*, for example, sustains the production of 'club goods', but these can only be used by the members of each specific network, and directed mainly towards the specific needs of the leading firm. On the other hand, the production of strategic resources by associations has to respond to the pressure and needs of the membership, and is mainly directed to short term problems. In this case, we can speak of 'categorical goods' suited to specific actors and with a short-term focus. Furthermore, there are goods that cannot be produced either by associations or individual firms without the assistance of local governments. For example, urban planning and transport, infrastructures and social services. Thus, although a low degree of political regulation, weak industrial relations and the delegation to private actors may have contributed to the development and the performance of local systems in Veneto, it could also endanger success in the long-term (Burroni, 2001). As for Tuscany, notwithstanding the active role played by local governments, it is not easy to provide the adequate supply of collective competition goods and to overcome political failures. Furthermore, the strong ties between local government and voters, and the need of political consensus, can also hinder the production of collective goods with a long-term orientation.

Summarizing, local systems can follow different pathways of local development and institutions can provide strategic goods in many diverse ways. The results of international comparisons on the *variety of national capitalisms*[11] are confirmed also at micro level: global pressures led to a divergence of organizational and local governance models among different contexts. There is also clear evidence of the importance of the action of formal institutions in supporting the competitiveness of local economies. Nevertheless, the two models here analyzed may have shortcomings that can hinder a long term competitiveness. Thus, the competitive advantage of local economies depends on how the above-mentioned diverse institutional arrangements will deal with the new challenges brought about by globalization and increased competition.

Notes

1 See Bagnasco (1977), Trigilia (1990 and 1992). On the concept of industrial district see Becattini (1990); on the recent change in industrial district see Rullani and Romano (1998).
2 On the concept of local collective competition goods see Crouch *et al.* (2001).
3 On the communitarian mechanisms of provision of collective goods see Dei Ottati (1994 and 1996).
4 See Bellandi and Russo (1994).
5 The financing of Law 46/82 is almost double for Veneto.
6 See Trigilia (1990 and 1992).
7 On the role of business association in the governance process see Schmitter and Streeck (1985); on the pluralistic model of governance and industrial relations see Crouch (1993).
8 On the institutional support to economic competitiveness both at local and at national level see Trigilia (1996).
9 See Sforzi (1994 and 1996).
10 On the concept of delegation to associations, see Schmitter and Streek (1985).
11 See Berger and Dore (1996); Crouch and Streeck (1997).

References

Anastasia, B. e Corò, G. (1996), *Evoluzione di un'economia regionale. Il Nordest dopo il successo*, Nuova Dimensione Ediciclo, Portogruaro.

Argentieri, A. (1997), *Industria e lavoro in Toscana e in Veneto: un'analisi comparata*, tesi di laurea, Facoltà di Scienze politiche, Università di Firenze.

Bagnasco, A. (1977), *Tre Italie. La problematica territoriale dello sviluppo italiano*, Il Mulino, Bologna.

Becattini, G. (1990), 'The Marshallian Industrial District as a Socio-Economic Notion', in F. Pyke, G. Becattini and W. Sengenberger (eds), *Industrial Districts and Inter-firm Co-operation in Italy*, International Institute for Labour Studies, Geneva, pp. 37-51.

Bellandi, M. and Russo, M. (eds) (1994), *Distretti industriali e cambiamento economico Locale*, Rosenberg & Sellier, Torino.

Berger, S. and Dore, R. (eds) (1996), *National Diversity and Global Capitalism*, Cornell University Press, Ithaca.

Burroni, L. (2001), *Allontanarsi Crescendo. Politica e sviluppo locale in Veneto e Toscana*, Rosenberg & Sellier, Torino.

Cooke, P. and Morgan, K. (1998), *The Associational Economy*, Oxford University Press, Oxford.

Crouch, C. (1993), *Industrial Relations and European State Traditions*, Oxford University Press, Oxford.

Crouch, C., Trigilia, C., Voelzkow, H. and Le Galés, P. (eds) (2001), *Local Production Systems in Europe. Rise or Demise?* Oxford University Press, Oxford.

Diamanti, I. (1996), *Il male del Nord. Lega, localismo, secessione*, Donzelli, Roma.

Dei Ottati, G. (1994), 'Trust, Interlinking Transactions and Credit in the Industrial District', *Cambridge Journal of Economics*, 18, pp. 529-546.

Dei Ottati, G. (1996), 'The Remarkable Resilience of the Industrial Districts of Tuscany' in F. Cossentino, F. Pyke, and W. Sengenberger (eds), *Local and Regional Response to Global Pressure: The Case of Italy and Its Industrial Districts*, International Institute for Labour Studies, Geneva, pp 37-66.

Freschi, A.C. (1993), 'Istituzioni politiche e sviluppo locale nella Terza Italia', *Sviluppo locale*, I, 1, pp. 71-118.

Piore, M. and Sabel, C. (1984), *The Second Industrial Divide*, Basic Books, New York.

Rullani, E. and Romano, L. (1998), *Il post fordismo: idee per il capitalismo prossimo venturo*, Etas Libri, Perugia.

Sforzi, F. (1994), 'The Tuscan model: an interpretation in light of recent trends', in R. Leonardi and R.Y. Nanetti (eds), *Regional Development in a Modern European Economy: The Case of Tuscany*. Pinter, London, pp. 86-115 (reprinted in: G. Becattini, M. Bellandi, G. Dei Ottati and F. Sforzi, *From Industrial Districts to Local Development. An Itinerary of Research*, Edward Elgar, Cheltenham, 2003, pp. 29-61).

Sforzi, F. (1996), 'Italy: A – Local Systems and Small and Medium-Sized Firms and Industrial Changes', in OECD, *Networks of Enterprises and Local Development*, Paris, pp. 99-113.

Streeck, W. (1998), 'The Internationalisation of Industrial Relations in Europe. Prospects and Problems', Cologne, Max Planck Institut fur Gesellschaftsforschung, Discussion Paper 98/2.

Trigilia, C. (1990), 'Work and Politics in the Third Italy's Industrial District', in F. Pyke, G. Becattini and W. Sengenberger (eds), *Industrial Districts and Inter-firm Co-operation in Italy*, International Institute for Labour Studies, Geneva, pp. 160-184.

Trigilia, C. (1992), 'Italian Industrial Districts: Neither Mith nor Interlude', in F. Pyke and W. Sengenberger (eds), *Industrial Districts and Local Economic Regeneration*, International Institute for Labour Studies, Geneva, pp. 33-47.

Trigilia, C. (1996), 'Dinamismo privato e disordine pubblico. Politica, economia e società locali', in AA.VV., *La trasformazione dell'Italia. Sviluppo e squilibri*, Storia dell'Italia repubblicana, Vol. 2*, Einaudi, Torino, pp. 713-777.

Index

Page numbers in *italics* refer to tables. *n/ns* indicates note/notes

accountancy 117, 118
agency 86
agricultural industry, Italy 154-5
Agro Nocerino-Sarnese (ANS) study, Italy 153-66
Amin, A. 4, 24
  and Thrift, N. 24
amorality
  amoral familism 153, 159, 167*n*
  amoral individualism 152
  libertarian geographies (LETSystems) 121-6, 127, 136-7*ns*
  see also morality
Anglo-American culture 20
associated services/industries 7, 13, 154-5
associative regulation 180, 188*n*
Audretsch, D. 57-8
authority *see* leadership
awareness, horizons of 36, *37*, 42, 45

biotechnology clusters 54-5, 56, 59
  Cambridge, UK 61-4
bonding and bridging 101, 104, 109
Bowring, F. 121
Burnett, R. 3, 6, 20
Burroni, L. 176, *178*, 179, 183, 186, 188

Cahn, E. 132-3
Cambridge Advanced Electronic (CAE) 67
Camorra 157, 158-9, 160, 161, 167*ns*
canning industry, Italy 154-5
career paths, music industry 21, *22*
chance events 4
civic engagement 143, 144-5
'civic voluntarism model' 149
cluster concept 4, 6-8

see also high-technology clusters; music industry clusters
cognitive embeddedness 8, 20
collapsed institutions 150-1
collective action *see* co-operation
collective goods, local 176, 179-80, 188*n*
competitive advantage 3-4
concertation of firms, local 176-7, 180
conflict and social capital 152
construction industry 42, 44
Cookson, C. 53
co-operation 75-7, 163-4, 176
  conceptualising trust and power 77-9
  examples, Ghana 79-88, 89*ns*
  sustaining 83-8
coping strategies 153
core-periphery relations, Israel 31
criminal groups 152, 157
  Camorra 157, 158-9, 160, 161, 167*ns*
cross-cutting (transverse) interrelations 149, 151, 152
cultural embeddedness 8, 20, 34
culture associations, local 16
Curran, J. and Blackburn, R. 30, 34-5

Dacin, M.T. *et al* 8, 20
debt, LETS Scheme 131
developmental institutions 150
'diamond model' 4, 5, 18, *19*, 24
diversion and social capital 146-7
Dodd, N. 117-19, 125
dynamics of clusters 18, *19*, 52, 57

educational provision, music industry 15, 16-17

Edwards, B. and Foley, M.W. 144, 145, 146, 149
embeddedness 4, 5
   ethnic entrepreneurs 30, 34-7, 40-5, 46
   music industry clusters 6-8, 20-3
employees
   Israel 40, 41-2
   Italy 156, 163-4, 181-3, 183
   UK 65, 66, 70
Enright, M. 6
entrepreneurs
   Israel *see* ethnic entrepreneurs (Israeli Arabs)
   Italy 163-5
ethnic entrepreneurs (Israeli Arabs) 29-31, 45-7
   Arab industry in Israel 31-3
   embeddedness 34-7, 46
   firms and networks 34-40
   over-embeddedness 40-3
   under-embeddedness 43-5
exclusion
   exclusionary networks 61
   'exclusive cohesion' 103, 104, 106-7, *108*, 109
   and social capital 147, 152

face-to-face interrelations 148, 149
Fairshares 133-4, 138*ns*
family relationships
   Israeli Arab entrepreneurs 40, 41-2
   Italy 162
   transaction cost analysis 95-6
   trust factors 84, 105, 106, 107
financial support
   Ghana 81, 82, 89*n*
      susu groups 79-80, 83-4, 85, 89*n*
   Israeli Arab entrepreneurs 33, 41, 42, 45
   Italian entrepreneurs 164-5
   Mexican microfinance group 98-9
   Swedish music industry 14
   UK, high-technology clusters 54-5, 56, 63, 64
'flexible specialization model' 175
food industry 44, 46, 154-5

Forss, K. 3, 6, 8-9, 12
Fukuyama, F. 95

Gambetta, D. 77, 95
Garnsey, E. 55, 61
   and Lawton Smith, H. 58
Ghana, co-operative groups 79, 88, 89*ns*
Ghana Private Road Transport Union (GPRTU) 82-3, 86
global media industry 11, 12, 23
government
   in 'diamond model' 4
   policies
      Israel 31, 46-7
      Italy 141-3, 177-80, 185, 186
      Sweden 23
      UK 51, 126
Granovetter, M. 7, 8, 34, 36, 75, 83, 84-5, 88, 96, 97, 145, 148
group enterprises
   Ghana 79, 88, 89*ns*
   Mexico 98-112

habits 84, 89*n*
Hallencreutz, D. and Lundequist, P. 4, 12, 18, 21
Hansatech 67, 68
Hesmondhalgh, D. 4, 10, 11
high-technology clusters 51
   alleviating congestion/dualities 69-70
   Cambridge, UK 60-1
      biotechnology 61-4
      information technology 59, 64-9
   concept of 52-8
   UK 58-9
horizons of awareness 36, *37*, 42, 45
horizontal interrelations 148, 149
Hultsfred agglomeration, Sweden 10

industrial district, definitions 175-7, 185, 188*n*
industrial relations, models 180-1, 186
industry and workers' organisations
   Swedish music industry 17
   see also trade unions; transport

associations and unions
information and communication
  technology (ICT) clusters 55
  Cambridge, UK 59, 64-9
innovation 53, 54-5, 57
  in 'traditional' sectors 70
institutions
  malfunctioning/weak 150, 162,
    164-5
  role in social capital 149-51,
    166n
  support structure 23, 24
interrelations
  bonding and bridging 101, 104,
    109
  and social capital 148-9, 161-5
Israeli Arabs *see* ethnic
  entrepreneurs (Israeli Arabs)
Italy
  Agro Nocerino-Sarnese (ANS)
    study 153-66
  'third Italy' 175
  Tuscany *vs* Veneto models
    177-85

Keeble, D. *et al* 58, 59
kinship relationships *see* family
  relationships
'knowledge/learning spillovers' 66,
  69
Krugman, P. 55

leadership 85, 86-7, 96
LETS Schemes 126-32, 137ns
LETSystems 121-6, 127, 136-7ns
Lilliestram, L. 14, 15, 20
linkages
  sales and purchasing 38, 39
  traded interdependencies 68
  vertical interrelations 148, 149
Linton, M. 122-3, 136-7ns
local collective goods 176, 179-80,
  188n
local concertation of firms 176-7,
  180
local culture associations 16
local currency systems (LCS) 116-
  19, 135, 136ns
  LETS Schemes 126-32, 137ns
  LETSystems 121-6, 127, 136-
    7ns
  Time Dollar Schemes 132-4
localized network of firms model
  176-7
Lukes, S. 78-9, 86
Lyon, F. 76, 77, 86

machinery and equipment, music
  industry 7, 12-13
majority-minority relations, Israel 31
malfunctioning/weak institutions
  150, 162, 164-5
Mega, UK 67, 68
membership stability 109-10
Menger, P.M. 12, 23
microfinance group study, Mexico
  98-112
Middleton, R. 5
mixed embeddedness 36, 37, 46
Moore, M. 97-8
morality
  limited-group and generalised 97
  moral geographies (LETS
    Schemes) 126-32, 137ns
  moral obligations 84, 86
  see also amorality
motor industry 56
music industry clusters 5
  concept of 6-8
  Swedish study 8-24, 25n

Narayan, D. 149, 151
National Council for Cultural
  Affairs, Sweden 14
Negus, K. 10, 11, 12, 20, 23
networks
  cluster concept 4, 6-8
  exclusionary 61
  firms 34-40, 176-7, 179-80, 183,
    185, 186, 187
  formal and informal 63, 65-6,
    161-2
  hard and soft 65
  monetary (LCSs) 117-19, 136ns
  social 24, 57
  trust 94, 96
non-governmental organisations
  (NGOs) 30, 81, 83, 86

Oaxaca *vs* Puebla, Mexico 98-112

Oinas, P. 8, 34, 35
Ostrom, E. 77, 85, 88
outsourcing 54, 56
over-embeddedness 30, 36-7, 40-3

palm oil processing groups, Ghana 80-1, 84, 86, 87
Pantoja, E. 145, 146, 147-8
peer pressure 87-8, 89n
Pinch, S. and Henry, N. 23, 56
Platteau, J. 77, 97
political economy, Italian regional and local 177-80
political embeddedness 8, 23, 35
politicians, Italy 157-61, 162, 163, 167ns
'popular music'
   definition 5-6
   see also music industry clusters
Porter, M. 4, 5, 6, 18, *19*, 24, 52, 53, 70, 76
Portes, A. 145, 147, 148
   and Landoldt, P. 94, 146, 147
   and Sensenbrenner, J. 147
power relations 77-9
   entrepreneurs' embeddedness 35-6, *37*, 44-5
   global intra-industry 23
   in groups 85-8
   multiple community currencies 124-5
predatory institutions 150
primary goods, music industry 6, 11-12, 13
public authorities, music industry 14
public educational institutions, music industry 16-17
Puebla *vs* Oaxaca, Mexico 98-112
purchasing linkages 38, *39*
Putnam, R. 76, 94-5, 142, 143-5

reciprocity 143
reflexivity, monetary networks 117, 119
regulation
   associative 180, 188n
   monetary networks 117, 118-19
       Time Dollar Schemes 132-4
research & development (R&D)

companies 60-1
Roelandt, T. and den Hertog, P. 55
Route 128 58-9
Rowlands, J. 77-8

sales linkages 38, *39*
SC *see* social capital
Schnell, I.
   et al 29, 31, 32, *33*, 38, 43, 45
   Sofer, M. and 29, 31-2
Scott, A. 10, 11, 20, 21, 24
   Storper, M. and 51
Scott, A.J. 29-30, 34
shame 87
short term self interest 75, 88, 89n
Silicon Valley 54, 55, 56, 58
skills, local currency systems (LCS) 130, 134
social agendas, LETS Schemes 127-8, 137ns
social capital (SC)
   dangers 146-8
   dynamic and contextualised 145-53
   four different situations 151-3
   interrelations 148-9, 161-5
   local currency systems (LCS) 121, 132-4, 136n
   Putnam's theory of 143-5
   role of institutions 149-51, 166n
   see also Agro Nocerino-Sarnese (ANS) study, Italy; microfinance group study, Mexico; trust
social cohesion 151
social construction of value 131-2, 137n
social inclusion 162
social networks 24, 57
social relations of reproduction 120-1, 136n
sociality, monetary networks 117, 119
Sofer, M. and Schnell, I. 29, 31-2
spatiality, monetary networks 117, 119
speciality inputs, music industry 7, 12, 13
'spillovers' 56, 66, 69
Standard for European Industrial

Classification (SIC/NACE) 8
Stockholm region, Sweden 10, 11
Storper, M. 4, 24, 56
   and Scott, A. 51
Stroud LETS Scheme, UK 129, 130, 131, 137ns
structural embeddedness 8, 20-3, 34
Sundsvall agglomeration, Sweden 10
surveillance 86, 133, 138n
susu groups, Ghana 79-80, 83-4, 85, 89n
Swedish music industry study 8-24, 25n
systemic nature of industrial production 3-4

technological innovations 4, 38, 163
   see also high-technology clusters
textile industry
   Arab Israeli 31-2, 33, 42, 44-5
   Italy 154
   UK 59
'third Italy' 175
third sector organisations, music industry 14-16
Thrift, N. 120
   Amin, A. and 24
Time Dollar Schemes 132-4
time, value of 130-1
trade unions 17, 180-1, 186
traded interdependencies linkages 68
transaction cost analysis 95-6, 112ns
transparency 83-4
transport associations and unions 82-3, 86
transverse (cross-cutting) interrelations 149, 151, 152

Trigilia, C. 149-50, 180
trust 77, 83-5, 143
   concepts of 94-8
   'exclusive cohesion' 103, 104, 106-7, *108*, 109
   factor analysis 102-9
   generalised 86, 143, 144, 166n
   'perceived distrust' 104, 107-8, 109
   'trust without mutuality' 103, 105-6, *108*, 109
   variables *101*, *112*
Tuscany *vs* Veneto, Italy 177-88

under-embeddedness 30, 36, *37*, 43-5
Uzzi, B. 35, 36

value
   definition 120, 136n
   social construction of 131-2, 137n
   of time 130-1
Veneto *vs* Tuscany, Italy 177-88
vertical (linking) interrelations 148, 149
voluntary associations, music industry 16

weak/malfunctioning institutions 150, 162, 164-5
welfare 152
women 31, 33, 80-1, 87
Woolcock, M. 76, 150, 151

Yeung, H. 23, 24, 34

Zukin, S. and DiMaggio, P. 5, 7-8, 20